THE CRAFT OF PSYCHOTHERAPY

TWENTY-SEVEN STUDIES

THE CRAFT OF PSYCHOTHERAPY

TWENTY-SEVEN STUDIES

I. H. Paul, PH.D.

JASON ARONSON INC.
Northvale, New Jersey
London

Library of Congress Cataloging-in-Publication Data

Paul, I. H. (Irving H.), 1928–
   The craft of psychotherapy : twenty-seven studies / I. H. Paul.
     p.   cm.
   Includes index.
   ISBN 0-87668-826-1
   1. Psychotherapy—Case studies.   I. Title.
   [DNLM: 1. Psychotherapy.   WM 420 P324c]
RC465.P38   1989
616.89 14—dc20
DNLM/DLC   89-17492
for Library of Congress   CIP

Manufactured in the United States of America. Jason Aronson Inc. offers books
and cassettes. For information and catalog write to Jason Aronson Inc., 230
Livingston Street, Northvale, New Jersey 07647.

For Edith

CONTENTS

PREFACE

This is my third book on the psychotherapist's craft, and just as the second—*The Form and Technique of Psychotherapy* (University of Chicago Press, 1978)—is a revision and extension of *Letters to Simon: On the Conduct of Psychotherapy* (International Universities Press, 1973), this one is a revision and extension of both of them. *Form and Technique* is a formal treatise, while *Letters to Simon* is an informal one, and the present book falls somewhere in between. It draws liberally from those books, yet there is much that is new in it—enough to justify the claim that it isn't merely a revised edition. Moreover, while there are substantial areas of overlap among the three books, the first is still a useful introduction to my views on therapy and the second remains a more complete coverage. The present book gives a detailed and closely argued examination of exact technique; it is more purely a study of the specifics of the therapist's craft.

The book owes its existence to Jason Aronson in more ways than the obvious one, for it was he who asked me to write it, advised me as to its content, and gave generously and enthusiastically of his judicious editorial acumen and moral support. I am deeply indebted to Dr. Aronson.

The debt I owe my students is evident throughout the book. What isn't evident, however, is the extent to which their views and their intellectual perspicacity have played a major role in forming its content. Over the past eight years I have asked my students to provide me with detailed critiques of my published work, and it was their constructive criticisms that significantly influenced my revisions and elaborations. That teachers learn from their students is one of those truisms that is true—and when the students are as good as mine, the teacher learns a good deal.

But I want to single out two students who played an especially significant part in shaping this book. One is Andrew Kuhn, whose incisive criticism of *Form and Technique* was instrumental in my decision to rewrite it. Andrew, more than any other student, showed me what was wrong with it—where the text failed to convey my views, where the arguments and rationales fell short, and where the spirit and tone were inept—and most importantly, he showed me how to fix it. He also edited much of the manuscript and provided fresh material for several of the "dialogues." My gratitude to Andrew is great.

The second student is Michael Lipson, and my indebtedness to him is harder to express. For it was he who carefully pored over the manuscript and gave it the kind of attention an author only fantasizes about getting. Doesn't every writer dream that a good editor will take his manuscript in hand and make sure every word and every sentence is right, excising every redundancy and obsessionality and offering phrases, sentences, and even whole paragraphs, that strengthen and freshen the text? Well, Michael was that dream come true. He is the quintessential student who both teaches and champions the teacher. It isn't fair to him that the reader will have no way of knowing how much of the book is his. Of course, I must take responsibility for it, and do, but his work is reflected on every page.

In the margin to a section that I thought might be overly obsessional, and after noting that he wouldn't change it, Michael added: "But it does remind me of Sir Walter Raleigh's poem in which he asks his own soul to go, after his body is dead, and—

> *Tell Wit how much it wrangles*
> *In tickle points of niceness;*
> *Tell Wisdom it entangles*
> *Itself in over-wiseness.*"

I. H. PAUL
City University of New York
at City College

1

THE PSYCHOTHERAPIST'S CRAFT

Twenty-seven Studies in Technique

A book's introductory chapter often amounts to an implicit dialogue in which the author anticipates the reader's questions and arguments. And the same is true for discussions within the body of a book, especially if they digress. Since this book presents many explicit dialogues between hypothetical patients and their therapists, and digresses often, I will take the liberty of allowing a hypothetical reader to break into the text with questions, challenges, and comments. For instance, I can imagine a reader asking—

Reader: Are you aware that Chopin composed twenty-seven studies for piano?
Author: Yes, but mine adding up to that number was sheer coincidence. I didn't count them up until I had decided to call them "studies" and include the number in the title. When I composed these simulations of events and exchanges that might occur in therapy, I called them "scenarios." But that never felt right, so I took to calling them "paradigms." A paradigm, however, is an abstract pattern or model, whereas my simulations are concrete and circumstantial. That's why I looked for another name and settled on "study."

1

Reader: "Study," however, is a bit inapt, isn't it? It calls to mind something scholarly, theoretical, or literary. One hardly expects specific events and verbal exchanges that might occur in therapy.

Author: Well, that's why I wanted the title to carry the number; I thought it would perhaps suggest something analogous to piano studies—concrete compositions whose purpose is to help us develop and maintain technical proficiency, where each piece is specific to a particular technical problem or a circumscribed set of problems.

Reader: Except piano studies aren't purely technical in nature, they are good music too. All of Chopin's certainly are, and so are many of Czerny's, thereby providing also for the development of musicality.

Author: Yet their chief purpose isn't to celebrate the art of music but to enhance the art of performance. And that corresponds closely to my studies for psychotherapy; they consist of specific pieces that provide us with opportunities to study the craft of conducting therapy. In their focus on the concrete and circumstantial, and their detailed examination of alternatives, exigencies, and short and long term consequences, they often have the character of talmudic lessons and commentaries. Their purpose, however, is to study technique—to articulate therapeutic goals and work out precise ways of translating them into explicit interventions, and then to rehearse and in some sense "practice" them.

Reader: They are designed, then, for beginners?

Author: Yes and no. It isn't only beginners who benefit from piano studies, experienced pianists, too, will master and practice them—if not also perform them in public. I have the temerity to believe the same might be true for mine. Although my principal student is a beginner, the studies are composed for students in the broader sense of the term—such as yourself, for instance—for I believe we can all benefit from the availability of studies in psychotherapy. We, too, need to sharpen and improve our technique; we too need to "practice."

Reader: In our case, however, "practice" is ambiguous. I take it you don't mean "engage in clinical practice."

Author: I mean it in the same sense that pianists use studies to practice their basic skills, I don't mean doing warm-up exercises to keep limber. What pianists achieve by practicing is what we therapists achieve by "performing." In effect, we have little opportunity to "practice" but must develop and perfect our technique in "performance." To be sure, ours isn't a performing art. Whatever species of art it is, however, ours is also a craft—a labor that demands technical facility.

Reader: Look here, I hope you aren't going to claim that technique is everything!

Author: When's the last time you heard anyone claim it was? And neither is it everything for pianists, or even for surgeons, and when's the last time you heard a piano teacher or a surgeon say it was irrelevant?

Reader: All right, but which techniques are we talking about? Psychotherapy, after all, comes in so many varieties and such diverse forms that the technical requirements for each have to be irreconcilably different. How is it possible to compose studies relevant to all of them?

Author: It clearly isn't. In fact, I could hardly hope to compose studies that would be relevant to very many of them. But piano studies also come in schools of pedagogy, you know.

Reader: You are now straining the analogy!

Author: Because I wanted to point out that my studies are designed for a "school" of therapy, the so-called dynamic or traditional school, and they are specific to a particular method within it. The format is one-to-one, the mode is verbal, and since the therapeutic process is inquiry that focuses on the patient's intrapsychic realm, and the therapist strives to maintain a nondirective and neutral position that extends to all aspects of the therapy's procedure, the method is a blend of psychoanalytic and nondirective therapies.

The clinical-theoretical underpinnings of the method are discussed at various places in the book, but there isn't a comprehensive description and full account of the therapy itself, of its substance and its drama—its "music." The book's aim is too limited for that. As form, not content, is the principal subject, the coverage is selective. Personality differences and dynamics, psychopathology and etiology, are mentioned only in passing; regression, emotional insight, reconstruction, working-through, acting-out, impasses and crises—phenomena that are central to all forms of traditional therapy—aren't given the attention they deserve. Resistance is studied in some detail, and so is transference, but they aren't examined comprehensively either. Instead, the focus is on technique: namely, the purely craft aspects entailed in conducting a particular form of psychotherapy.

And neither do the studies cover all the technical aspects of this method. Since my aim was to examine matters intensively rather than extensively, and I wanted to be as concrete and detailed as possible, the studies focus on those issues of procedure and format that I believe are the most fundamental. You see, I wanted to write not only "on" technique, or even "about" it, I wanted to write a technique as explicitly as I could.

Reader: How feasible a goal is that?

Author: For a therapy that relies substantially on the verbal mode, I don't think it's all that unfeasible. After all, the mode is isomorphic in its spoken and written forms. To be sure, the translation of spoken into written language is hardly free of serious limitations. Spoken language is expressive of a variety of nonverbal signals, such as voice tone and texture, inflection and tempo, and whenever we talk face-to-face there are bodily gestures, too. Most of those aspects of communication, however, can be described adequately enough. And although writing about psychotherapy may have serious shortcomings, it is free of the inherent limitations of writing about music or surgery, where the modalities are qualitatively different from each other. Their techniques can only be demonstrated and practiced under supervision.

Reader: But isn't apprenticeship also the best way for us to acquire our technical know-how? Surely you don't intend to downplay the role that supervision plays in our training.

Author: I intend to play up the role of didactic study. And the reason I am rising to the defense of technique is because it so often is challenged and deprecated. Many teachers of psychotherapy regard technique as an arid and useless formality, mechanical and inhuman, a way of keeping distance and playing an empty role—therefore it *shouldn't* be taught. Some regard it as a necessary evil, subservient to understanding— they believe our technique emerges quite naturally from a knowledge of the dynamics of human experience and behavior together with a knowledge of the dynamics of psychotherapy— therefore it *needn't* be taught. And for some, there is no such thing as correct or good technique, all therapists must fashion their own out of the ingredients of their individual personality and then tailor it to their patient's particular personality and problems—therefore it *cannot* be taught.

Reader: And with all those points of view—

Author: —I disagree.

Reader: That's no surprise. But in order to teach technique, you need reliable criteria on which to base an assessment of their soundness and validity. Where do we find such criteria? Ours, after all, isn't a science.

Author: Then bear with my analogizing a moment more, and consider the scale and the arpeggio. Their relevancy lies in the prominent role they play in classical music and pianists' need to play them fluently and automatically in order to free themselves to pay attention to the esthetic meaning of the music itself. There are traditional criteria for "good" scale and arpeggio work, criteria that are neither arbitrary nor unreliable. There is a correct, or optimal, fingering for each scale, a fingering that is based not on intuition or esthetic considerations but the structure of the instrument and the anatomy of the performer. In a meaningful sense of the term, a "science" of scales and arpeggios exists. This doesn't mean we overlook the fact that playing scales and arpeggios can never be fully uniform. There are idiosyncrasies of hand that require deviations, and idiosyncrasies of instrument that require modifications. And the music will make a significant difference too; the same scale can be fingered one way for Mozart and another way for Debussy. But these considerations don't attenuate the value and necessity of our acquiring the skill of playing scales and arpeggios in the standard ways. Deviations and modifications are, after all, predicated on those standard ways, and every pianist must learn them at the level of a skill. The same is true for every surgeon. And the same is true for every psychotherapist. We, too, must know how to pass the thumb under the third and fourth fingers smoothly, fluently, and automatically, in order to devote our full attention to our patients and to the work that really counts.

Reader: Ah yes, "the work that really counts!" What *is* the work that really counts in psychotherapy? In order to do *their* work that really counts, pianists have to know music, understand the esthetic principles and artistic purposes of Mozart and Debussy. It also pays to know how musical instruments are constructed and understand the human motor system.

Author: All of that is altogether necessary and altogether insufficient—they must also acquire the craft of playing. Similarly, it isn't enough for surgeons to know anatomy and physiology, they have to know how to operate—they must have technique. And similarly, I believe it isn't enough for us to know psychology, the way our behavior is organized and gets disorganized, the way our emotions, needs, and motives are integrated and get disintegrated, the way our phenomenal world is structured, and the like, and neither is it sufficient to understand the dynamics of personality change or behavior modification. We must acquire the technical skills of doing therapy—we have to learn the craft.

Reader: Okay, you've made your point—though you haven't answered my question. Still, I think it's worth mentioning that we therapists aren't like surgeons whose technique must take such great precedence, and neither are we like musicians who cannot begin to play any music without a certain level of skill and facility. Your analogies are limited in their relevancy.

Author: Yet they are relevant enough, I believe, because conducting therapy is part science and part art, and both parts rest on a foundation that is secured by technique. That, at any rate, is the working hypothesis for this book.

Reader: I suppose you are now going to argue that we should work like pianists and surgeons do, or perhaps like repairmen and healers.

Author: On the contrary! Once I am finished arguing in favor of technique, I quit using analogies and do an about-face. I argue that we should work like nobody else, only like psychotherapists. I'll do it under a new section heading—

On the Therapeutic Process

Teachers are prone to develop a conception or theme around which they organize their pedagogy, and the teaching process tends to elicit underlying convictions and give voice to silent opinions. Perhaps for those reasons, I came to profess that therapy be construed in a way that sets it apart from all socially familiar interpersonal and professional interactions, and therapists take a stance that doesn't borrow significant features from other professionals who provide human services in our society. In short, we work in a way that is unique. Here's how I formulate it: psychotherapy is potentially a unique and distinctive event, and psychotherapists may define themselves as unique and distinctive professionals.

A further thesis that stemmed indirectly from the fact that matters of theory and conception can be expounded and argued, case histories and clinical events recounted and analyzed, but techniques can be actually taught and "practiced" is this: psychotherapy can be relatively unstructured and yet unambiguous; a therapist can remain nondirective and neutral and still function actively and effectively. In fact, it has become my strong conviction that the efficacy of an average-expectable course of therapy will be significantly enhanced when we therapists remain as nondirective and as neutral as we can feasibly be, giving our patient little, if any, guidance and counseling, as well as little, if any, evaluation and reinforcement. Under those conditions, we may participate actively in the vital processes of therapy, and thereby promote its effectiveness.

Reader: And the method that embodies those theses and actualizes these potentials is of course the therapy I'll read about in this book. But isn't that psychoanalysis?

Author: As we rely on the interpretive mode of intervention along with the principal conceptions of psychoanalysis's clinical theory, you could still call it that. There are, however, differences that many analysts would regard as crucial. The method's thoroughgoing nondirectiveness requires, among other things, a significant alteration of the "fundamental rule."

Reader: Patients aren't directed to use the couch?

Author: That *is* a directive.

Reader: They aren't given the free-association instruction either?

Author: No. If they want to use the couch or free-associate, that's fine. They aren't instructed or advised to, that's all. But if the therapeutic process is carefully established and supervised, the patient might discover the benefits of free-association, and it wasn't necessary to define it as a task. The same is true for the use of the couch, of dreams, of childhood, and the rest. I'll tell you soon what instructions we do give, and why. First, let me explain the way I construe the therapeutic process.

Every psychotherapy can be defined in terms of two sets of behaviors, those of the therapist and those of the patient, and many definitions pivot on their interaction. But the interaction of two sets of behaviors can only be defined in terms that are quite different from those of each one—the interaction itself cannot be described at the same level of abstraction as its component parts—and this makes those definitions rather vague and formalistic. Therefore, I prefer to define therapy in a way that makes no reference to any interactional processes. Instead, I use a two-part definition, where one part takes account of the distinctive behaviors and intentions that describe the therapist, and the other one rests on the concept of the "therapeutic process," which denotes the psychological experience that the therapy affords the patient. Such a two-part definition is, I believe, accurate and also adequate. It has the advantage that we can nest one of the parts within the other, so that our behaviors and intentions as therapists are construed in terms of their principal function—specifically, the facilitation of the therapeutic process and the promotion of its full development.

Reader: If I understand you correctly, this formulation requires you to spell out our methods and goals as therapists, and as they are functionally organized around a ruling construct—what we're calling the "therapeutic process"—that's what has to be defined formally.

Author: Yes, that's the point. And my definition of the therapeutic process takes four propositions. The first defines it as an intrapsychic and mental process, as distinct from an interpersonal and behavioral one; the second grounds it in the act of discovering, as distinct from learning; the third specifies that it doesn't encompass everything that happens in our therapy—it's the core event but not the sum-total of the patient's behaviors and experiences; and the fourth invokes the concept of ego-autonomy. These propositions are discussed and exemplified during the course of the book, so I needn't explicate them here. I do, however, need to describe the process, and it can be done with a few broad strokes.

The therapeutic process refers to the work our patients engage in as they express and explore their inner and outer realities, as they strive to articulate and understand their behavior, their self, and their mind. The work consists of reflecting and introspecting, reminiscing and recollecting, reorganizing and reconstructing. The realm of outer reality is never slighted, but the process tends to focus on the inner reality of affects and emotions, of impulses and wishes, of needs and conflicts, of attitudes, beliefs, and values; and a special emphasis is placed on experiencing individuality and autonomy, as well as on the sense of volition. The process is grounded in the complementary acts of understanding and being understood; it's an activity of self-inquiry that strives to articulate, explore, comprehend, and discover.

Reader: But isn't that overworking it? Does it make sense to subsume all of those phenomena and activities under a single construct?

Author: My rationale rests on the observation that the separate aspects of self-inquiry tend to coalesce in practice and become closely interrelated as the therapy develops.

Reader: The same is true for the "analytic process," isn't it?

Author: Yes. In fact, analysts would regard the description of the therapeutic process as a good enough depiction of their "analytic process." That process, however, is often construed in a narrower and more specialized way, requiring, for instance, genetic reconstructions, and resolving experiences and symptoms into their component parts and determinants. Furthermore, the analytic process relies on the work of free-association; it therefore tends to be a more passive-receptive and contemplative experience than the therapeutic process sometimes is.

Reader: So our patients aren't in analysis?

Author: Not necessarily. But in fact they may be. You see, not only are the two ruling concepts fundamentally alike, but a course of our therapy can be indistinguishable from a course of classical analysis. Our patients may slip naturally into the free-association mode, their symptoms and habits may become subject to analysis and working-through, their conflicts and fantasies may be brought to the surface, a transference-neurosis may burgeon and be resolved, and the rest. There is nothing we do to prevent all of this from happening, and there are features of our method that are fully consonant with its happening. How closely our therapy will approximate psychoanalysis, and whether it will instead take on some key features of other forms of traditional psychotherapy, such as those that can fairly be labeled Humanistic and Existential, depends largely on the patient and on the circumstances of the therapy.

Reader: We're so nondirective that our patients get to choose the kind of therapy they want—and hopefully, need?

Author: In a sense, yes, but within certain specified limits. One of them is implied in our very nondirectiveness—so if they wanted Behavior Modification, for instance, they'd have come to the wrong place. But the way we define the therapeutic process sets a number of significant constraints on our patients, as it also does on us, and this leads us back to the question of technique.

Reader: Your eagerness to get back there is a bit obvious. I trust you don't consider your treatment of these conceptual matters here to be exhaustive.

Author: No indeed. But any treatment of them would sooner prove exhausting—to both of us—than truly exhaustive. I won't ignore them in what follows, but I don't intend to deal with them in detail.

Reader: Fair enough. Get on with it.

The Technical Requirements of the Therapeutic Process

Author: Because of the emphasis on uniqueness, but chiefly because of the way we construe the therapeutic process, our form of therapy requires of us an exact technique, and its constraints allow relatively little latitude with respect to our personal characteristics. In many forms of therapy it matters a great deal who the therapist is—what personality traits and special talents he or she has—which means their technical requirements cannot readily be acquired. That the same is not true for ours, or at least not so true, is an important advantage.

Reader: You mean it doesn't matter what kind of person I am?

Author: Within certain parameters, no, it shouldn't—if you adhere scrupulously to technique.

Reader: I find it hard to believe that even if I'm an insensitive dolt I'll be able to do good therapy, no matter what technical rules I follow.

Author: Take it as a given that therapists need empathy, intelligence, the ability to communicate understanding. Charisma and even intuition, I would argue, are not essentials; a fair degree of patience is. But the point I'm trying to make is that your personality characteristics are not what will make psychotherapy work or not. Technique will.

Reader: And what exactly do you mean by "technique"?

Author: Aside from considerations of timing and tact, I mean details of wording and phrasing, as well as details of inflection and formulation. Such details matter, and in my opinion they matter significantly and substantially.

Reader: Yet therapy takes so long and involves so many verbal and nonverbal exchanges. There are competent supervisors who listen less to the details than to the larger sweep of sessions.

Author: Yes, there is plenty of justification for that. Nevertheless, a whole can be significantly different from the sum of its parts even when the parts are contributing significantly to that whole. In psychological phenomena, the parts, even the smallest ones, can be intrinsic to the shape and form of the whole. At any rate, I am convinced that every detail of our conduct as therapist counts, both in itself and cumulatively, and I'm never surprised when patients recall a precise detail of what I said, or exactly how I said it, and claim it had a significant impact on them.

Reader: Then what about individual differences in style and temperament? Isn't it, after all, true that each of us has to find the way of working that suits her or him best?

Author: Many teachers would use that argument in taking exception to the kind of pedagogy that is reflected in this book— especially insofar as I so often tell my students exactly what words to use. It is one thing to suggest that they convey this or that message to a patient, it's quite another to put the words into their mouths. So first let me disclaim: my position on this matter is not as rigid as it may sometimes appear to be in the book. Yet I must admit to finding nothing wrong with suggesting to therapists—whether they are students in the narrow

or broad sense—exactly what to say. For not only do I believe
that words matter, and matter significantly, but I find that
agreeing on a precise way of wording an intervention can be
very useful. For one thing, it can free us to devote our full
attention to understanding the patient.

Reader: And that's part of the work that really counts, I
gather. But what if the words aren't easily learned, if they don't
seem natural and congenial to us, won't we be distracted by the
effort it takes to find them? And won't this detract from our
ability to pay full attention? Furthermore, while our work can
benefit from the discipline of self-consciousness, an excessive
degree of it can be disruptive—and the requirement to speak in
ways that aren't habitual can easily intensify our self-
consciousness.

Author: Therefore it's necessary to acknowledge a degree
of latitude in the matter of style, and allow for a range of
individual proclivities, provided we don't lose sight of the fact
that the words we speak play a vital role in psychotherapy, and
close attention must therefore be paid to them. And while
different therapists may choose different ways and words to
express the same idea, each way must bear scrutiny for its
surplus meanings and unwanted implications. Conducting
therapy requires a great precision of communication on our
part; that is one of its basic craft aspects. And I won't resist the
temptation to claim that the ability to communicate accurately
and the ability to understand accurately are likely to be positively correlated.

The Technical Requirements of This Book

Similarly, I face the task of writing with clarity and at the same
time judiciously. Remarkably few assertions about an enter-
prise like psychotherapy can stand free of substantial qualifica-
tion; every technical principle and supporting rationale, every
guideline and rule of thumb, brook important exceptions and
crucial conditions. Perhaps it was little more than my obses-
siveness, but the early drafts of this book were encumbered
with so many parenthetical asides and digressions that the
result was a turgid text. Whether enough of them are gone, I

can't say, but my goal was to enhance readibility without oversimplying or distorting my views.

It isn't easy to write explicitly on technique without slipping into a dogmatic posture. It is especially difficult when the technique applies to a form of therapy that puts a premium on the uniqueness of the therapeutic experience for a patient, and also when that uniqueness is predicated on the distinctive way a therapist has to behave—and keep from behaving. Insofar as the therapy's technical requirements are based to such a substantial extent on interventional modes that have to be avoided, and they include among them modes that are used deliberately and freely by experienced practitioners, there are several kinds of risks in advocating them. On the one side stands the risk of exaggerating, so as to bolster the advocacy; on the other stands the risk of blurring the focus, so as to keep from seeming inflexible. And when I challenge practices that are so widely accepted—

Reader: Such as?

Author: —Asking patients direct questions which turn therapy into an interview, for instance, or making what I call "diagnostic" formulations which tend to confront the patient. When I debate their value, there is the risk of misrepresentation and oversimplification. Yet, despite these dangers, I have chosen to be forceful in argument. The degree to which I may appear to be rigid is partly due to the limitations of my literary technique.

And it may also be due to the fact that I have chosen to organize much of the discussion around the work of my students. This, too, was largely literary convenience; I needed material on which to base my discussion, I wanted concrete examples for the purposes of critical examination, and I didn't want to fabricate all of them. Since I had given the studies as class assignments in a course on psychotherapy at City University of New York's clinical psychology program and used them as the basis of seminar-type discussion over the course of six years with a total of 146 students, I had a rich store of material available.

Reader: Untouched by editors' hands?

Author: Actually, no. Besides some modifications of grammar and syntax, I've made more extensive editorial changes, some of which are significant. And if you find that the

examples presented in the book show a surprising but not, I
hope, tediously uniform style, this is because the examples are
the work of my own students, in the first place, and also
because I have replaced certain types of locutions with others.
Consider the following interpretation:

> I am struck by your having said you felt angry at your
> brother. I can't help wondering if you wanted to hurt him.
> It sounds as if you thought he was being cruel to you, so it
> occurs to me that you needed to retaliate for it.

Notice how the remark seems to define the speaker as the
passive one—the one who "is struck," who "can't help" wondering, to whom ideas "occur"—and as someone who listens to
the "sound" of things, and passively at that. Do we ever want to
convey that message? Sometimes, perhaps, but for the most
part these locutions are spoken automatically and without
consideration; they are little more than verbal habits. Believing
as I do in the relevancy of detail and the power of words, I place
great store in the locutions with which we frame our remarks.
Since I'm convinced they can matter and are likely to have
significant reverberations—especially when they are spoken in
psychotherapy—I draw my students' attention to them at every
turn. But to do that in this book would make for excessive
repetition. Therefore, if I wanted to examine the interpretation's
content and not its form, I would present it in this edited form:

> I gather you felt angry at your brother. I wonder if you
> didn't want to hurt him. Perhaps you thought he was being
> cruel to you, and you wanted to retaliate because of it.

Reader: "I gather" is okay—how come?
Author: So is "I take it." Those words acknowledge our
effort at understanding the patient and contribute to the sense
of the interpretation being *offered* to him rather than imposed
on him. And they are free of passive reverberations.
Reader: I notice you say "he" and "him." Why not "she"
and "her"?
Author: Just habit. Nevertheless, I do want the book's text
to avoid the grammatical implications that all of us are male
and so are our patients. Yet the pronomial *he* is very helpful;

reliance on the plural becomes stilted after a while, and to write *he or she* grows awkward. One way I've chosen to solve the problem is to rely on the first-person, both singular and plural; another is to contrive to make the gender of *our* patients entirely irrelevant. Instead of arbitrarily designating this patient as *male* and that one as *female,* I consistently—and purely for the sake of grammatical convenience—designate every one of them as *male.*

Reader: Their gender matters not at all?

Author: I have contrived matters so that it doesn't. I hope you will find that substituting a female patient for a male one, both in the studies and the illustrations, won't make a significant difference. Moreover, unless otherwise specified, I always have in mind the so-called "average-expectable" patient.

Reader: Well, I don't get it. Something as basic as gender . . . I guess if you've contrived it so it doesn't matter, you've cooked up some pretty contrived examples. Or are you really saying there's an area, an important area, of both content and technique over which gender issues just don't matter—an area so vast that the essentials of psychotherapy can be written about with no reference to gender? And anyway, why didn't you use "she"?

Author: I'll use it for my students. Do you mind if we get started with psychotherapy?

The Basic Instruction

Therapy begins in diverse ways. The patient often starts out by telling us *his* reasons for seeking it. Sometimes he initiates a discussion of fee and schedule; occasionally he begins with questions about therapy. In any event, our chief technical problems at the outset are these: how to introduce him both to us and to our therapy's format; how to set the therapeutic process in motion; and how to do them with a maximum of clarity and a minimum of ambiguity. We may therefore want to give him a set of guidelines and instructions. Even when formulated didactically, they are bound to be directives—but is there a sensible and feasible alternative? Can a patient be given an unambiguous orientation to therapy that doesn't come down to a set of directives?

Suppose he began with a request for orientation, asking us: "*What is the procedure here?*" If we wanted to avoid any instructions and setting of rules, we could say something along the lines of "There is no procedure here." But can we expect the average patient to be satisfied with that answer? Isn't he too likely to be puzzled, if not incredulous, at the implication that there could be no procedure? And even if we wanted him to discover it by himself and shape it according to his needs so we answer: "How you proceed here is largely up to you," we still have to be ready to define the terms and boundaries of the method's unstructuredness. And whether or not we deem it appropriate to spell them out fully at the outset, these are important considerations that have to be carefully thought through in advance.

In order for us to do it on these pages and with a minimum of digression, restricting ourselves to the fundamental issues and their main technical implications, we will have to agree on some assumptions. The main one is that psychotherapy—our partic-ular brand of it—can begin right away. Accordingly, we need to assume that our patient wants a traditional therapy and be-lieves it can be of benefit to him, that he has been referred to us by a colleague who assessed his suitability, and we have sufficient reason to rule out the need for conducting a diagnostic interview of our own. We aren't dispensing with an independent assessment, mind you, we are basing it on our observations of his behavior during the initial sessions. In other words, we're assuming that we had ample basis to believe that therapy could responsibly be inaugurated during the initial session. The chief task we face, then, is how to orient him—how best to answer the question, whether asked or not, "*What is the procedure here?*"

Instead of courting perplexity with "There is no procedure," or resorting to the nondirective "It's largely up to you," we could give a description of the way we conduct therapy, perhaps adding what our main rationales are. However, while this is something we will want to do, it won't always be feasible to do it right away. Our patient might have pressing things on his mind and be in the wrong frame of mind for a formal discussion. He might have strong feelings about starting therapy. He might be apprehensive and anxious, excited and relieved; he might have doubts, misgivings, and conflicts, and a need to express them. If that's the case, we might prudently assume that he wasn't in a good position to listen to a didactic description. No matter how sensitively given, it might be untimely.

And for those reasons—and under the "average-expectable" circumstances for our "average-expectable" patient—a succinct and relatively informal instruction is likely to be our best option for a starter. We can offer a simple formulation that conveys the essential feature of our therapy's format and provides him with the widest and most feasible latitude to begin the way he wants and deems appropriate. I call it an instruction— The Basic Instruction—to avoid any implication that it isn't a directive. But it is minimally directive. It informs more than instructs, and in my experience it provides an adequate preliminary orientation without striking too dissonant a chord. Here's how it's worded:

You can talk about the things you want to talk about. It's up to you. I will listen and try to understand. When I have something useful to say, I will say it.

Reader: Some patients might hear a hint of asperity in "When I have something to say I will say it."

Author: Patients can and do have many sorts of reaction to any or all parts of the Basic Instruction, and we should be listening carefully for them. Later I'll be examining some typical responses in detail. For the moment, though, I'd like to focus on the instruction itself—what it says and doesn't say.

Reader: It seems like your basic psychoanalytic approach.

Author: With significant modifications. Note that the Basic Instruction doesn't direct the patient to say what is on his mind, it doesn't ask him to share his thoughts or express his feelings and neither does it invite him to speak about himself. He can do any, all, or none of these things—"It's up to you." Neither does it say "I want you to" or "You should"; it says "You can," which means "If you choose to."

Reader: Do we have to speak the lines verbatim? Would "You can tell me the things you want to tell me," for example, make a significant difference?

Author: Not necessarily. Whenever I offer a script in these pages—and I'll do it as often as possible—I mean only to exemplify concretely, nothing more. It's the rare message, after all, that is fully conveyed by words alone; context always makes a significant difference. What counts is the core message and its being communicated with as few unintended implications and unwanted connotations as possible. And the Basic Instruction's core message is that the patient is free to decide for himself.

Reader: No mention is made of self-inquiry—how come?

Author: Because we want him to feel free to do it or not. Of course, if he knows that traditional psychotherapy is a place for self-inquiry, making no mention of it won't matter. But the Basic Instruction deliberately avoids defining it as a task.

Reader: But isn't the instruction open to a variety of interpretations when our patient is naive about therapy?

Author: Yes, and that's fine. Those interpretations, as they emerge, will play important parts in the therapeutic process. The same is no less true for a sophisticated patient, who might construe the Basic Instruction as no different from psychoanalysis's "fundamental rule." The fact remains, however, that we've made no mention of self-inquiry. I regard this careful avoidance of defining the therapeutic process as an especially important feature of the Basic Instruction. We especially do not want to be setting the patient a task, which we'd inevitably seem to do if we said that self-inquiry was the point of psychotherapy. Let self-inquiry evolve as the therapy develops; let the patient discover how therapeutic it can be, and thereby take it on as a task for himself.

Reader: That's a pretty ideal state of affairs, isn't it? And doesn't it overlook the active role we play in promoting the therapeutic process?

Author: So I won't lay any more stress on it here. What I mean to emphasize is this: by virtue of the fact that the Basic Instruction's task requirements are minimal, we define ourselves as those who set no task—limits yes, flexible boundaries too, but nothing that qualifies as a task. And even if it merits being called a task, the task set by the Basic Instruction has the important characteristic of being incapable of evaluation. It obviously has that characteristic for us, the ones who set it. What can it mean, from our vantage point, to succeed at it or fail? Since the requirement is to say whatever he chooses, we cannot charge a patient with not fulfilling the Basic Instruction if he doesn't say what he "wants to" but instead, for instance, what he feels he "should" or "has to." We can construe "want" in its broadest sense—and we need to, because it reduces the Basic Instruction's task requirements to a practical minimum.

Reader: You mean that even when, session after session, week after week, the patient brings in nothing but trivial anecdotes or dull details of his work, we have no right to object?

Author: To object? Not at all. To interpret, perhaps, but probably more sparingly than many analysts would—and never from the perspective, implied or explicit, that by talking about those things in those ways the patient has violated the therapeutic contract. Again, we'll take this up in some detail later on, and I discuss it explicitly in a Dialogue on Resistance and Neutrality at the end of the book.

Reader: What about when the patient is silent? Isn't that a violation of the Basic Instruction?

Author: Strictly speaking, no.

Reader: But in practice? It isn't easy to imagine psychotherapy proceeding effectively in the face of utter silence.

Author: Yet, short of silences that are "utter" or excessive—and that's for our clinical judgment to determine—the Basic Instruction also allows for the decision not to tell and to be silent. Silence, however, is a complicated issue for us; I am reluctant to discuss it here and now. I'd rather rest with the assertion that when he falls silent our patient isn't failing at anything—not from our vantage point, he isn't.

Reader: But of course that might not be true from his. In fact, to the extent that he has construed the Basic Instruction as setting him the "task" of deciding what he wants to talk about, he might well take his own silence as a sign of failure.

Author: That's true. But not only is this something on which we can work together, the work itself can become integral to therapy in ways that benefit him vitally. This, too, I will be writing about later. Now I want to introduce you to the basic and fundamentally important distinction between—

Business and Narrative

When the patient said *"What's the procedure here?"* our response, the Basic Instruction, was predicated on the assumption that it was a "business" question. That's why we responded the way we did, no differently than if he had said "*What is your fee?*" and then went ahead to inquire about our policy in regard to billing, payment, the filling out of insurance forms, and the like. We might have inquired into his financial resources and billing preferences; we might have asked whether his insurance required us to write a report on his psychological condition; but we deal with these matters in a "businesslike" way. And what this means, chiefly, is that we don't interpret or explain. We proceed on the assumption that such issues, especially when they arise early, are not the stuff of therapy. They may be vital to the therapy's integrity, but they aren't integral to the vital work of therapy—not at this point, in any case.

But if he said "*Why am I feeling so tense and nervous sitting here?*" we would respond quite differently. This may no longer be a question of *business,* it may count as *narrative,* and it might indeed count towards the vital work of therapy. Accordingly, we wouldn't deem it necessary to "deal with" this question in a direct and businesslike way; we might choose to deal with it the same way we intended to deal with his recounting of his life history, his description of his problems, and the like. This means we might respond with silence or interpretations; what we should not do is respond with any questions of our own, for we don't want to initiate an interview. And that, in turn, is because we are going to draw a sharp distinction between what I've chosen to call *business* and *narrative.*

Business refers to matters such as fees and schedules, of course, but I broaden the category so that it encompasses a wide range of practical issues, and I keep the boundaries as elastic as possible so that they can be stretched to conform to all working requirements that pertain to us, in particular, and to our particular patient. Business, in my opinion, must include everything that we and he regard as relevant to the necessary conditions and structural format of the therapy. If we believe that more than one session a week is a necessary condition, that clearly counts as business; but it can also count as business if we have difficulty hearing him because he speaks too softly, or we find it hard to listen to him because he chooses to pace the floor. Similarly, if the patient believes that more than three sessions a week will be be impractical for him, it can count as business; but so can his conviction that a fifty-minute session may not be long enough, or that we must refrain from smoking. And if he is distracted by the way we dress, or tells us that a picture hanging on the wall disturbs him, we can—repeat, *can*—choose to construe the matter purely as business. For I believe the potential value of a broad and flexible definition of business is so great as to justify the technical guideline "When in doubt, count it as business." This is especially important if we are working within the framework of a therapy as nondirective as ours. Whenever we work with a business matter, we must try to be as direct as possible.

Reader: Don't business and narrative often blend, so that one becomes incorporated with the other? What do we do then?

Author: Judge which has priority, and treat it accordingly. Within the framework of our guideline, we should be inclined to lean towards business—especially when therapy is in its early stages. Moreover, treating an issue as business often prevents it from burgeoning into narrative.

Reader: But doesn't that do exactly what we don't want to do, quash significant material?

Author: In the short run, it may. If that doesn't positively drive the patient out of therapy, however—and handled properly, it shouldn't—the material will resurface. To the extent that there is a trade-off, I believe it's more useful to have questions about the frame of the therapy, so to speak, settled clearly and relatively quickly than to attempt to deal exhaustively with all the responses the patient might be having to the prospect of doing therapy in this specific way.

Reader: The assumption being that we'll be hearing plenty about that when the therapy gets under way?

Author: Yes. And there's another consideration; switching from the business mode to what I'm calling the narrative mode can be done in a straightforward fashion, but moving from narrative to business is more problematic, as will become clearer in the next two chapters.

Reader: But what is our rationale for reliably distinguishing the modes at all?

Author: Our chief rationale is based on the distinction between the interpretive mode and the interviewing mode. So long as we face an issue that belongs to business, we cannot be reluctant to investigate it, and interviewing will often be the only way. This will entail, at the very least, our asking direct questions, which is dissonant with our otherwise nondirective stance, but what other choice do we have? We can make it clear to our patient that only when such practical issues arise will we ask him such questions. We can emphasize that our need to have such answers is restricted to matters like these; and we can—and should—respond to his answers and statements as forthrightly as possible. Being direct and being directive can be quite sharply distinguished. It is one thing to tell a patient directly that we need a piece of information or some time to think about a request he's made, it's another to deflect him, or buy the time, with counterquestions and interpretations.

Reader: Yet it seems to me there are serious technical problems associated with sustaining the distinction between business and narrative.

Author: We'll meet them in Chapters 2 and 3. But in the meantime I want to emphasize that the viability of a dynamic form of psychotherapy, especially when it is framed in a nondirective format, depends greatly on the following guideline: When the material is narrative we must eschew the interviewing mode, and when it is business we must eschew the interpretive mode. Our basic rationale centers on the concept of neutrality and the fact that matters of business cannot always be approached with the same degree of neutrality we can usually apply to matters of narrative. Personal preferences and requirements inevitably enter into it—for example fees, or the question of smoking—and to maintain neutrality about them strains us and our patient's credulity in unnecessary ways. As we want to maximize our neutrality and keep it from becoming ambiguous, we should restrict it to matters that are unequivocally narrative—and not mix narrative with business.

Reader: You've raised the hoary problem of neutrality. I trust you're planning to persuade me that not only is it desirable but it's possible.

Author: Repeatedly, but hopefully not ad nauseam. Right now I will limit myself to one claim. My clinical experience has persuaded me that neutrality is viable and reasonable only when it is confined to the patient's narrative—or to put it another way, when I can protect it by limiting it to that domain. The best way to achieve this goal is to broaden the definition of business and then prevent its distinctiveness from becoming blurred.

Reader: There's nothing in the Basic Instruction about neutrality, I notice. How do we communicate to the patient our intent to be neutral?

Author: In the first instance, by treating the issue of neutrality itself as business. In other words, we have to clarify the matter for him and explain it fully if necessary, because whether he fully accepts it, much less believes it, or no, he has to know that we are trying to be neutral in respect to the content of his narrative.

Reader: And how do we go about convincing him of that?

Neutrality with Respect to Content

Author: When he first hears it, the patient might react to the Basic Instruction with incredulity, wondering whether there weren't certain appropriate topics for starting therapy. Even after he hears our reply—"I would prefer you told me the things you want to tell me"—it's easy to imagine him perplexed, having taken it for granted that a therapist would suggest topics and ask questions. We could now explain our nondirective position and tell him that we intend to work without preconceived ideas about what would be best for him to talk about during the sessions.

Reader: But even if he accepts the explanation, can we assume the matter is settled? Let's say that he proceeds to speak about something he apparently "wants to" speak about, either because he planned the topic beforehand or because he judges it appropriate for therapy. That doesn't mean he necessarily believes that we are truly neutral with respect to content, or even that we should be.

Author: That's right. To assume that he's grasped the import of the nondirective format will most likely turn out to have been mistaken. The more prudent assumption is that he believes he will be given direction and guidance at certain times and in certain ways. Typically, this belief surfaces in the form of an avowed expectation during the later sessions, especially when he's finished telling his problems and recounting his life history. But it might emerge right away in one form or another, as soon as the Basic Instruction is given.

Reader: I'll play the role of patient. *"Won't you at least tell me what I should want to talk about? Surely it has to make a difference what I talk about!"*

Author: That's what I had in mind. Please go on.

Reader: *"Do you mean to say you actually don't care what I talk about, whether I decide to talk about 'useful' things or not? Look here, surely it's going to make a difference to my well-being what I talk about!"*

Author: And you might end with an outraged—

Reader: *"If I want to waste my time here, I'm perfectly free to? Oh, fine! What's it to you, after all; you get paid whether my talk is useful or not."*

Author: Your challenges should be anticipated. They present us with complex and subtle technical problems. The Basic Instruction Studies were composed to help us solve and practice them.

Reader: But you won't leave me hanging like this! *"Look, do you really mean it when you say you have no expectations with respect to what I talk about and no preconceptions about what would be most beneficial? What if I choose to talk about the weather or deliver a disquisition on species counterpoint, won't you regard such topics as irrelevant? Aren't you going to intervene with a remark implying that such talk is not useful? Don't you have some basis for believing that certain topics are likely to be more germane than others, more beneficial? And if so, isn't it duplicitous, if not also unethical, to keep those convictions to yourself?"*

Author: Though you speak as patient to therapist, I'll reply as Author to Reader. Every therapist has convictions about the differential fruitfulness of topics, commonly called "material." Based on an amalgam of practical experience and clinical theory, those convictions are likely to encompass a variety and range of topics. We may believe, for instance, that our patients stand to benefit from an exploration of their childhood, of their development; we may believe that a balance is best struck between the past and the present, between the intrapsychic and the interpersonal, between the affective and the cognitive; we may believe that night dreams and daydreams are valuable for uncovering conflicts and memories. That list can easily be extended. My point is this: our form of psychotherapy doesn't require us to abandon those convictions. The Basic Instruction doesn't even imply that we foreswore having them. Just because we want our patients to choose their own topics doesn't mean we have no preconceptions.

What our therapy *does* require of us in respect to such convictions is a kind of holding them in abeyance; we have to keep them from diminishing or diluting our fundamental non-directiveness. This means, at the very least, that we don't inform our patient about them. But more than that, we try our best to keep them from influencing his choice of topics in such a way as to maximize the occurrence of the types of material we believe are likely to be the most beneficial, and that is no simple achievement. In fact, because the ways in which we can shape his behavior and steer his narrative are so manifold and subtle, and because it is altogether unrealistic to expect that our interpretations won't reflect a selective bias, and also because certain of them—interpretations of defense and resistance, for instance—will necessarily imply that certain topics are more germane to therapy than others, the achievement can only be regarded as an ideal goal: worth striving for but impossible to attain.

This is a critical question for our form of psychotherapy, perhaps its key problem or dilemma. Can we effectively supervise the therapeutic process from a position of neutrality? Can we participate effectively in the work of therapy without at the same time being directive? My overriding conviction is that the question can adequately be answered at the level of practice, the level of form and technique; it doesn't need a theoretical resolution. There's no denying that perfect neutrality is a perfect theoretical fiction—and even if it weren't we couldn't achieve it without severely constraining our work. But in practice, I believe it is altogether possible to achieve a level of neutrality that is significant and effective. Moreover, there are steps we can take against reinforcement effects, when they assume significant proportions.

At the very least, as I mentioned, we don't tell the patient what our convictions are. At the very most, we face a conflict of interests. On the one side stands our conviction about the differential fruitfulness of topics, on the other, our conviction about the profound ramifications of allowing him to talk about what he wants to. We can, of course, resolve that conflict by making a choice, but we can attenuate the choice by construing the two convictions not as being in conflict but as nested within a larger coherent conviction: namely, that in order to yield its beneficial results, a topic must freely be chosen—the choice must not be made under the aegis of an externally imposed task. And to support that larger conviction, we accept this working hypothesis: whether it is the weather or his childhood, species counterpoint or his marriage, whatever topic a patient chooses to talk about will reflect something authentic, meaningful, and salient for him; the choice will prove relevant in the short run, if not also valid in the long run. Therefore not only will it serve the therapeutic process, but he also stands to benefit from understanding it.

Reader: If I understand you, we construe the choice of topic as reflecting a wish and intention, perhaps a hierarchically ordered set of wishes and intentions. So when he speaks about the weather or when he speaks about his childhood we do the same thing: try to comprehend the choice and discover its meaning. But speaking about the weather might reflect a wish to test us, if not also an intention to sabotage the therapy. Is that no different from telling us about his childhood?

Author: In respect to the way we work with narrative: yes. Whatever the wish, whatever the intention and expectation, we listen in order to understand; and when we think we've understood—and judge it useful to share that understanding with him—we offer an interpretation.

Reader: Which raises two key questions: what do we mean by *useful?* and, what do we mean by an *interpretation?*

Author: Let me defer the second question until the next chapter. My answer to the first question is given and examined at many places in the book, but for the purposes of this discussion I want to point out that we might judge it useful to offer the patient an interpretation if the issue at hand is resistance, or if we deem it prudent to conceptualize the issue as a form of defense directed against therapy. Accordingly, insofar as they count as resistance and satisfy that criterion of "useful," our patient's wish to test us and his intention to sabotage therapy can be the basis for our interpretation.

Reader: And you're going to tell me that the same is true for his wish to provide us with historical data and his intention to expedite the therapy, because they, too, can be construed as resistance?

Author: Short-circuiting the therapy can be a form of sabotage, yes. To be sure, the two "resistances" differ in certain important respects—their blatancy, for one—and that makes an important practical difference for the ways we can articulate them and help the patient understand their purposes. But otherwise it needn't make any difference. Only for the sake of this argument can we assume that his reason for beginning with his childhood history embodies a significant resistance. It might instead be based on a desire for a classical psychoanalysis and he had reason to believe it was the appropriate way to begin. The same applies to free-associating, recounting dreams, and the like. I don't want you to think I would challenge such decisions and reasons; I would want only to understand them.

Reader: And if they weren't "good" reasons—based on misinformation, for instance?—

Author: —I'd choose to direct an interpretation at them only if I also had reason to believe they were subserving a resistance. In other words, our own convictions about the differential fruitfulness of topics must be held in abeyance until the therapy itself is in jeopardy.

Reader: Assuming we were dealing with forms of resistance, doesn't it then follow that we might even welcome their blatant expression, inasmuch as such an expression gives an early opportunity to clarify the format and orientation of our method? After all, if his resistance was manifested by *good patient* behavior, such as recounting the details of his childhood, we might face a greater problem interpreting it to him in a plausible way.

Author: And that's what I had in mind for the claim that the difference can be largely practical, or technical; it may involve considerations of timing and tact, nothing more.

Reader: Nothing more! Technique may not be everything, but you promised me that it was a great deal.

Author: And the studies, I hope, will fulfill that promise.

Reader: All right, then let's see if I can sum things up so we can get on with them. Our form of therapy requires of us a full

faith in the therapeutic efficacy of a patient's choosing freely
what he will talk about during the sessions. This means we
have to work both from the surface of his consciousness and
from the matrix of his decisional and volitional processes. Our
chief problems, then, are how to vouchsafe those processes,
how to safeguard the patient's freedom and autonomy, and how
to establish and promote the therapeutic process. And these are
problems that can be solved only by exact technique.

Author: Thank you. Let's now practice the Basic Instruction Studies.

2

THE BASIC INSTRUCTION

Instructions for the Basic Instruction Studies

For these studies you are to assume that this was the beginning of a course of psychotherapy, the first session perhaps. Your task is to continue the dialogue between the therapist (T) and patient (P) by composing several more exchanges. Your continuation should exemplify your understanding of the issue and the optimal way of dealing with it. The studies are independent: each one is of a different patient. You can assume that schedule and fee arrangements have already been made.

Study 1
But You're the Therapist!

T1: You can talk about the things you want to talk about. It's up to you. I will listen and try to understand. When I have something useful to say I will say it (The Basic Instruction).

P1: *You mean it's altogether up to me to decide what I should talk about here?*

T2: Yes.

P2: *And it doesn't matter what I talk about?*
T3: What matters is what you want to talk about.
P3: *But you're the therapist, surely you must know what would be most useful for me to talk about!*
T4: ____

What is the best and most "useful" T4? Should we stay with the Basic Instruction by reiterating and perhaps amplifying it, or should we address the patient's challenging incredulity and thereby acknowledge a transition to the narrative mode? Practitioners would probably regard the latter as our better option. The patient seems to have understood the Basic Instruction; his questions convey skepticism and disbelief more than puzzlement. Moreover, when we hear his skepticism and disbelief (and perhaps overtones of mockery in his *"But you're the therapist"*), we are keeping our promise to listen and understand him.

When therapy is so young, however, the interpretative mode carries an especially heavy burden. Over and above their content, interpretations show the patient how we work, defining the way we use them and the role they play in the therapy. If it's an interpretation, T4 will be the first one we've made, and we don't want to start off on the wrong foot. All of our early ones need to be formulated with special care. In the context of this study, where the patient is arguing with us, an interpretation runs several kinds of risk. It might be taken as contentious or defensive; instead of hearing it as our attempt to understand him, he will hear it as an attempt to defuse his challenge and win the argument. Our more prudent course, then, is to stay with the Basic Instruction—for another exchange or two, at least—and use the opportunity to amplify it. That's what my students tend to do.

But that, too, has to be done carefully. We want to amplify rather than modify; we certainly don't want to distort. And the Basic Instruction lends itself to a variety of modifications in letter and spirit, some of which amount to significant distortions. Consider, for example, the following T4 that a student suggests: "I will be able to say more useful things when you talk about what you want to talk about." It's a subtle modification but a significant one. It implies that our nondirectiveness serves our needs, not the patient's, in that its purpose is to understand him. Not only isn't it altogether true, but he would probably

argue that this purpose could better be satisfied by his answering our leading-questions and speaking about topics we
recommend.

Adding the qualifier *important,* which many students do, is
an appealing modification of the Basic Instruction. Unfortunately, it's a distortion that isn't even subtle; it does nothing
less than inject a fresh task requirement—namely, to say
important and / or *meaningful* things. Not only does this add
a strong directive to the Basic Instruction, it undercuts its basic
intent. Consider the following continuation from this angle:

T4: No, I don't know what you think about, what's
important to you; those are the things that are useful.

P4: *But shouldn't I talk about my parents, or my
dreams, or sex?*

T5: Are you assuming that I think it's important for you
to talk about those things?

P5: *Yes. Aren't they the kinds of things that will help
you understand me?*

T6: I don't think your parents or your dreams or your sex
life are necessarily important; they may or may not
be. I hope to come to understand you by your
choosing to talk about those aspects of your experience that you deem important.

Notice how the question "Important in what way?" remains
hanging, so that the patient is likely to fall back on his original
query—this time in the form of *"How should I know what's
important?"* And notice the radical difference between T6 and
the Basic Instruction.

If I chose not to address the patient's incredulity and decided
instead to elaborate on the Basic Instruction itself, I would try
for a continuation that gave me the opportunity to emphasize
that I wanted to give him no advice. A student does it this way:

T4: Anything you decide to talk about will be useful.

P4: *But can't you advise me as to what is most relevant?*

T5: I intend to give you no advice or direction as to what
to do or say either here in therapy or outside of it. I
can appreciate the awkward position this places you
in.

That's fine—except "Yes, but I'd prefer not to," should preface the notification at T5, and the closing remark is quite unnecessary. Although it was apparently intended to be supportive, that remark can too easily be taken as an attempt to defuse the patient's challenge. (And he might even resent being told he was in an "awkward position.") Instead I would try to move toward the challenge by inquiring into his "*most relevant*," as follows:

T5: Yes, but I'd prefer not to, because I intend to give you no advice or direction as to what to do or say either here in therapy or outside of it. I'm not sure, however, that I understand what you meant by "most relevant."

P5: *Well, you said that anything I talked about would be useful, but I can't help believing that there are certain things that will be more useful than others.*

T6: I see. Your thought is that everything cannot be equally useful.

P6: *Exactly. That makes no sense to me.*

Since it made sense to me, and that can be taken for granted, I don't have to respond. I can wait and see how the patient resolves the problem. Will he continue his challenge? In what form? Or will he acquiesce to my nondirective stance?—and in what form will he do that? In any event, I haven't done anything to defuse his challenging incredulity. The main shortcoming of the following continuation is that after articulating the challenge, the student doesn't let us stay with it when the patient bristles at our interpretation:

T4: I believe it would be most useful for you to talk about what you want to.

P4: *You've said that already. Can't you give me an idea of what to talk about?*

T5: It seems you're trying to get me to tell you what to do.

P5: *What do you mean "get"? All I'm saying is that you have more experience in this sort of thing.*

T6: Perhaps you are testing me in a way. You want, in other words, to see if I will really refrain from directing and advising you.

P6: *Look, is this going to be a battle of wills? Are you going to sit there resting on your principles or are you going to try to help me?*

T7: I believe I can be of most help to you by not giving you advice and direction, but rather by listening and trying to understand.

Instead of retreating to the Basic Instruction, I would try for a tactful remark that articulated his challenge and didn't deflect attention from his incredulity. T5 has moved into the realm of narrative, after all, so I would respond to *P6* this way: "I take it you believe that my method will not be helpful to you." (A student offers this variation: "You're finding it hard to believe that I am not being willful and that I truly believe this method will be helpful to you.") However, I would have tried to avoid the struggle in the first place by not offering that confronting interpretation at T5; my response would simply be "Yes, but I'd prefer not to."

The study invites a confronting approach, which in my opinion should be turned down. Confronting interpretations can be useful, and they may occasionally be necessary, but they run so many risks in respect to the therapeutic process and our role definition as therapists that they have to be used with great circumspection. Moreover, this early in therapy they should rarely be attempted. Consider the following example, and notice the element of censure in it:

You seem rather persistent. And since I've already said that it isn't appropriate to the therapy to give you directions, perhaps you want to find out if I mean what I say, or if you can get me to change my mind.

How is our patient supposed to respond? Isn't he likely to insist that he wasn't being "persistent," merely incredulous? And will he not feel misunderstood, if not also put down? Even if he accepted the interpretation as correct, he might feel embattled and defensive, and something of an argument could ensue. As it does in this continuation:

T4: But I have just met you for the first time today. How would I know what's useful for you to talk about?

P4: *Do you mean to say you have no theory that you go by, no idea of how therapy should begin?*

T5: I'm not saying that. All I ask is that you understand the instructions I gave you earlier.

P5: *Which tells me nothing.*

T6: Which tells you everything you need to know, as I see it.

It's hard to imagine how the patient will continue; he appears to be backed into a corner. The next example gives a vivid illustration of the problem. The student comes on very strongly, with remarks that are very confronting, and with the result that we have the last word, while our patient is apparently left speechless.

T4: You seem to be contradicting yourself. You said, did you not, that I'm the therapist and I would know what would be most useful for you talk about?

P5: *Yes, that's what I said.*

T5: And yet when I told you my only instruction was for you to talk about the things you want to talk about, you disregarded it. On the one hand you say that I am the expert and that you will do what I say; on the other hand, when I say something you disregard it.

P6: *I heard your instruction. I just thought it would go more smoothly if you told me which things might be more important to talk about.*

T6: Then you didn't hear the instruction, or you didn't believe I would stick to it. It's up to you what you talk about. I think, though, that you feel two ways about me, as your contradiction indicates. You feel I'm the healer who knows what's best for his patient; you also feel that I may not be so expert, because you don't take instruction—my "medicine"—too seriously.

No matter how warmly it was spoken, T6 is an unnecessary attack and should be replaced with silence or "In my experience what's important to talk about is what you want to talk about." The point, after all, has been made and the patient has not said he disagreed with it. He is no longer leveling the challenge he made at *P5*. He is saying, in effect, that he used to think it might be better the other way. Such features of communication are important; we must listen carefully to our patient's words and not disregard their meanings, most especially their surface meanings. *P6* can also be construed as an apology and acknowledged as such: "You are apologizing, I take it; you felt my remark was a challenge."

To be sure, it isn't uncommon at any stage of therapy for interpretations of any kind, even fully empathic and tactful ones, to be taken as criticisms and for the patient to react to them as if he'd been judged. Those unintended and unwanted side effects cannot entirely be avoided. Although there are steps we can take to attenuate them, we can also take pains to avoid interpretations that carry too strong an implication of evaluation—and those that confront and diagnose the patient are especially prone to these implications. Therefore, I would "play" the study as follows:

T4: I gather you believe it's going to matter what you choose to talk about here, and that I should know what you need to choose, because I've had experience with therapy.

P4 *Yes. What else can I believe?*

T5: Then let me take it a step further. Perhaps you are thinking that I do know what things you should talk about, only I refuse to tell you what they are. And this is making you feel outraged—perhaps because you feel it's unfair of me.

P5: *Of course! What the hell else am I supposed to feel?*

T6: I didn't mean to imply you had no reason to feel outraged. And neither did I mean to say you shouldn't believe that I knew what you should choose to talk about. The main reason I'm pointing out what it is you think and feel is because I am trying to understand your thoughts and feelings: that is one of the main things I will be doing in therapy.

P6: *Okay, I get it. But I still think you're playing games with me.*

And *P6* will continue however it has to, but the therapy may be off to a good enough start.

Study 2
But What Good Is That?

T1: You can talk about the things you want to talk about.
It's up to you. I will listen and try to understand.
When I have something useful to say, I will say it
(The Basic Instruction).

P1: *You mean it's altogether up to me to decide what I
should talk about here?*

T2: Yes.

P2: *And it doesn't matter what I talk about?*

T3: What matters is that it's what you want to talk about.

P3: *But what good will that do me? I mean, if I just talk
and talk—what good is that?*

T4: _____

Until *P3*, where the challenge is leveled more squarely at our
method, this study is identical with Study 1. In the context of
P3's challenge, however, a reiteration and amplification of the
Basic Instruction is not responsive. Students do it anyhow. But
if they preface their reiteration with an empathic interpretation—such as "I gather you are puzzled about what will go on
here"—that, it seems to me, is responsive enough. Compare it,
however, with this variation: "I can appreciate that you are
puzzled about what will go on here." The difference is small, yet
it could be significant, because this formulation casts the
interpretation in a supportive frame, and a gesture like that,
although it aims to be "understanding," can too easily backfire.
The message usually comes down to "What you are now
experiencing is altogether expectable / natural / normal / ratio-
nal, so please don't worry about it." The patient might well
resent the reassurance. And the message is significantly different from the one we hope to convey when we make empathic
interpretations. It implicates a quite different meaning of "understanding." (I will discuss this issue soon.)

P3 can also be taken as an expression of doubt—will a
therapy that allows him to *"just talk"* do him any good? A
student addresses the point directly: "I guess it's difficult to see
how just talking will do any good." Another does it indirectly
but probably as effectively: "I believe you are asking me what
part I will take in the therapy." My inclination would be to

emphasize that he was challenging this type of therapy, experiencing a sense of disbelief—perhaps even of outrage—and I'd add:

> Leaving it entirely up to you what you talk about, how can that be an effective way of doing therapy? That's your question, I take it.

If he simply agreed in a way that continued to press the question, I'd have the recourse of falling back on my professional experience. Of course it can be taken for granted that I wouldn't be using a method I didn't believe in, and if that wasn't obvious to the patient, it might mean that something more was afoot. What might emerge, however, is either that he cannot accept the validity of the method in general or he wants to question its suitability for him. The latter would give me the opportunity of introducing the idea of a trial period, which means defining the beginning sessions as an opportunity for him to judge the therapy's validity and suitability. And students do suggest a trial period at T4. For example:

> I appreciate that it's hard for you to see how this may be helpful before you've tried it out. Why don't we consider our first week or two of sessions as a kind of trial period, and at the end of that time perhaps you will have more of an idea whether you think this way of working together can be helpful to you.

Although they occasionally raise more problems than they solve, trial periods are usually useful and sometimes necessary. Expecting patients to commit themselves to an unfamiliar form of therapy, as well as to a therapist whom they know only by credentials and perhaps recommendation, is expecting a great deal. A trial period can go quite far in helping them decide whether to make the commitment.

If it's to be a reasonably brief one, the trial period itself might be insufficient to establish the method's therapeutic usefulness. But it may be sufficient time in which to determine whether we and the patient understand each other, and it can be useful if we spoke often enough and offered interpretations whose main purpose was to show him the way we work, the way we empathize, articulate, and explain. We might also try for some interpretations that he is likely to find interesting and evocative.

Two further points: (1) routinely suggesting a trial period isn't necessary, for it's generally better to wait until there's good reason to believe the patient has the need for it, when the trial period is the solution to an actual problem or question; (2) establishing clearly when the trial period is over and when the commitment to therapy is made can be important, for otherwise the beginning of therapy might remain ambiguous and unrepresentative.

The following continuation calls for a T6 suggesting a trial period:

T4: All the good in the world.

P5: *What the hell do you mean, "All the good in the world"?*

T5: I believe your therapy will be most useful to you if you talk about anything you want.

P6: *But I can talk to my friends, and it doesn't cost me money.*

T6: I already gave you the basic instruction for it; that is how I do therapy.

Why such a curt and nonresponsive T6? Where does it leave our patient? Suggesting a trial period might not have been altogether responsive but it could prevent an impasse.

If, on the other hand, I judged that saying "I take it, then, that you have reason to believe that therapy for you will require being told what to talk about," was more responsive, and the patient had concurred, then I would have to decide whether or not to treat the matter as business—in other words, no differently than if he had asked me to reduce his fee. That, of course, would mean I was going to give serious consideration to making the necessary accomodation. But it should go without having to be said that I was prepared to make feasible and judicious modifications in my procedure, and if my patient needed to be told what to talk about, if that was a condition for his continuing in therapy with me, then I might have no other good option than to go ahead and do it. (Though for our patient in the above example it's too late for that because the treatment would no longer be "therapy" in my eyes.)

Another option for a continuation to Study 2 is a clarification question. Is it, after all, clear, or clear enough, what the patient has in mind? Students think it isn't, and their T4 consists of questioning the meaning of his *just talk and talk.*" That's a good idea because it might elicit the admission, or recognition, that he meant it in a mocking way, and might lead to a useful exploration of his feelings about therapy. But the question "What do you mean?" must be used judiciously; excessive and indiscriminate use of it can transform the session into an interview and define us as troubleshooters, if not also as one who doesn't comprehend.

Nevertheless, I draw a sharp distinction between questions that ask for information and questions that ask for meaning. The latter, for one thing, are not directives to explore, they are directives to explicate—"Tell me what you meant to say (say it another way)." For another, they subserve our intention to comprehend what our patient is telling us—"Because I'm not sure I understand." Thus, they are business questions, not narrative questions, insofar as they are grounded in the Basic Instruction rather than the patient's narrative. To avoid duplicity—namely, the use of the clarification question as an indirect directive to explore or expand—it is necessary that we truly not have understood, if not entirely then at least in the sense that his utterance was open to several constructions, and we were not sure which one he intended. In fact, we can often ask the question with an interpretation that speculates on the meaning—"I gather that what you meant is—" However, calling such remarks "interpretations" may provoke a reader to ask—

Reader: Why would you call such bland remarks "interpretations"?

A Definition of Interpretation

Author: Calling them "interpretations" implies a broad definition of the term, namely, any attempt on our part to articulate a patient's thoughts, wishes, intentions, and feelings.

I advocate that broad definition because I believe we can usefully count as an interpretation every remark that addresses what is on his mind.

Reader: Even if it doesn't seek to explain why it's on his mind? And even if there was no reason to believe it was opaque or hidden, obscure or disguised, preconscious or unconscious? How can that be *useful?*

Author: I haven't said that every interpretation will serve the fundamental purpose of promoting active and free self-inquiry in an equivalent way; content and form, as well as context, count substantially. But the interpretive mode defines us as someone who intends to understand, and it does it in a basically different way than the interviewing mode. Most importantly, it does it in a way that has at least the potential of becoming relatively free from significant directive properties.

Reader: Wait a minute! Doesn't an interpretation imply the directive "Pay attention to this!"?

Author: Yes, it clearly does. But if the interpretation had the same focus of attention as the patient's deliberations had— if it addressed his actual thoughts, intentions, or feelings—then the directive to pay attention becomes inconsequential.

Reader: But surely an interpretation can be more than a fully empathic articulation. Doesn't it raise new issues and fresh considerations, draw novel connections, and suggest different ways to understand? Can't it try to deepen and broaden the scope of his attention?

Author: Insofar as it went beyond addressing what was on his mind, or what formed part of his phenomenal experience, and especially insofar as it offered an explanation, the directive to pay attention and take into consideration can indeed assume significant proportions. Whether it does or doesn't depends largely, however, on its timing. That is the subject of Chapter 5, and I won't discuss it here beyond making these two claims: an interpretation of any kind can be timed in a way to keep its attention-deflecting properties at a minimum, if not at a point of relative insignificance; if and when our basic format has carefully and patiently been established over time, our patient can be substantially free to "ignore" an interpretation. To be sure, a well-timed question needn't necessarily deflect. But a true question—namely, one that asks for new information—is more likely than an interpretation to command, if not also deflect, attention, and rarely can it be ignored the way an interpretation can. A direct question virtually demands a direct response.

Reader: At the very least, however, an interpretation implies the question "Is this true?"

Author: Yes. In fact, to proffer it in a questioning voice— "What do you think of the possibility that . . . ?" is a technique I advocate in Chapter 4 where we examine different types of interpretation, and I explain the distinction between those I call "empathic" and "diagnostic." What I want to emphasize here is that if the interpretation resonated with his self-inquiry, the question "Is this true?" doesn't necessarily deflect the patient's attention. And insofar as it did ask a question, no directive other than "Correct me if I am wrong," need be implied. "Am I understanding you correctly?" is our basic question—and we can make it clear.

Reader: But we can do the same for direct questions: make it clear that our only reason for asking was to understand the patient. Moreover, isn't it advantageous insofar as the query avoid speculating and thereby the possibility of error?

Author: I don't see anything wrong with speculating, if it's done judiciously; and neither do I believe that making an "error" is so terrible. Moreover, the act of speculation defines us in a distinctive way; it defines us less as the one who *does* understand than the one who *seeks* to understand. More importantly, perhaps, it defines us as the one who understands *sometimes* and *some things,* not someone who understands *everything.*

To be sure, these differences can be quite subtle, but I believe they can also be quite significant. I think it's fair to claim that the interviewing mode, especially when it asks why-questions— "What are, were, or will be your reasons for . . . ?—can imply that we are steadily wondering why, that we are bent on baring our patient's purposes and reasons, and we thereby define ourselves as someone who strives to discover the motivational bases of his behavior and experience.

The interpretive mode, in contrast, needn't imply that kind of ubiquitous interest. We define ourselves as someone who sometimes has a hunch about why and who seeks to confirm those hunches when he or she believes it will be useful to share them with him. We won't be asking out of a special interest in motivation per se; only when we have an insight about his motivation, an insight that might be useful for his efforts at self-inquiry and discovery, will we "ask the question." Last, but by no means least, is the fact that when we speculate instead of interrogate we don't put him in the position of having to respond "*I just don't know why.*"

Reader: All right, then let's return to the study.

Author: My students refrain from offering an interpretation that articulates the element of mockery in *P4*—

Reader: Excuse me for interrupting, but I am struck by . . . No, let me say this correctly. I have noted the similarity between the style of notation you are employing—*P4* and *T4*—and the notational system that is used in chess.

Author: It happens to be quite coincidental.

Reader: Again!

Author: I think so. Although my discussion of the studies has an element of "our move—his move," I do not in fact believe that the adversarial game-playing mode is appropriate for us. Chess puzzles that require both sides to cooperate at arriving at the solution might fit us better, but the game-playing element remains. My use of the notational system is purely in the service of convenience.

Reader: Okay, I get the message! You were saying that students refrained from offering an interpretation that articulated the element of mockery in *P4*—*"just talk and talk."*

Author: Either they didn't hear it or they intuitively recognized that the risks were simply too great for this interpretation, it was likely to be too confronting, and chances are, too speculative as well. If it turned out to be correct, the patient might feel caught more than understood, and if it turned out he was unaware of having poked fun, he might feel embarrassed.

Reader: But hold on! Are you being *that* inconsistent? Why is it okay to hear his challenge in Study 1 and not okay to hear his mockery in Study 2? Why in the one case will he feel understood while caught in the second?

Author: There are two grounds on which to resolve this kind of inconsistency: one is clinical judgment, the other is clinical tact. Tact, when applied to our behavior as therapists, has a number of meanings. The meaning that applies here pertains to our capacity for provoking feelings—feelings such as shame and embarrassment, for instance—that can put a patient into an awkward and uncomfortable position. If he experienced such feelings as a result of what he himself was saying and disclosing, it's one thing; it's quite another if the feelings resulted from something we said or did. And if articulating his challenge in Study 1 resulted in such feelings, then it was indeed tactless for me to have done it. My decision must have been based on the intuition, or call it a prediction, that it just wasn't going to have that result. And intuition, of course, is never infallible.

Study 3 examines the consequences of our having offered an affect interpretation, probably somewhere close to T4, and it's an interpretation that can tactlessly provoke feelings. It isn't an interpretation that I recommend. In fact, I have strong reservations about the ubiquitous "You are (were, will be) angry." Moreover, giving it this early in therapy is bound to be untimely. Still—we did it, so let's see what we can do about it.

Study 3
It's Embarrassing!

T4: I think you are feeling angry. And I think it's because you expected me to be telling you what to talk about here. Ask you questions, for instance. So, by not doing that, I have put you in an awkward position, and that makes you angry.

P4: *Yes, you're right. I always get angry when I feel embarrassed. And it is embarrassing, you know, to have to talk about anything that just comes to mind.*

T5: _____

T4 is an interpretation of our patient's reaction to the Basic Instruction, and the study asks us to listen carefully to the response. He accepted the interpretation; he translated our "awkward position" into *"embarrassment"*; and—he altered the Basic Instruction! And that's what merits our attention: the alteration. To be sure, we are certainly interested to learn that embarrassment makes him angry, and we have good reason to expect that his being embarrassed to speak his mind is going to figure importantly in therapy. But our attention should be commanded by the fact that he apparently believes he must free-associate, for it goes to the heart of our therapy's format.

What is the best way to attend to the matter? Perhaps treating it as business with this kind of T5:

I want to point out to you that you don't have to say anything that comes to mind. I said you can talk about the things you want to talk about.

But it isn't our only option and may not be the best one. We can attend to the matter with a simple interpretation that is equally direct: "I take it you believe you have to talk about anything that comes to mind." It is more open-ended, it can open up more lines of exploration; it might, for instance, lead to the following P5:

Yes, I do. I know you said I should talk about whatever I wanted to talk about. But I know myself pretty well by now—I'll end up talking about anything that just comes to mind. That's because I'm a person who has no control when it comes to talking. I'm a blabbermouth. I'm always putting my two feet into my big mouth.

Focusing attention on the alteration itself with a mild confrontation, such as "Are you aware that you've changed the instruction I gave you?" is a third option. After all, in the heat of his feelings the patient might have lost sight of that fact. Still, even if some important narrative were to ensue, it will have been evoked by us and by a remark that was likely to embarrass him even further. Confronting remarks always run the risk of provoking feelings of embarrassment, and when therapy is young the risk is especially great.

Our patient, however, was embarrassed to begin with, wasn't he? This too invites our attention since it raises two questions: why does he get angry when he is embarrassed? and, how come he was embarrassed at learning that we weren't going to tell him what to talk about? We might be tempted to look for a way that addressed these questions at the same time as we articulated the alteration of the Basic Instruction, and there are probably good and interesting ways to do this. But I wouldn't try very hard to find them. For one thing, they are likely to require formulations that are too complicated. For another, it'd be mixing business with narrative, which I believe is rarely a good idea. The line between business and narrative—again, especially when therapy is young—has to be kept clear and sharp.

Accordingly, I believe our best option is to start with an empathic interpretation that draws the patient's attention to the way he changed the Basic Instruction and allows him to explore its meaning. The embarrassment can wait. Yet, by offering interpretations that implicate his fear of being judged and evaluated, students structure their continuations entirely around the issue of embarrassment. A typical T5:

Perhaps you expect that I will judge what you say, and I'll think unfavorably of you if you don't say the right thing.

While it addresses a central issue of therapy, our fundamental neutrality, it fails to acknowledge that our patient is contemplating the free-association method. In fact, students also go right along with him:

T5: Perhaps you are concerned because you feel you have to tell me about particular thoughts you are embarrassed about.

P5: *Do I really have to tell you everything?*

T6: While the decision is up to you, I believe it can be useful in the therapy if you do.

P6: *Now I'll feel embarrassed if I do tell, and embarrassed if I don't.*

T7: This implies that you expect me to judge you. I don't intend to do that.

However, students also acknowledge the alteration. One begins with a supportive remark followed by a reiteration of the Basic Instruction—"I can appreciate your anger and embarrassment. You can tell me things you want"—and then has the patient say:

You mean you don't expect me to tell you everything that comes to mind? I thought that's what you did in analysis.

This provided the opportunity to clarify the format of our therapy and explain how it differed from the "*analysis*" he expected. Instead the student responds: "I find it more useful to leave it up to you to choose and decide." At the very least we could have articulated the expectation in order to facilitate an exploration of the important subject. So we might have said:

Yes, there are forms of therapy in which you are expected to say everything that came to mind. But this is a form of therapy in which you say what you want to. Of course, if you want to say what comes to mind, you are perfectly free to do it.

And here's a continuation that gave us a similar opportunity:

> **T5:** You seem to be under the impression, then, that you are supposed to say everything that comes to mind.
> **P5:** *Well, yes. Isn't that what therapy is all about?*
> **T6:** You may talk about whatever you wish here.

This time, however, we might have responded with a somewhat different T6 from the one I suggested above. Our *P5* now has overtones, and I would be inclined to sound them out first by asking for clarification. ("I'm not sure I understand what you mean.") If the patient answered that he meant only to say that he thought therapy required the free-association method, I would tell him that it wasn't true for all forms. ("The free-association method is commonly used, but not all therapists require it.") And by saying no more than that, and holding in abeyance a reemphasis of the fact that he is free to use it if he wishes but the decision is his, I would be giving the patient a chance to tell me about his views and feelings on the matter.

Students do raise this issue, but then they evade it out of an eagerness to get into the narrative mode and offer explanatory interpretations. In the following continuation, the student allows the patient to do the evading and then hits him with a diagnostic interpretation:

> **T4:** Although you speak as though you're agreeing with me, you appear to be saying something quite different—namely, that you feel forced to say certain things.
> **P4:** *Oh no, not at all! It's just that if you think I'm angry because I don't speak up, then I feel as if I have to reassure you that I'm not. I'm just embarrassed mainly.*
> **T5:** Perhaps it is more reassuring to you to think of yourself as embarrassed. It may even be frightening to be angry.

I label T5 "diagnostic" for several reasons, not the least of which is because it simply isn't "empathic." But I use both terms in their broadest sense, where they refer not to the act of placing a behavior in a nosological category or the process of empathy itself, but rather to the way they address "mental content." (This issue is discussed more fully in Chapter 4.)

A formulation is diagnostic insofar as it imposes an explanation from the outside, so to speak: it takes the vantage point of an outside observer. And it is best exemplified by an interpretation (like the first sentence of T5 above) that explains the function of the patient's behavior. ("Thinking of yourself as embarrassed serves the function of reassuring yourself.") Aside from being very diagnostic, in this sense, that T5 interpretation is also very premature. Most importantly, however, the student seems to be ignoring the patient's attempt to set the record straight, while at the same time losing sight of the fact that he feels *"forced to say certain things."*

As I've already mentioned, if we've only pointed out to him that he altered the Basic Instruction, we've already made a confronting remark. It could, however, be justified on the grounds that the issue at hand was the format of therapy. And while it doesn't exactly "invite" the patient to wonder why he did it, a mild confrontation does "allow" him to—if he wants to, that is. Students have us raise the issue of why, and sometimes in an inferential way, mainly by focusing attention on his embarrassment. Here are three T5's that exemplify this approach:

> You want me to take the responsibility for choosing a subject to talk about. In this way you might avoid saying anything embarrassing—or if you do, it won't be so embarrassing, because it was my idea.

> It seems to me that you would like me to demand that you speak about whatever occurs to you so that it would be my fault that you are talking about things that embarrass you.

> Perhaps you are not sure how safe it is here to talk about things that might be embarrassing.

Each of them is fine, but only for T6 or 7. At T5 the alteration had to be noted. Nevertheless, a student finds a way to start out with an empathic interpretation that results in the patient's noting the alteration, and then offers an explanatory formulation:

T4: You feel under some pressure to talk about things you may not want to talk about.

P4: *Yes I do, but then, as you say that, I see the contradiction. I mean, I can say just what I want to. Well, what I want to tell you is that I wish I knew what I wanted to tell you* (laughs embarrassedly). *I guess this is such a new experience for me.*

T5: Perhaps that is the reason you changed things. You would feel less embarrassed if I instructed you to say everything, wouldn't you?

And finally, here's one that takes a nonconfronting, noninterpreting businesslike approach, but still, by virtue of the patient's initiative, makes a smooth transition to the narrative mode:

T5: I'm not sure I know what you mean by "have to" talk about anything that just comes to mind.

P5: *Well, I have to say what's on my mind, right?*

T6: You don't "have to." It's up to you to say whatever you want to say.

P6: *Oh! Well, what if I don't have anything I want to say, then what will you do?*

T7: It's up to you to remain silent if you want. I could be wrong, but you seem disappointed that I am not going to make you talk.

P7: *Yes. I don't know why, though.*

T8: I wonder if you feel it might be easier for you to tell me things you felt that I was forcing you to tell me. Maybe you feel embarrassed, not because you "have to" talk about things, but because you "want to."

P6 deserved a better answer; T7 isn't altogether responsive. "Nothing special," would be responsive enough, and we could then wait for his thoughts on the subject. (I might even ask for them.) Is he concerned about being silent? Does he think I will do something "special" when he falls silent? Next, I would divide T8 into two parts and save the second sentence for further developments. "Maybe that's one of the reasons you changed the instruction," could take its place. Nevertheless, as it stands, the continuation leads to a sensitive exploration of the defensive basis of the alteration.

If we draw his attention to a defense, a patient often reacts with the defense itself. If we tell him he is angry at us, as we did in this study, he often reacts with more of the same. That's what happens in the next study, and the technical problem is how to work with a patient's anger without merely defusing it.

Study 4
How Should I Have Known You'd Leave it up to Me?

T4: I think you are feeling angry. And I think the reason is that you expected me to be telling you what to talk about here. I would ask you questions, for instance. So, by not doing that, I have put you in an awkward position—and that makes you angry.

P4: *But how the hell should I have known you'd leave it all up to me? I've never been in therapy. All I know is what Harry told me. His therapist tells him what to do, asks him lots of questions and everything. So why the hell shouldn't I be expecting the same treatment?*

T5: ____

The patient is indignant. But over what? Over his frustrated expectation (which we have suggested to him with apparent accuracy) that we behave like Harry's therapist? Or is he indignant over the interpretation itself, because it implied that he had no right to such an expectation? Even if it turned out to be not as valid as the former, the latter should command our attention. To be sure, both issues are relevant to therapy in important ways, but the second one is germane to a feature of our therapy—namely, the undesirable judgmental implications that inhere in our interpretations, which I believe must be given a special priority.

The first question pertains to our nondirectiveness in general, while the second has specifically to do with our neutrality in respect to the interpretive mode. And in view of the fact that we ventured an early interpretation (the fact that we had some qualms about it is beside the point), we must seize the opportunity to repair the damage, so to speak. We should therefore respond in a way that takes account of the likelihood that our patient was reacting not only to the content of our interpretation but to its implied criticism as well. Few students do that. Let's take a critical look at three attempts.

The first begins in an unfortunate way: "It was quite natural for you to expect the same treatment." That's a piece of flagrant diagnosis whose function is purely supportive. If I wanted to concur with the patient, I would do it more directly, saying "I see no reason why, either." Formulating it supportively *might* mollify the patient (although it probably won't), and I wouldn't want to do it. Moreover, I'd worry that the implication of "natural" might return later in the "treatment" in a way that will make me regret having used the word. At any rate, the student now has the patient formulate his complaint in its most direct form: *"Then why did you chew me out for being surprised at the way you operate?"* This offered an excellent opportunity to explain a vital aspect of the interpretive mode, and our response might be:

> I didn't mean to chew you out for being surprised. In fact, I'm going to be trying my best never to criticize or judge you in any way, although it won't always be possible to keep my remarks from sounding that way.

What the student has us respond is: "For some reason you are seeing my description of your embarrassment and anger as 'chewing you out,' almost as if my saying that you feel these emotions is the same as my saying you are out of line, bad." To be sure, this interpretation can be read as an indirect rendition of the response that I suggested, but it can also be read as a further piece of scolding. "For some reason" carries the distinct implication that, whatever the reason, it is not a good (or "natural") one.

The second example begins well, although the final sentence is dispensable:

> **T5:** It seems to me that you feel I'm scolding you. That I expected you to know what type of therapy this would be. And you are even angrier because of this.

P5: *Why shouldn't I be? You are putting all the blame on me. You should have told me what to expect.*

When? But the student overlooks the problem and responds instead with a disclaimer followed by a diagnostic interpretation to which the patient responds contentiously:

T6: I didn't mean to scold you or imply that you should have known the rules. I only wanted to point out my impression that when your expectations don't materialize you become embarrassed, angry, and perhaps feel that it's the other person's fault for putting you in that position.

P7: *Well, I was put in that position. I only had Harry's therapy to judge from.*

T7: And you feel I should have saved you from the embarrassment you experienced by being more explicit in my instructions.

This interpretation is responsive, but it fails to raise the important point: He is reacting to the interpretations as if they were criticisms.

Our third example handles the situation quite well:

T5: I can certainly understand that your expectations would be based largely on whatever information you've been able to get about therapy from your friends. You seem to feel, however, that I am criticizing you for expecting the same treatment from me that Harry gets from his therapist.

P5: *Damn right!*

T6: When I said you were feeling both embarrassed and angry, I did not mean that these were bad or wrong ways to feel, merely that it might be helpful to you to realize what, in fact, you are feeling.

That was good and to the point. What might be edited out is that "merely," and what might be added is something to this effect:

I know that you can hear a criticism and value judgment, when I point out to you that you are angry. But when I say you are feeling such and such a way, I mean only that I believe it's true and that it might be helpful to you to recognize it. I *don't* mean it's bad to feel or act that way, that it means you're a bad person or anything like that.

Insofar as it pertains to two important practical matters, the unavoidable but unintended implications of valuation that inhere in our interpretations and the extent to which we'll be striving for neutrality, this is a piece of business that we need to address early (and often) in the therapy. And it's what I have in mind whenever I write in these pages that there are steps we can take against the non-neutral implications of interpretations. But let me repeat: it is still good technique to avoid interpretations that are especially prone to such implications. (And I return to this issue repeatedly throughout the book.)

Now let's look at some examples that interpret our patient's indignation as stemming from a wish that we behave like Harry's therapist. Although they bypass the issue of neutrality, they do respond to an issue that is germane to therapy and examine it in a useful way. However, they tend to begin with a didactic remark to the effect that different therapists have different methods, and in the context of our patient's indignation, a didactic approach can be particularly inappropriate. For one thing, it can lead too easily to an argument. A response like "Not all therapists work the same way, and some don't ask leading questions," might lead us to the following exchange:

P5: *I know that! But I expected you to work like Harry's therapist, because it makes a lot of sense to me. Why doesn't it make sense to you?*

T6: Yes, it makes sense to me, too. A lot of therapists, however, prefer to work differently and not ask questions or tell their patients what to do.

P6: *So what? I'm sure a lot of therapists do all kinds of things. But I picked you. And I'm beginning to think maybe I've made a serious mistake.*

Admittedly, that is fairly extreme. Yet, given the patient's indignation, I don't think it is farfetched to imagine things already being that close to an impasse.

"Never argue with a patient" is a good rule of thumb. And if he's in a fighting mood, even a businesslike response can provoke an argument. Consider the following continuation, which begins with a repetition of T4's interpretation and then switches to the business mode:

T5: Is it possible that you're angry because I won't tell you what to do?

P5: *Well, let's just say I want the same treatment everyone else gets.*

T6: In order for this type of therapy to be useful for you, you must decide what you want to say in the sessions.

P6: *Would it hurt if you told me just once so I can get the idea?*

T7: Probably not, but it wouldn't help either.

The patient was asking us to try out his (or Harry's) method, presumably because he judged it might be better for him. Without contesting that at T6, we could simply have restated and clarified the point with "I take it you believe that way would be better for you because you feel you need the guidance." If he went on to persist that we tell him what to talk about ("*just once*"), we would have the option of acquiescing (although it would be disingenuous, if not worse, to then say: "Okay! Tell me why you believe you need my help in that way"), or we could ask him whether he'd be willing to accept a trial period of our method. At all events, however, we must assiduously avoid implying that our type of therapy is better than any other, especially Harry's. To convey the message "This is the way I choose to do it," is quite sufficient. Notice how T7 carries the distinct implication that Harry's therapist's method is without much merit.

Study 5
The Autobiography

T1: You can talk about the things you want to talk about. It's up to you. I will listen and try to understand. When I have something useful to say, I will say it.

P1: *After I spoke to you on the phone last week and we made the appointment for me to begin today, I sat right down and began writing my autobiography for you. I've been working on it for about an hour every evening before I go to bed, and I figure it should take another few days to complete it. So I'll give it to you next time.*

T2: _____

Our T2 is bound to be predicated on how we construe *P1*. Is it
narrative or is it business? Deciding in favor of one doesn't, of
course, rule the other completely out; we can start in one mode
and keep open the option of switching into the other at some
point. But which would be the better choice to start with? Given
that the patient has simply made an announcement (although
it's hardly a simple one) and hasn't confronted us with a direct
request or question, we may be inclined to opt for the narrative
mode because moving from narrative to business is generally
less problematic, and often more effective, than vice-versa. On
the other hand, given the therapy's extreme youth, we may
prefer to regard the issue purely as business and not even
contemplate a move toward narrative.

As I've emphasized in Chapter 1, when faced with a business
matter in the framework of a therapy as nondirective as ours, it
is vitally important that we try to be as direct as possible. I also
emphasized the importance of being especially cautious and
circumspect when the matter becomes incorporated into the
work of therapy, when it blends with narrative, and I advocated
a certain reluctance to let it go too far in that direction. My chief
reason was this: we cannot be reluctant to investigate a business matter, and interviewing will usually be our only way of
doing it.

The first question to consider is whether a nondirective
orientation mandates that we must or must not accept the
autobiography. I believe it doesn't. So long as we construe the
matter as business and not narrative, our decision can be
influenced by our particular preferences in conjunction with
our clinical judgment. For instance, we might want to guard
against feelings of resentment over the imposition on our time,
or we might instead welcome the opportunity to have the
autobiography's information; we might want to take account of
any potential "manipulation," or instead put a higher priority
on positive motivational aspects; we might be concerned about
defensive and resistive implications instead of implications for
mastery and synthetic function. The possibilities and considerations are many and diverse. But I am not going to discuss them
here, because my intention is to exploit the study in the
interests of exploring some fundamental features of our form of
therapy. Although it isn't typical for a patient to offer us his
autobiography, I have found this study especially useful for

analyzing the process definition of therapy and the role definition of the therapist. It also highlights some of our basic
technical issues, particularly those that occur at the interface of
business and narrative.

If I had no qualms about reading the patient's biography,
there'd be no technical problem. Similarly, if my decision was to
refuse it, I would have to work with his reaction, but the issue
itself isn't likely to be problematic. In neither case is there any
reason to expect that my response was going to distort my role
definition or introduce a note of fresh ambiguity into the
therapy. Quite the contrary, as it gave me an early opportunity
to explain the way I prefer to conduct therapy, the issue might
help clarify and articulate my role definition. If, however, I
wanted to avoid an a priori position, and instead make a
decision on the basis of the patient's motives, expectations, and
feelings, then I would face at least two technical problems. The
first is how to secure that knowledge without unduly compromising my nondirective position; the second is how to formulate
my decision in a way that doesn't distort my role and introduce
further ambiguity into the format of therapy. The former raises
the key question: Must I resort to interviewing or can I achieve
my goal with clarification questions and interpretations? The
latter raises the question of neutrality and the limits of our
format's unstructuredness.

Before turning to these technical problems, let me mention
one reason for deciding against an a priori rejection of the
autobiography: there is no way of knowing whether it won't
cause the patient to abort the therapy. Moreover, if that happened, I would not be justified in maintaining that he was
therefore unsuited for it. Our format's reliance on the verbal
modality needn't be construed as imposing such a limitation,
and I don't think that reading the autobiography outside the
session (or even within it, for that matter) is so dissonant with
the spirit of the method that it must never be done. That it is
dissonant, I don't dispute, because I do believe that the therapeutic process stands a better chance, all things considered, if I
don't read it. But the dissonance isn't so serious as to rule it out
no matter what. It boils down, as do so many technical matters
in psychotherapy, to a weighing of relative priorities.

My approach would be that although the therapeutic process
stands a better chance if I didn't read the autobiography, I may

have to read it in order for the process to stand *any* chance. Therefore, I need to find out how necessary it is, and for that reason I will have to learn more about the patient's position. What purpose does he think it will serve? How strong is his need to have me read it? What will be the ramifications of my refusal, and also of my acceptance? Moreover, as I want to learn those things without influencing the matter for him, it may be necessary (at least for a time) that I keep him from knowing my reticence. But I couldn't simply remain silent at T2, for such a silence would clearly imply that reading the autobiography raised no special problem; he might then surmise that I was fully prepared to do it, and go ahead and complete the document and hand it to me next session. My short-range goal, therefore, is to find a way to pursue the matter, and it will have to be away that keeps not only my options open but his as well.

I am going to discuss the technical problems by examining three student continuations to this study and then two "model" continuations of my own. Let me say in advance, however, that the problems of avoiding an a priori position might turn out to be so intractable that we will necessarily conclude that the issue must be treated purely as business. In that event, the only acceptable T2 is either silence (saying in effect "It's okay with me") or a gesture of acknowledgment to the same effect, or else a remark that says No and explains why. In the meantime, however, we will proceed under the assumption that a T2 which satisfies my requirements exists—and our only problem is finding it.

In Example 1 the student elects the option of accepting the autobiography, but begins, nonetheless, with an interpretation. Regardless of which option they've chosen, most students do begin with an interpretation, and then they compose continuations that explore the matter diversely. Many construe *P1* as a sign of the patient's eagerness to expedite therapy, and some uncover defensive implications; many explore his expectations about therapy, and some uncover misunderstandings. The most popular T2 is: "You are assuming that once I have all the facts about your life, I will be able to proceed with therapy and help you resolve your problems."

To this kind of interpretation the patient can respond with a mere Yes, but students put more words into his mouth at this point, thus skirting the problem of how to follow it up. But if he responded with a mere Yes, we would have to decide whether to remain silent (which in this context could imply the directive "Tell me more") or whether to complete the interpretation with "I take it you feel an oral autobiography would not be as good." This remark, however, could be taken by the patient as casting doubt on the soundness of his reason. (And the same is also true for the T2.) In fact, any interpretation that addressed his reasons runs this risk. For if, instead of a mere Yes, he responded "*Isn't that evident? Why do you draw it to my attention?*" we could then readily reply "Yes, I did think that was one of the reasons; I thought it might be useful to focus attention on it." He might pursue the question, asking: "*Useful in what sense—to raise doubts in my mind?*" To be sure, we could now say "No, I didn't mean to raise any doubts; I thought it would be useful because it may deal with your beliefs about how therapy is going to proceed." That, after all, is always useful, isn't it? Yes, except would we have done the same if *P2* had been "*I've decided to tell you my biography*"? That, you see, is the sticky problem. In any event, and however carefully handled, this approach is quite likely to put us in the position of having to say whether or not we regarded the autobiography as "useful." The first example shows us the problem.

Example 1

T2: You believe I will be able to understand you better if you provide me with a *written* autobiography?

P2: *Well, there's so much to say, and a therapy hour goes so quickly. And besides, it must be hard to keep all the dates and details straight. Don't you want it?*

T3: If you feel it's important and will be helpful to your therapy, of course I will read it. However, I would like to explore some other issues that possibly may be important also. How had you hoped we would use the autobiography?

I interrupt to point out that *P2* contains two interesting points, and we could have commented on one of them before responding to the direct question. It doesn't necessarily follow, after all, that having a written autobiography is going to simplify the task of keeping all the dates and details straight, and this could be said. But the student gives priority to the direct question; to do otherwise would run the risk of seeming to parry it. (And my remark could come across as a quibble.) The answer she gives, however, fails to respond accurately. An accurate response has to address the question *"Don't you want it?"* "Yes, I will read it" ignores the *"want."* In an important way, it could even be evasive.

So what I might do at this juncture is take the opportunity to spell out my neutrality with respect to content, and tell the patient "I don't intend to want anything of you—beyond telling me the things you want to tell me, talking about what you want to talk about." Moreover, since the hallmark of psychotherapy is authentic and accurate communication, and since my response begs the question, I would add "I take it, however, that you want to know whether I will read it." For otherwise he is too likely to respond *"Yes, I appreciate that you won't tell me what you want or what I should talk about, but what I'm asking is whether you will read the autobiography—wasn't that clear?"* And it clearly was.

In any case, the issue would now squarely be joined, and I would have to respond directly. So the question Yes or No must be faced. And anything other than a Yes or a No is bound to be an error. Any kind of "maybe" is fraught with potential pitfalls, and any sort of hedging-with-qualifications would introduce unnecessary complications. Consider the conditional clause with which the student began her T3, and transform it slightly into "If it's important and will be helpful to your therapy." That's a risky kind of condition to introduce because it raises the questions: Who will make the judgment? and how? Similarly, "I would rather not, but I will if it means a lot to you," might be entirely accurate (although not as accurate as ". . . if the therapy depends on it"), except that it places the burden of responsibility on the patient to prove its importance; it sets him a task to fail or succeed at—to demonstrate the value of an autobiography. Moreover, a struggle of wills, or a difference of judgments, might ensue, which is not only unnecessary but inimical to the spirit of psychotherapy.

Therefore, once he has put the question (and bear in mind

that this is a first session and we are working with a new patient), there is potential hazard in not giving a direct answer, and the student would have avoided the hazard if her T3 were not hedged by the opening clause. I realize that the sense of the clause is "*since* you feel it is important," but even so the remark would be better without it. And T3 should have ended with the acceptance. Saying yes was altogether sufficient; directing him back to the question of what function the autobiography will have, serves no useful purpose. (In fact, allowing him to react to the acceptance could be useful.) As it stands, T3's third sentence can be construed as an attempt to undo an error. It's as if the message was "That was unfortunate although necessary, now let's get back to business!" And the way she gets back to business is to begin an interview. Why not define the autobiography as business in the first place and do it then? In fact, notice how the continuation itself actually moves ahead to underscore the advantage of doing it that way.

P4: *Well . . . You have to know all the details of my life in order to begin helping me, don't you? I thought if I got it all down on paper it'd give you a head start, and I wouldn't have to go over it all again. I mean, I know it, it's you who has to catch up.*

T4: So you feel the biography can substitute for talking about your earlier experiences?

P5: *Well, I've gone over them again and again, what's the sense of talking about them?*

T5: I have the impression you'd prefer not to talk about them.

P6: *No, it's just a question of efficiency.*

T6: Just efficiency?

P7: *Well, I guess some of them are rather unpleasant . . .*

Consider T5, what a large leap it takes from *P5* where the patient is questioning the value of taking time to give us the facts of his life, when he can instead write them for us to read. That's a fair question. It isn't uncommon for a patient to feel he was wasting valuable time whenever he recounted an event for our benefit. We can, of course, regard it as a necessary use of session time, and we may also believe he might learn something new for himself during the recounting. But we cannot simply ignore the point the way T5 ignores it, and substitute a rather tactless kind of interpretation—a confronting remark for which there isn't a shred of evidence. And finally, when the patient disagrees, saying it was just a question of "*efficiency*," to challenge his opinion with that kind of T6 has little merit. It says "I don't believe you!" and "Come off it!" It can only put him in an embarrassed and defensive position—and it was wishful thinking to expect of P7 that it would reflect useful therapeutic work. (Yet notice, nonetheless, the direction in which things are moving: the interview that was initiated in T3 may end with his deciding that the autobiography wasn't such a good idea after all.)

Our second example starts right off with an interview. Instead of conjecturing a motive, we ask for it—which is the core distinction between the interpretive mode and the interviewing mode.

Example 2

T2: I'm wondering why you decided to write your biography for me.
P2: *Well, don't you want to know all about me?*
T3: I am interested in knowing what you want to tell me. I'm wondering what made you decide to write it.

P2 is a beautiful illustration of the hazards of asking why. The patient counters with his own why-question! In this instance, the counterquestion begs for clarification; as it stands it is plainly impossible. So our T3 could have asked after the meaning of "*all about me.*" He probably has in mind the "important" facts, and he is wondering what we believe they are; or perhaps he wants to know what facts we need before we can begin to say "useful" things. Whichever question it was, the answer could be that we have no way of telling in advance. I might choose to say so in these words: "No, I don't believe I have to know certain things about you in order to be useful in therapy." And by offering him useful interpretations, I would do my best to prove it as soon as possible.

At any rate, the student has the patient obligingly repeat his original answer, adding one element to it that has a double meaning, and then he puts the direct question (as he did in Example 1):

P5: *Well, so you would have all the information; so you would have a better picture of me and understand me better. Don't you want it?*

T6: I want it if you want to give it to me.

That was an interesting way of saying yes! We seem to have said "I want it *because* you want to give it to me, not for its usefulness." On the other hand, judging from the rest of the response, a more plausible reading is "I will take it if you still want to give it to me, after I have exposed your true motive for wanting to give it to me," because the rest of the response can be read as a flagrant piece of dissuasion:

T6: (continued) But I'd like to share a thought I have. You seem to be working hard on this biography, and one possible reason may be that you want to please me and give me not only a better picture of you, but also have me think better of you.

This interpretation happens to be an excellent exemplification of an important misuse of the interpretive mode, inasmuch as its purpose is something other than to make a contribution to any self-inquiry the patient might be engaged in. Even if it were entirely correct, it is entirely untimely. It explains something he's entirely uninterested in having explained. A good interpretation doesn't do that. Neither does it subserve, as that one can be suspected of subserving, any motive other than under-standing and exploration.

That's why our T2 plays such a pivotal role. Not only does it set the tone of the entire exchange, it establishes the way we will work with the patient and with the problems he will bring to therapy; it concretizes what we meant by "useful." For instance, if it was a remark that served little more than the purpose of buying some time—and I'm referring to such T2s as "You've been spending a lot of time on it," and "It sounds like a lot of work"—then we've defined ourselves as someone who

marks time (if not kills it) with idle and pointless comments. I'm
not talking about gratuitous remarks; they do have a role to
play in therapy. They *can* facilitate the therapeutic process. But
in order to do that, they must fall into step with the patient's
narrative and not change the subject or impose a new idea.
Moreover, if we've taken a wait-and-see approach because we
have no a priori position (which is the option I am exploring
here), we must find a response that might elicit the information
we need, and it may have to be a rather gratuitous remark.

A reiteration of the Basic Instruction can also serve a wait-
and-see purpose, and students choose it for their immediate
response. This gives me the opportunity to point out that
"when in doubt repeat the Basic Instruction" isn't *always* a
good rule of thumb. It is a good way to deal with many issues
that arise early in therapy, but their context can determine its
meaning. In the context of *P1*, responding with the instruction
simply conveys the message "No, I will not read your biography"—and saying so directly is much better than using the
instruction for the purpose. Repeating the instruction after the
demurrer has been expressed is all right (a student does it by
prefacing her reiteration with "I don't believe it would be in the
best interests of therapy for me to read what you have written,"
which is a tactful way of saying no), but using it as a shield is
not.

Nevertheless, observe the way our third example uses the
Basic Instruction. The student reformulates it in a way that
forthrightly says no. Her reformulation has merit; it defines her
as someone who means what she says. And notice how the
businesslike continuation keeps focusing attention on the way
she works in therapy. I think that's a good approach to take. A
comparison of *P3* and T4 highlights the way the patient focuses
on the autobiography's usefulness for him, and the therapist
doesn't challenge him but focuses on its lack of usefulness for
her.

Example 3

T2:   When I said you can tell me what you want to and I'd
listen and try to understand, I meant it quite literally.

P2:   *You mean you don't want the autobiography?*

T3: I mean that reading something you've written is not the way I think I can be most useful.

P3: *But I'll be much better able to give you all the important information about myself if I write it all out systematically.*

T4: I feel that I will understand best if you *talk* about what you want to.

P4: *But won't it be much better if I write things down? I mean, that way I won't forget things or block.*

T5: Perhaps talking about what you want to is something you don't feel entirely comfortable with.

T4, however, is unresponsive and quite curt. It could benefit by being prefaced with "I know that an autobiography can be a good way to give me all the important information about yourself, but—" And since the reason an oral biography would serve us better is far from evident, the patient deserves an explanation. His *P4*, in fact, seems to be a request for one. He persists in his belief that it will be efficient for him, and seems to be missing the therapist's main point. Then, at the height of the argument, she falls back on the interpretive mode—exactly the wrong time for it! Making the switch from business to narrative may be less problematic than doing it in the other direction, but still it has to be done at the right moment. T5 wasn't the right moment. Any interpretation at T5, unless it simply articulated what the patient meant to convey, or perhaps said something about the argument itself, is bound to be bad. Trying to win an argument by making a diagnostic inference is the epitome of parlor analysis, defining us as the confronting one, if not also the one who takes unfair advantage. (This patient will not feel free to level a challenge or argue any more—unless, of course, he enjoys being diagnosed.)

Okay, then where do we stand in our quest for the perfect T2? Is there one that doesn't define the autobiography decision as business? (Can T2 be an interpretation which isn't overly speculative and confronting, which doesn't impose an extraneous issue on the patient, direct or judge him, and at the same time affords him the opportunity to explore the issue in a meaningful and potentially useful way?) When I composed the study I was confident there was. I no longer am. I can best explain why by discussing two T2s in detail. Then I will present two full continuations that I composed and examine them in the light of my own, as well as my students', criticisms of them.

Two interpretations for T2 might satisfy my requirements. One addresses the implications of the autobiography for the therapy (what it means in respect to the patient's attitudes, intentions, and expectations vis-à-vis his therapy); the other addresses its implications for me (what it means in respect to his intentions and expectations vis-à-vis his therapist). The first can be formulated:

> I gather you are doing it so that you won't have to review your life history here.

Is this remark completely gratuitous? I don't think so, because the patient might conceivably respond:

> *No, I am planning to review my life history here. I thought it might be useful for you to read it beforehand so that you could prepare questions to ask me or point out areas I omitted.*

Moreover, since it focused on an evident purpose of his decision, the interpretation could lead him to consider its motivational basis as well as defensive implications. Whether the remark is sufficiently neutral, however, is debatable. Still, if he had responded "*Yes, that's the main idea; are you implying that it's a mistake to write it out instead of reviewing it here?*" I could disavow having intended that implication, adding:

> I asked because I wasn't sure whether you intended it to take the place of reviewing your life history here, or that I would read the autobiography outside the session so that you could use your time here to speak of other things.

But notice: not only has it led us away from the defensive implications (his but, alas, not mine), I might as well have begun with the more straightforward T2, "And I take it you will be expecting me to read it" (the second option I'll examine shortly).

Suppose, however, the patient had responded by emphasizing the efficiency of his plan, saying:

Exactly, it will save us a lot of time; no point wasting time going over all the facts here. And you're going to need to know my life history, isn't that so?

What are my options now? How can I pursue the issue without injecting any evaluation or direction, without admitting that I was questioning the decision and feeling reticent about accepting the autobiography? The chief danger here is in criticizing him. An interpretation like "You regard it as a waste of time to review your life history during the sessions; I take it, therefore, that you don't expect to learn anything new and important while you are doing it," could easily be heard as a reprimand. In fact, any interpretation will now imply some criticism. And if he responded *"Yes, I guess that's what I believe,"* and then added *"I take it from the tone of your remark that you do not agree,"* I'd have to say Yes, wouldn't I? How could I possibly do otherwise? And if he had said: *"You're right, I'm sure that's what I do believe and I didn't realize it,"* was I not implying that he should have?

Another possibility is to speculate that he believed we were going to work this way: he would give me the facts and then I would give him their explanation. Even if it turned out to be an accurate guess, it isn't hard to imagine his reacting with embarrassment and resentment (*"When you put it that way it sounds kind of childish and mechanical"*), and I would have to take responsibility for it by saying "I think you feel I've scolded you. I've said you have no right to make those assumptions and expect therapy to work that way." That might indeed be useful, but I certainly couldn't say that he wasn't right, that therapy was in fact going to work that way. Furthermore, his response clearly showed me that my interpretation was tactless.

Then what about my second option for a T2—"And I take it you will be expecting me to read it?" Is that also potentially tactless? Yes, it is, and my second "model" highlights the fact. But my first one is predicated on its being quite gratuitous instead.

Model 1

T2: I take it you'll be expecting me to read it, and not during the session?

P2: *Naturally. That's why I'm writing it.*

T3: And you believe my reading it will help the therapy, I gather?

P3: *Yes. It will save us a lot of time. I won't have to tell you everything about my past, you can read it. It's the efficient way.*

T4: I can see that having me read your biography will save time for you and make it unnecessary for you to review your life history here. That could be efficient from your vantage point. But I want some time to think about it, because I'm not altogether sure it will be efficient from mine.

P4: *Why wouldn't it be?*

T5: For one thing, I work best when I listen to you, when I can hear the things you talk about and can clarify those things both for myself and for you.

P5: *I see.* (falls silent)

Notice how I questioned the autobiography's value for me, yet didn't commit myself as to whether or not I was going to accept it. The patient is probably reconsidering its advisability, and I won't interrupt his silence and influence the course of his deliberations. If, after some thought, he said he wanted me to read it, despite my having cast doubt on its usefulness, and he put it forthrightly: *"Look, I appreciate that it might not be so efficient for you, but I really want to finish it and have you read it anyway,"* I would say "Yes, I will," and nothing further. But if he was tentative and conveyed a sense of doubt, if he showed concern over seeming to incur my displeasure, or if some other issue of this kind now came up, then I would forestall my decision and comment on those developments. If his response was simply *"Okay, I see your point, and I understand how it might not be such a good idea, so I'm going to drop it,"* I would respond in a way that didn't influence the decision, and silence is probably my best option for that purpose. But if his response was simple indecision—*"Look, I don't really feel strongly about the thing one way or the other, and I want you to say whether you think it's a worthwhile idea or not"*—I would respond with "I believe that for me to read it isn't likely to be very helpful" (and be strongly tempted to add "But

I still prefer to leave the decision up to you"). The model, however, continues on the assumption that the patient broke his silence with a recounting of the events that led up to the decision.

P5: *(continued) I was surprised when you said I could start therapy this week. It wasn't an easy thing for me to decide to go into therapy. Last year, when I was having a rough time in school and at home, too, I thought about it. But I figured it was too expensive and I could work things out for myself. And when I was working during the summer, things did get better, and I thought all I had to do was make myself a schedule, plan my life better, so that I wouldn't fall behind in my schoolwork again. I did make a schedule and everything but it didn't work out, and before I knew it I was in the same mess again. And then my mother got sick and things at home got impossible. And my friend Henry went into therapy. . . . I wanted to go into therapy with his therapist but he said it wasn't advisable, and he gave Henry your number to give me. But he said it would probably not be possible for me to see you right away, and when you said I could start today, I was . . . a bit surprised. But it's what I wanted, because things have been really rough, and . . .*

T6: And you felt under a lot of pressure?

P6: *I sure did! And getting help is really important to me now. So I don't want to mess it up, like I mess up everything else.*

T7: So you felt excited and hopeful when I told you we could begin this week, and that's when you made the decision to write your autobiography?

T7's chief purpose is to steer the patient back to the autobiography. I have a special reason for being directive in this way: I don't want him to leave the session with a sense of ambiguity about the autobiography and perhaps the conviction that I had advised him against writing it.

P7: *Well, I guess I was sort of excited, though. . . . But I realized it was important and I should do therapy right. That's when I realized that you didn't know anything about me and I would have to give you all the facts, and it would waste a lot of valuable time, doing that. So I got the idea of writing my autobiography for you.*

T8: I understand. But it isn't entirely clear to me what you mean by *waste,* when you say it would waste a lot of valuable time.

P8: *Well, Henry told me his therapist said he wouldn't be able to tell him anything until he knew a lot about him. And that makes a lot of sense to me.*

T9: I gather, then, you're eager for me to tell you things as soon as possible. And you have reason to believe that once all the facts are in, and not before then, will I be able to start saying useful things to you.

P9: *Henry's therapist hasn't said two words to him yet, and he has been seeing him for two months! Anyhow, what can you tell me before you know a lot about me?*

That's an important question, perhaps a loaded one, and perhaps there's a challenging edge to it. But in the context of this exchange, acknowledging anything more than the fair question *"What sorts of things are you going to be telling me?"* is pointless. And since I have imposed the issue, for me not to answer it would be wrong. I will choose an answer that has several goals, one of which is to show him the sorts of remarks I'll be making and how I construe "useful." I am therefore going to offer him an interpretation, and it will necessarily be a speculative one. Notice, however, that it doesn't come out of the blue; some evidence for it can be found in what he has already told me.

T10: Well, I can suggest that you probably have mixed feelings about the matter. A part of you is sort of excited by the prospect and the anticipation of what I will say, but another part of you dreads it. Is it possible that my giving you a full explanation and analysis one day also frightens you? So maybe you

decided to give me all the facts right away to get the
. . . uh . . . the ordeal, let's say, over with as quickly
as possible.

P10: *I guess that's pretty much . . . pretty much correct,
I guess.*

T11: Let me mention, however, that I don't intend to do
that. I'll try to say useful things while you're
speaking about the things you want to speak about,
but I won't be giving such full explanations and
diagnoses.

P11: *I see. So . . .*

T12: So I guess you're wondering whether you should
finish the autobiography and give it to me.

P12: *Yes. I gather from your remarks that you don't
think it's such a hot idea.*

T13: Yes, I do think it might not be the best way to
proceed here. At least from my point of view, it
might be better if you told me the things you
wanted to tell me.

P13: *So you're saying I shouldn't?*

T14: Yes and no. I realize that my having told you that it
won't be so efficient for me to read it, and having
also suggested that one of your reasons for doing it
is to get the ordeal over with as quickly as possible,
has made it difficult for you to decide to go ahead
with it. But I don't want it to be impossible or even
too hard for you to do it anyway. I prefer to leave the
decision up to you.

And that's where my first continuation ends—on something of
a problematic note. My final remark could sound duplicitous; it
could also leave the patient in an awkward position. But was
there a better option? (And this isn't altogether a rhetorical
question.) I examine the question in my second continuation,
which is predicated on his reacting to my T2 with more feeling.

Model 2

T2: I take it you'll be expecting me to read it, and not
during the session.

P2: *Well, you can read it . . . You can read it whenever you can.* (flushes slightly and smiles sheepishly) *You know, I didn't think of that—that you would have to read it on your own time. . . .*

If he now continued with *"But that isn't asking such a helluva lot, is it?"* I could answer that it depended on how long it was, adding "And there's another consideration: I will have to study it in order to remember everything you've written." If he went on to ask if that wasn't part of my job—*"Wouldn't you be doing that anyway?"*—I could say "It may be easier for me to remember the things you tell me here than for me to remember the things I read about you; I can ask you questions about things I don't understand as we go along." Alas, however, this amounts to protesting the imposition on my time and attention, and it could have implications I'd have reasons to regret. But I was generous with myself and didn't let the patient continue that way. I had him pause instead. And then I used the opportunity to interpret his feeling.

T3: Are you feeling embarrassed because you didn't realize that I would have to read it on my own time?
P3: *Yes, and it's something I do all the time. I fail to take the other person into account. I'm always imposing on people. I should have phoned you back and asked you whether you wanted me to do it.*

This is much too good an opportunity to let slip. I think it is technically correct to respond as if he actually had asked the question.

T4: I can tell you what I would have answered. I would have said—because I intend to try never to tell you what to do and what not to do—that it's up to you.
P4: *So I would've gained nothing by asking? Then . . .*
T5: Then what am I making a fuss about?
P5: *Exactly! I thought you were implying that I should have asked whether I would be imposing on you if I gave you my biography.*
T6: I didn't mean to imply that.

P6: *But I . . . but you said that if I had asked you, you would've answered that I should do it if I wanted to. And just before you said I should have asked you. No, I guess you didn't say that in so many words. But you implied that I should have, didn't you?*

T7: I can see why you think so, but I didn't mean to. What I'm saying—and it's something I need to make clear to you because you had no way of knowing it before you came here—is that I'm going to try never to tell you what to do. That's what I meant when I said it was up to you.

P7: *Look, I know you said I should talk about whatever I wanted to talk about—and I sure didn't expect that. It doesn't make much sense to me, either. I can't see what good it's going to be if I just talk and talk. There must be certain things I should talk about.*

T8: I take it you have in mind the things you've been writing in your biography.

Was I back in Studies 1 and 2? Shouldn't I have played this *P7* the same way I played their *P3*s? I don't think so. Context, after all, makes a difference, and this was not the best moment for an exploration of those issues. (Bear in mind also that I had no way of telling how extended the exploration was going to be.) It was time to get back to the autobiography. For one thing, it was I who had imposed the topic of its usefulness, and I now want to make sure the matter is resolved before the end of this session. For another, asking about meaning needn't be done right away; it can wait. After the matter is resolved, I can return to the neutrality issue by reminding the patient of his earlier statement. ("Let me ask you about something you said before—")

P8: *Sure! I figured you needed to know all about my past and everything. So I figured if I wrote it out for you, you could read it and then you could tell me what things I should talk about. Otherwise I'd just wander aimlessly all over the place—which I've been doing all my life anyway and it hasn't got me anywhere. Come to think of it, that's not true. It got me here! . . . I really need help, and . . .*

T9:   And you feel a need for me to tell you what you should do.

P9:   *Yes.*

T10: I gather the main reason you decided to give me your biography is so that I would be in a better position to guide you, at least during the sessions.

P10: *And you're not going to do that, eh?*

T11: And you feel that if I didn't tell you what to talk about, if I just allowed you to talk about whatever you want to talk about, I wouldn't be of use to you.

P11: *Well, it could make sense for some people, I guess, but not for me. Look, I've been doing my own thing all my life. My parents are these big liberals and they believe a kid should . . . Oh, you know what I mean. And look what a mess I've made of everything! They should've given me more guidance, is what I think. And that's why I'm such a selfish person. And inconsiderate. I never take the other person into account—like I didn't even think about the fact that you would have to read my whole biography on your own time. That's typical of me. And I know it. And I should . . . I mean, I want to change it. But. . .*

T12: But you feel I'm going to have to be active in helping you change it. And I seem to be taking the same position your parents have taken, leaving things up to you.

P12: *Yes, and that's ironic, isn't it? . . . Look, let me get straight on something. You're saying that everything's going to be up to me here. That means I can . . . I can do what I want, right?*

I will now pause for a moment before responding to the question. I'll do it for several reasons, one of which is to consider whether to ask a clarification question. (What is the *everything* my patient had in mind? In what sense did he mean "*I can do what I want*"?) But instead I will interpret the question in a way that focuses attention on the issue at hand. I'll be steering the conversation, thereby being directive, of course. But the issue at hand is a business one, and I am straddling the line between interviewing the patient and "supervising" the therapeutic process. If he'd been engaged in narrative alone, I wouldn't want to be that active. (During a narrative, my activity is aimed more at "facilitating" the process than supervising it—a subtle, but in my opinion significant, difference.)

T13: ... Are you wondering if what I said before, when I pointed out to you that I'd have to read the autobiography on my own time, meant that you weren't free to ask me to do that?

P13: *Sure. I figured you were saying that I shouldn't give it to you. But look here, if it's up to me—if things are really up to me—then it follows that . . . that if I really wanted you to read the damn thing—*

T14: Then I would, yes, because I also prefer to leave that up to you.

P14: *I see. That's interesting. I am free to impose on you and be inconsiderate.* (impish grin) *And how about if I wanted you to tell me what I should talk about here?*

T15: ... I could do that also.

I paused to make sure I had to respond. The pause also gave me the chance to choose my words carefully, and it might convey to the patient the care with which I chose them. The sense of my answer is: I would if he wanted me to, if he believed it was necessary for him. Bear in mind that I've already made it amply clear that I preferred not to, that I believed he might benefit more from therapy if he did the choosing. What I am doing therefore is defining myself as someone who is rigorous but not rigid, someone who doesn't back him into a corner, who can be "manipulated," and who maximizes his freedom. There will be ample opportunity in the ensuing sessions to establish the limits of my position and the boundaries of my willingness to accede to his requests; at this early juncture I want to minimize the risk of an impasse.

It seems quite likely that he was testing me. (His impish grin might be taken as a signal.) I might therefore have said "I take it you're testing me, perhaps teasing me, to see how far I am willing to go in allowing you to call the shots here." This remark, however, is a diagnostic kind of interpretation whose form is confronting. Such interpretations tend to cast a patient into a passive position and define us as keen observers and troubleshooters. So if I did regard it as timely to address his provocativeness, I would formulate an interpretation this way: "I think you're meaning to keep me from taking your question seriously; part of you wants me to dismiss it as just teasing." It seems to me such a formulation is less evaluative and more empathic, and it's tactful.

But because the issue at hand was more salient, I decided to make no reference to the testing. My intention, after all, was to define the therapy and myself as clearly and unambiguously as I could. Moreover, I see little merit in "using" an interpretation, no matter how correct, which might be perceived by him as serving the purpose of getting me off the hook. Consequently, I chose to address his question directly, bypassing for the moment its provocative intent. And it is, after all, an important question. Isn't he weighing a commitment to an undertaking that will have profound ramifications for his well-being?

> **P15:** *That's even more interesting; you're willing to leave all decisions to me, even the decision not to make my own decisions!* (smile) *This is quite strange. I must ask my logic professor about it. But it adds up to my having to decide what I really want, doesn't it? And it's not going to be easy, I assure you, because it happens to be exactly the kind of problem that's been messing up my life. Maybe I should tell you . . . I mean,* (sheepish grin) *maybe I want to tell you something about it.*

And it seems to me, that whatever decision he eventually makes about the autobiography, he is well started into psychotherapy. Did I contrive too pat a correspondence between the nature of his presenting problem and the nature of the therapy itself? Of course! But I did it because autonomy happens to be the therapy's key theoretical concept. (And where is it written that a teacher has to avoid such ulterior motives?)

3 _____

BUSINESS

Instructions for the Business Studies

Each study presents a single remark by the patient. Your task is to offer three different responses, silence excluded, and then evaluate each one in terms of its advantages and disadvantages. You may assume that each patient was given an adequate orientation to psychotherapy during his first session. This is now the beginning of the third or fourth session, and it began with an extended silence.

Study 1
How Old Are You?

In saying *"How old are you?"* our patient did two things: he asked us a direct question, and he asked us a personal question. The former requires of us an a priori policy regarding requests for information; the latter requires a policy on the issue of impersonality. Each can be treated as business, but I will examine them separately. The prickly problem of impersonality will involve us in an extended discussion.

    Countering a direct question with the direct counterquestion "Why do you ask?" is something of a cliche, and my attitude toward it should be obvious by now. Responding with silence, however, is tactless, especially the first time or two that our patient asks us a direct question. Our best option, in my opinion, is to define the matter as business and respond accordingly:

> Before I answer your question I want to tell you how I plan to respond when you've asked me a question.

Then we tell him what our policy is. Mine is worded:

> From time to time you may want to ask me a direct question, the way you did now, and what I'll usually do is not answer it—not right away, at least.

This policy can be supported by several interrelated rationales that differ in their focus, though each relates to considerations of timing and the potential effects of our answer on the therapeutic process. If the patient asked me for mine, I would frame a rationale in these terms:

> I don't answer right away because I may want some time to consider whether the answer I could give you would be useful for the therapy.

This explanation is simple and to the point, unencumbered by extraneous issues that might invite argument. To be sure, the patient might say: "*But on those occasions when you don't need any time for consideration, will you answer right away?*" I could respond:

> Sometimes I'll answer right away, but not always. I might wait a few moments to give you a chance to say more about the question.

This touches on an alternate rationale that can be framed in terms of the possibility that once his question was answered, his reasons for having asked it, along with his feelings about the matter, may be thrust into the background. He will then be reacting to the answer; it will have taken precedence over the question. This rationale, too, can be formulated in terms of the therapeutic process, but not without difficulty. For one thing, it implies that whenever the patient wants to ask a direct question, he has to consider his reasons for it before expecting an answer—and that, of course, is a directive. For that reason I'd be hesitant to use the rationale, and would resort to it only if the patient found my first one inadequate. But at all events I'd be careful to keep from suggesting that his motivation for asking the question was going to determine my answer—namely, the reason I wait is in order to hear his reason—for I want to avoid the implication that I am going to judge it in any way. (If it turned out to be a "good" question, I'll answer it, and my not answering meant it was a "bad" one.) Maintaining my neutrality is more valuable for him in the long run than any short-term benefit he might derive from my answering or not answering his direct questions.

Another reason for waiting is that I want to maintain a degree of autonomy of my own. I, too, want to feel free to decide when to speak; I don't want to be forced into speaking (or, for that matter, into silence); I don't want my patient to learn ways to "shape" my behavior. This rationale, however, has to be qualified and limited, and rarely can it be shared with a patient. For one thing, it is also based on my expectation that there will be times when I am going to be taken by surprise, and whenever I am surprised at something he says or does (such as ask me a direct question) I will want to say nothing. My most prudent action at such moments is to keep silent. For I see no value to the therapeutic process in my expressions of surprise; chances are good that any remark I'd make, even if it were a good one (which isn't very likely), would breach my neutrality.

And the important technical point of this study is that practically any kind of interpretation that went beyond a simple clarification of what the patient meant to be asking is bound to be untimely because it will violate the requirements of neutrality. Even the simplest elucidation of his reason for asking the question can carry unwanted implications. In fact, not only do I think it's a good rule of thumb never to give an interpretation if we are taken aback, I believe the same applies when a direct question has been asked. Thus, "I gather you are wondering if I am old enough/too young/too old," which most students offer as an advantageous option in this study, is untimely. Responding with an interpretation is generally an error (in the light of my rule of thumb), but it is especially wrong if the issue

of direct questions hasn't yet been carefully dealt with in a
businesslike way.

Having done it, however, we face two decisions: whether or
not to answer the question, and whether or not to interpret it.
Students believe there's an advantage to exploring the patient's
concerns before telling him their age ("I will answer your
question in a moment, but first—") and they initiate an exploration with either an interrogation or an interpretation. Students also answer first and inquire after. Whichever way they
choose to order their responses, they apparently believe that he
stands to benefit from an inquiry into the matter, because they
approach it, in some degree, as narrative too; they offer interpretations that are to varying degrees empathic, explanatory,
diagnostic, and confronting. But I won't examine them in detail,
because I want to discuss the larger issue of impersonality at
length.

Before leaving the problem of direct questions, a general
point: whatever course we chose to follow, our primary concern
must be to protect our neutrality. We have to be vigilant with
regard to the potential reinforcement effect of discouraging—or
for that matter, encouraging—our patient to ask us direct
questions, for we want him to feel perfectly free to ask us not
only direct questions but personal ones too. Whether this goal
will be achieved by offering him interpretations that he finds
interesting and useful, or whether it will be better achieved by
abstaining from interpreting, is a matter for clinical judgment.
This early in therapy, however, I believe our prudent choice is to
take the conservative position and save our therapeutic work
for matters that are unambiguously narrative. Now let's turn to
the big question of impersonality, because I can hear a reader
impatiently asking me—

Reader: Are we going to tell the patient how old we are?
Author: It depends on whether we regard it as a business
matter. Our approximate age shows, of course, but there can be
a range of uncertainty.
Reader: And our patient apparently wants to narrow it.
Author: Yes, and what if he'd asked for the exact birth-
date? The question we face is whether our exact age is personal.
The larger question, however, is twofold. How impersonal
should we want to be, and how impersonal *can* we be?

Reader: But I have a prior question. Why should we want to be impersonal in the first place?

On Impersonality

Author: My answer to that question is framed around the requirements of neutrality. I see no way around the conclusion that as we intend never to evaluate our patient and pass judgment on him, as we try to keep from being a source of extrinsic reinforcements, from taking sides and the like, we have no choice but to remain impersonal. For if he knows we're a pacifist, how can he be persuaded that we aren't judging him when he advocates war? If he learns that we believe in the sanctity of marriage, how can he behave adulterously without incurring our valuation? And if we've told him our tastes in music range from the Renaissance to the baroque, he might have to defend a love of Tchaikovsky.

Reader: But we can stay neutral despite anything he may know about us personally, can't we? We do, after all, have attitudes, opinions, values, and tastes. Doesn't our task remain the same whether or not he knows what they are?

Author: From our vantage point, that's quite true, but perhaps not from his. Two questions can be raised from his vantage point. Of what use is it for him to know personal things about us, and won't knowing them complicate his task of "accepting" our neutrality and working securely within it? Moreover, our form of therapy doesn't require us to be personal. It requires of us a degree of warmth, a degree of enthusiasm, along with our empathy, sensitivity, tactfulness, and ability to listen, but none of this means we are being personal.

Reader: Sure, but only according to that particular definition of "personal."

Author: However defined, impersonality is a feature of the method that my students challenge the most—especially when I spell out the extent to which I might strive for it. For I don't stop at refusing to divulge whether I am happily married; I might choose not to tell a patient whether I am married at all. And I might refuse to divulge whether I had seen a movie, even if it was a movie to which he had important personal reactions that he planned to explore during the session, and if he didn't have to describe the movie he could devote more time to his reactions. Yet for me to tell whether I saw it could—repeat, *could*—amount to having revealed something personal about myself, and therefore I might—repeat, *might*—choose not to.

Reader: Your intention to remain impersonal can extend that far!

Author: Yes, it can. But it doesn't have to; some distinctions and caveats must be considered. Insofar as it pertained to knowledge alone, my having seen a movie differs from my marital bliss. And my store of factual information may be personal but it can have implications for my neutrality that differ from other aspects of my life and personality. So if he asks whether I've seen *Citizen Kane* or do I know Mahler's Ninth Symphony, I might choose to tell him.

Reader: Even if you thought it might be a loaded question?

Author: By "loaded" I take it you mean the extent to which its intention is to learn something about me personally. Yes, I might tell him even if I thought it was. Otherwise, you see, I'd be back in the business of evaluating and judging—namely, "I'll tell you only after I've satisfied myself that your need for the information is legitimate."

Reader: So we can draw the line at factual knowledge by excluding it from the domain of "personal," and that, I take it, resolves the problem.

Author: Not fully. In order to analyze the problem further, we need to draw a distinction between those of our personality features that have a direct bearing on our ability to understand our patient and those that have none. His personal questions, especially at the beginning of therapy, are usually directed at our professional experience and credentials. Are we competent enough? is the underlying question. Often, however, they are also directed at our personal experiences and our personal "credentials." Are we compatible enough? is the question. And the question might be accompanied by a concern over whether his life-style and experiences will be comprehensible to us. Discounting inquiries into our professional training, orientation, and experience, which should of course be fully answered, a variety of nonprofessional questions such as *"Do you have children?" "Are you a devout Catholic?" "Are you knowledgeable about music theory?"* can be asked, and these be construed as questions about special competency.

If he was having problems with his children, a patient might believe that a parent was likely to understand him better than someone who was childless. If he is a devout Catholic, he might believe that only a devout Catholic could comprehend his feelings and experiences. If he's a composer with work problems, he may want a therapist who knows something about music theory. These are legitimate questions, but only up to a point, and up to that point they can be answered in a way that preserves a sufficient level of impersonality.

For supposing my patient believed that a childless, non-Catholic and unmusical therapist wasn't likely to understand his problems, I can acknowledge his belief and explore it carefully. But I can do both without taking a position on the belief itself—without dismissing it out of hand, and also without losing sight of the fact that my being a parent doesn't ensure my ability to understand his particular problems, that my not being Catholic might have little bearing on my ability to understand his religious experiences and feelings, and that even if I knew a good deal about music theory, my knowledge might be insufficient for the degree of sophistication he could bring to bear on it. So finding out those personal facts about me won't serve its intended purpose, and the question at issue will remain unanswered.

Reader: Then how do we answer the question at issue?

Author: It's rarely easy. Ideally, he and I should share in arriving at an answer. A trial period is often the optimal way, but in cases where aspects of special competency aren't likely to become significant until later on in therapy, I might choose not to rely on it and instead invite the patient to interview me.

Reader: Interview you? Even if it amounted to a kind of examination, could you take it without compromising your neutrality?

Author: Why not? If I tell him I am well acquainted with the problems of parenthood, and familiar with the rites of communion, and knowledgeable about counterpoint, I haven't, after all, told him anything that is so personal. Even specifying the extent of my knowledge won't cross the line. "Yes, I know the four species and Fux's classical rules," is significantly different from saying "I studied counterpoint for two years when I was a student at the McGill Conservatory." It's the difference between what I know and how I came to know it.

Both are personal, yes, but the former remains exclusively in the domain of my factual knowledge, and that much I can share with him. The same is true for "I know the problems of parenthood," in contrast to "I know them because I have four children of my own," and "I am not a Catholic but I grew up with Catholic friends."

So I believe that the question "Where do we draw the line?" can be answered: "I draw it at the boundaries of my factual information or knowledge. I define my personality as a therapist in a way that limits it to my personal experiences, to my opinions, sentiments, and tastes." And the reason we exclude them is because those aspects of our personality are generally irrelevant to our effectiveness as therapist for an average-expectable patient; they need not interfere with our ability to understand him nor with our capacity to supervise his therapeutic process. But the same isn't true for our knowledge. Our ability to understand can be significantly enhanced or impaired if we are, or aren't, sufficiently informed about aspects of his experiences.

Up to a point, therefore, what we happen to know can matter a great deal, and that point depends on our patient. If he has a psychological problem with counterpoint and needs to explore it in detail and depth, we may need to understand counterpoint. To the extent that we don't, we will have to ask him for clarification. In itself this needn't be a handicap for him, for he can benefit during the course of his explanations by discovering new things about what he had been taking for granted. Yet the possibility remains that our grounding in music is so lacking that his explanations won't suffice, and it's that possibility that has to be taken seriously.

Reader: Haven't you overstated the problem to make the point? The illustration, after all, is very specialized.

Author: I chose it on purpose. Counterpoint is a subject few nonmusicians are likely to know much about. The average-expectable therapist can be expected to have a fund of common knowledge—operationally defined as whatever is fit to print in the *New York Times*—but will be uninformed about a wide range of topics that are known to the average-expectable patient. This, however, doesn't obviate the fact that what he or she knows can matter. And it can matter in a way that has a lot to do with neutrality, because the problem, unfortunately, isn't fully resolved by drawing the line at knowledge.

Reader: Hey, I hope you're not going to tell me that distinguishing between a familiarity with the writings of Thomas Pynchon, say, and a personal opinion of those writings won't satisfy the stringent demands of neutrality!

Author: I'm afraid I have no choice. Knowledge, after all, is selective; it bespeaks values and interests. Since we can no longer expect to know everything—not even everything in the *Times*—the selections we make are revealing. If a patient knows I've read *Gravity's Rainbow* but not *Airport,* knows I recognize John Cage but not John Lennon, he has learned something about my literary and musical tastes, hasn't he? In short, that we "happen to" know something, or not know it, does say something personal about us.

And I see no way around this difficulty. We can, of course, weigh each of his personal questions to estimate whether the balance is on the side of divulging personal information for the sake of ensuring a level of understanding, or whether it's more on the side of learning personal things for transference purposes. We can also translate the question into *"You're asking whether I understand."* And since we freely ask him for clarification anyway, instead of answering the personal question, we can tell him that we'll ask whenever we haven't understood. But this cannot apply across the board, and there will be occasions on which he will need to know in advance whether we will be understanding him.

Reader: All right, so let's just go ahead and tell him whether we're familiar with the book, or movie, and run the risk of a "flaw" in our neutrality! The same "flaw," after all, will undoubtedly develop when he speaks on a subject in a way that presumes our familiarity with it and we don't ask for clarification.

Author: Which boils down to the hard fact that considerations of feasibility set obvious limits, and there has to be a substantial artificiality to limits that are based exclusively on what we choose to divulge. To refrain from telling a patient whether I am married is one thing, but don't I wear a wedding ring? And how about my clothing, the way I cut my hair and decorate my office, don't they reveal a great deal about me? And isn't my personality reflected in a wide range of nonverbal behaviors, expressive gestures, and the like? To argue that I can know my so-called "stimulus properties" isn't germane here; every therapist must take pains to know them, the one who doesn't strive for impersonality no less than the one who does. To be sure, I can try to keep them as minimal and as blandly nondescript as possible. I can doff the wedding ring, wear nondescript clothes and hair, decorate blandly and convention- ally. But there are limits. Furthermore, if a patient wanted to learn about me personally, there are ways he can—look me up in the professional directories, for instance—so why not spare him the trouble? Isn't it artificial to insist that he must find things out for himself? That merely tests his resourcefulness and shifts the burden of feasibility onto his shoulders.

And we must also take account of the fact that the question of feasible boundaries applies not only to us but to our patient, too. On my part, if I could keep him from knowing my gender, I would; but since any attempt to conceal it would obviously create fantastic problems for both of us, it has to be judged unfeasible. The same is true, in different degrees, to everything about me that shows: my speech dialect, my expressive ges- tures, my approximate age. But on his part the limits of feasibility may be broader than that which shows. My marital status may not show but he may have ways to find out. And let's suppose he puts it this way: "*I have a need to know whether you are married, and I don't care to understand that need or make it go away. If you refuse to tell me, I'll go to the library and look you up. So your refusal will cost me time and effort.*" I might judge it unfeasible, ultimatum or no, not to comply, because the practical implications and side effects for him would be too far-reaching. That, of course, is largely a matter of judgment, and it's going to depend on who my patient is and the stage—and state—the therapy is in. But it can be formulated in terms of feasibility, which is my main point. Similarly, with respect to the movie illustration, he might say:

If you don't tell me whether you've seen it, I will listen very carefully to your remarks about my reactions in order to discern whether you're familiar with the movie. I don't care to understand why I'm going to do it, but I'm going to do it. I will be preoccupied with your remarks.

And even if you are able to choose your words so care-
fully—which will put a big constraint on you—I will be
distracted. So it would keep me from being distracted if
you simply satisfied my need to know whether you saw
it.

And even if he didn't articulate all those different factors, I
might judge that feasibility, from his vantage point, required
me to tell him whether I had seen the movie.

In fact, I can envisage circumstances in which I would tell
him even if he hadn't asked. For instance, say he was describing
the movie in a way he wouldn't if he knew I had seen it: I can
imagine interrupting with "I gather you're describing the movie
to me because you don't know whether I've seen it or not." This
might raise the question of his reluctance to ask me personal
questions, and thereby serve a useful therapeutic purpose. But
my intention wasn't to change the subject; I was trying to
address the question of feasibility in a businesslike way. And in
the end it comes down to a matter of clinical judgment. The fact
that it reveals something personal about us notwithstanding,
there is no a priori way to decide whether we should divulge
information or not.

Reader: But isn't there a point beyond which the minimal
requirements of neutrality cannot be satisfied, when the patient
knows too much about us and therefore will be unable to work
effectively enough within the format of our method?

Author: Yes, and that point, too, is a matter of clinical
judgment. Just as neutrality is a relative achievement, an ideal
position at best, so is impersonality. Which of course doesn't
justify abandoning all attempts at it. Having granted that the
line has to be artificial is not the same as contending that it is
futile to draw it. Moreover, we can share the problem with our
patients; we can explain our position to them, concede that
there's a substantial arbitrariness to the degree of our impersonality, and promise them we will rely on our judgment to
keep that arbitrariness to a minimum.

So the line, in my opinion, can feasibly and sensibly be drawn
at what we divulge verbally—provided we exercise clinical
judgment in each instance rather than follow a rule, and
provided we draw a distinction between being impersonal and
personality-less. For the term personality can be construed

broadly, to include attitudes, opinions, values, tastes, even interests and hobbies. More narrowly, however, it includes only our behavior as it is presented to the world—appearance, manners, demeanor, emotionality, and the like. In the narrow sense, being personality-less would entail a nondescript appearance and bland demeanor, and there can be little merit in that. Not only would it take extraordinary effort, which is bound to show, but it would necessarily fall short of any useful standard. Moreover, the requirements of neutrality—as distinct from those of "blank-screen" theory, for instance—do not call for it. Neutrality's requirements are fully satisfied by maintaining a nonselective position. They are satisfied not by being personality-less, but by using our personality in nondiscriminating and nonselective ways.

Reader: What on earth does *that* mean, "using our personality in nondiscriminating and nonselective ways"?

Author: It's a clumsy way of putting it. I mean, say you are emotionally warm and demonstrative, it's an aspect of your personality: then you can behave warmly demonstrative towards your patients without at the same time having violated your neutrality. The critical point is that you remain warmly demonstrative throughout, without significant regard to what they are saying and how they are feeling. If they are despondent or elated, if they are feeling bitter or vindictive, if they are angry at you or resentful—you are still warm and demonstrative. In other words, you avoid, or at least minimize, variations that are reactive.

Reader: But that is asking an awful lot. That kind of uniformity and nonreactiveness, it seems to me, has to be difficult to maintain, if not quite impossible.

Author: Yes, but only if the level of your warmth and demonstrativeness is very high to begin with—and also, to be sure, very low. So you may have to temper it, that's all. The same applies to other expressive aspects of your personality. If you are an enthusiastic person, you need to make sure to maintain the same degree of enthusiasm throughout, and too much of it, as well as too little, can make the task more difficult.

Reader: You select those illustrations deliberately, I gather. You mentioned before that our form of therapy requires of us a degree of warmth and enthusiasm, to go along with our empathy, sensitivity, tactfulness, and ability to listen.

Author: They can be beneficial to the therapeutic process, and I see no reason why they will vitiate our neutrality.

Reader: But isn't there bound to be a difference between our neutrality and our impersonality in the degree to which they put a strain on the patient's sense of credulity? Despite our conscientious efforts to maintain neutrality, despite the care we take to time and formulate our interventions so that they remain nonjudgmental, the patient may find it hard, if not impossible, to fully believe it. And he will cling to the conviction that we are valuating and criticizing him, only hiding the fact.

Author: Yes, that's often the case. Even if he appreciates the profound benefits he derives from having such reactions hidden from him—and most patients do come to appreciate it— he may be unable to shake the conviction that the reactions are there.

Reader: And isn't he is quite correct? We can hardly be expected to remain perfectly neutral.

Author: Of course. Relative neutrality is the most we can strive for. But deliberate impersonality is quite different. For one thing, it isn't so hard to achieve—not at the level of divulging personal information, at least. For another, that we have a personal life, with convictions, opinions, tastes, and values, is never in question, and patients will accept the fact that it's going to be kept from them. They may balk at it. They may recognize no special benefit to them and therefore protest it. But my experience has been this: the relevant issue is special competency and compatibility, which is a business matter, and once that issue has been resolved, patients gradually come to appreciate, and also value, the benefits and advantages of our impersonality.

For inherent in the dynamics of psychotherapy is the fact that our impersonality comes to serve a vital function for our patient. His not knowing us in a personal way provides him with a profound freedom in therapy. He is free to admit every shameful secret, every humiliating experience, every embarrassment and degradation, without running the risk of incurring criticism and deprecation. And the same also applies to "good" experiences—feelings of pride and victory, for instance—they, too, can be inhibited from full expression when another person's interests are at play. That's a fundamental rationale for impersonality. It's an integral aspect of our basic position. If the optimally functioning therapeutic process depends on freedom and autonomy, then we must remain both neutral and impersonal.

Study 2
I Had a Dream Last Night.
Do You Want Me to Tell it to You?

In discussing ways of responding to a direct question, I argued for the option of treating it as business. That was also an option when our patient, in the Basic Instruction Studies, asked for guidance on what to talk about. In this study he is doing both, asking whether we want him to tell the dream he had, so the option is doubly available. We can translate his question into a request for our professional opinion: "Are you asking me whether I believe that dreams are likely to be especially useful for you to examine here?" (And the same can be asked about the review of childhood events, of sexual experiences, and the like, and can also pertain to the use of the couch.) If he agreed with this interpretation, or if his question had taken that form in the first place, we could respond conservatively by saying that there's no way to know it in advance.

However, while this may be our best option, it isn't our only one. There are circumstances that mitigate the directive force of any notification. In certain cases it may be quite possible to say something about the expectable value of dreams without at the same time directing the patient to bring them in. For instance, in response to our patient's direct question we might say "I gather you believe it, and you want to know whether I believe it too." (That's to make sure he *does* believe it, and perhaps it will also reveal the nature and strength of his belief.) Then we can say something like "It has been my professional experience that dreams are sometimes (or usually, or often) useful." And if we thought he might take that as a breach of our nondirectiveness, we could add "I don't mean to be giving you any advice or direction." The element of directiveness remains, of course, but it can be quite minimal. And if we believed that dreams had great potential significance, it may be well-compensated for. That's the rationale for treating the matter as business.

In response to this study, few students suggest as one of their options a remark that invites the patient to say what he thinks of dreams. On the other hand all students include the key phrase "It's up to you" among the options, and they tend to rate it as the best. In fact, "It's up to you" occurs frequently and regularly in their continuations to all of the early studies, probably because it conveys the nondirective message so succinctly. Too often, however, is it used mechanically, in an evasive, nonresponsive way. This study provides a good paradigm of a situation in which the key phrase feels altogether right for a response—only it isn't. Our patient is too likely to persist with:

> Yes, I know it's up to me, but that isn't what I asked you.
> I asked whether you wanted me to tell it to you.

While fully appropriate to a variety of situations that arise early in therapy, "It's up to you" is sometimes quite beside the point. It can fail to address the question. Consider this version:

> I'd rather not say whether I want you to tell it or not.
> Instead, I prefer to leave it up to you.

It seems like an altogether innocuous variation on "It's up to you," and also manages to respond to the question, except, I don't regard the variation as so innocuous. It can imply that we do have certain "wants" (with respect to dreams, at least) but refuse to share them with him. Whenever we intend to respond with the Basic Instruction, our safest course is to repeat it without paraphrase or alteration. (Although in the present context there's nothing wrong with saying "I want to leave it up to you whether you tell the dream or not"; it takes account of the patient's question.)

Students also suggest variations on "You need my permission to tell me the dream." Aside from the fact that it runs an appreciable risk of being wrong ("*No, I didn't ask for your permission; I asked whether you wanted me to tell you the dream,*" is too likely as a counter-response, and we've gained little, except maybe provoking a feeling of resentment over-having been misunderstood), that kind of interpretation has the disadvantage of being overly confronting. Responding to a question with a confrontation is always poor technique because of the implicit message "So you shouldn't have asked."

The following responses are also given by students:

• "Do you want to tell it to me?"—which is little more than fencing.

• "Your bringing it up suggests that you'd like to tell it to me."—which has a gamelike flavor.

• "If I answered your question I'd be telling you what to talk about, and that is something I've said I'd rather not do."— which is a direct response, provided, of course, the issue had already been adequately dealt with.

But responses such as these are likely to be premature because they take the patient's words too literally. His question, in my judgment, isn't self-evident. Aside from the possibility that his *"Do you want?"* was little more than a figure of speech, the question can reflect a number of different concerns. He might be wondering, for instance, whether it was too soon for dreams, whether it would be better if he told more about himself first. (Bear in mind that if he responded to our what-do-you-mean-question with the counterquestion *"Why do you ask? Isn't it perfectly clear what I meant?"* we could mention that meaning.)

Students prefer to select one or another of the possible meanings and cast it in the form of an interpretation. This is often a good technique, but rarely is it good in response to a direct question. When a patient asks a question, he wants an answer, not an explanation, and an unwanted interpretation is never a good one. Moreover, this circumstance calls for a request for clarification, not a speculation. We have no evidence to go on, and speculating from normative or theoretical grounds alone is potentially tactless. Direct steps to find out what he meant by the question are therefore appropriate, and they will have the added advantage of defining us as someone who takes his words seriously.

The same is true for many kinds of questions he might ask early in psychotherapy—for which this study is a prototype— particularly questions about how best to proceed during the sessions. "It's up to you" is sometimes beside the point, and "I'm not sure I understand what you mean." is often to the point.

Study 3
I Am Bothered by Your Sitting There and Staring at Me.

Again we have the option of seeking clarification. And if he responded with *"Isn't it perfectly plain?"* when we've said "It isn't clear to me what you mean by staring at you," we can explain:

> Well, I'm not sure whether you are referring to the fact that I am maintaining eye contact with you or whether it's the way I'm doing it that bothers you.

Perhaps he was experiencing a sense of pressure and expectation from us, or a sense that our gaze (*"stare"*) was critical. He might even think we can see what's on his mind, so he was bothered out of a sense of vulnerability. Or maybe it was our silence or inactivity that bothered him. But again, suggesting any of these possibilities is premature because they are overly speculative interpretations that may impose an extraneous issue. To be sure, mine was speculative too, but it stayed closer to *"staring."* My students, however, are more daring. For example:

> I take it you mean you would rather I didn't just sit here and stare—I should be active?

I would worry that he might have been bothered by the staring alone.

Students do include clarification as one of their three options—for example: "What would you want me to do?" and "I am wondering what it is about this that bothers you" (which I am perhaps too generously counting as questions aimed at clarification)—but they tend to restrict their options to interpretations. They interpret *"bothered"* as "angry" and relate it to the silence; they interpret *"staring"* as "scrutinizing" or "evaluating"; they focus on self-conscious and vulnerable feelings. All of them are intelligent guesses, but guesses nonetheless, because there is only a single piece of evidence available, the opening silence, and it provides little basis for anything more than a guess.

Students also invoke the opening silence in their interpretations, thereby incurring additional disadvantages. Consider this example:

I wonder if this is a possibility: that what is really bothering
you right now is the fact I have remained silent so far.

Notice the implication that we know better what is "really" at
issue; the patient is wrong if he thinks it's the staring. We are
inviting a dispute. And countering with "But I am not staring,"
which students also suggest, might merely provoke an argument that centered on the definition of *"staring."* Even a
tactful, empathic formulation like—

I can appreciate your feeling bothered. This situation is a
new one for you and takes a while to get used to. But I don't
mean to stare, I only mean to listen and try my best to
understand.

—could lead to a disagreement.

But my main reason for including this study among the
Business Studies is not to give me another chance to belabor my
students. The study raises an intriguing question that has
important ramifications: namely, should we respond by modi-
fying our glance and reducing our staring? And I believe we
should. Responding that way means that we construed the
patient's remark as business instead of narrative—this despite
the fact that he hadn't requested a change in our behavior but
merely noted his feeling. And that, in turn, means we are going
to respond neither with silence nor with a speculative interpretation but with the following do-I-understand-you-correctly interpretation: "I gather you are asking me to stop staring at you
the way I am." Then, after he presumably answers in the
affirmative, we will simply and unapologetically say: "I will try
to stare less."

My students never suggest this as an option. When I advocate
it, they express surprise that I don't regard such a response as
acquiescing to "manipulation" and that I wouldn't invoke the
familiar psychoanalytic injunction against it. When I refuse to
acknowledge this injunction for our form of therapy, and then
question its rationale, they answer on the grounds that our
autonomy is violated when we acquiesce to such a request.

I begin my rejoinder by reminding them that our patient's
autonomy needs to be protected as well. Then I emphasize that
we cannot be free in the same ways he is. We are not free to be

late to sessions, for instance, or to express our emotional reactions. We are in fact under many constraints when conducting psychotherapy—and one of them is the constraint against preventing him from influencing our actions. The key question is what considerations should determine how and when we shall allow it.

Our first step is deciding whether to construe the issue within the boundaries of business, so that it belongs together with such requests as changing the appointment time and shading a light bulb that was shining in his eyes, and can be extended to removing a piece of office decoration he finds disturbing, or even wearing clothes that are less offensive to him, and reading his autobiography, and staring. Many teachers would recommend a first step that aimed at finding out what lay behind the request—in other words, treat it as we would a direct question. But they would advocate taking this step no matter what the nature of the request is—and that, I believe, is unwarranted, because we would seem to be judging not only the importance of the request to him but the soundness of his motives. To be sure, we are interested in his motives and feelings, and perhaps his fantasies too, and there's the possibility that our direct response will thrust them into the background. But there is also the possibility that any other kind of response, by virtue of provoking fresh feelings and fantasies, will do the same. Consequently, when it comes to requests for action on our part, as distinct from information, I recommend that we delay making a decision only when the nature of the request has a significant bearing on the format and procedures of therapy itself.

In my judgment, the chief consideration is whether the therapeutic process might be impaired or impeded, either from the patient's vantage point or from mine. So if the light bulb that bothered him had no relevance to the process itself, I would go right ahead and acquiesce without first finding out whether his reason was "legitimate." If my way of dressing has no bearing on my ability to conduct therapy, and it wasn't going to be especially inconvenient for me to alter it, I would do it. And the same is true for "*staring*": if I need to "stare" in order to listen the way I listen best, then that would count as a significant request and I'd delay responding to it until I found out how important it was to him. If, however, that isn't the case, and the "staring" has little relevance to my ability to listen and understand, I would make the accommodation without first satisfying myself that he had a "good" reason for requesting it. Protecting our neutrality is far more important, I believe, than safeguarding ourselves against manipulation. And the ruling rationale is always the integrity of the therapeutic process.

Neutrality and Caring

Reader: But I wonder if you aren't bending over backwards to keep your neutrality from shading into indifference. By acquiescing to the patient's requests for "action," as you put it, weren't you motivated by a wish to show him that you cared?

Author: Neutrality can indeed shade into indifference, and it is something we have to be extremely careful about. It goes without saying that if it amounted to indifference, our neutrality would be ethically untenable. Fortunately, therapy provides us with diverse opportunities, which in turn provide us with diverse ways, to show our patients that we care—and I see nothing wrong in taking advantage of those opportunities.

Reader: What kinds of opportunities, aside from acquiescing to their "manipulations," do we commonly have?

Author: The principal one relates to their need to be heard and understood, and the ways we gratify those needs do reflect a profound aspect of caring. Moreover, I believe patients also have the need—how shall I put this?—the need for therapy itself to be protected against breaches of integrity. They need for us to be consistent and rigorous, and in that way care for their therapy.

But our caring needn't stop there; it can extend from their practical needs, that we gratify in a straightforward way, to their idiosyncratic needs that we gratify in a considerate way. A willingness to be "manipulated" in the interests of those needs can be a tangible expression of our caring attitude, and I don't believe there's any need for stringency in regard to such actions, so long as the first priority remains with the therapeutic process. We can be flexible in meeting our patients' needs, and where we "draw the line" can be based on their particular requirements in conjunction with ours. We are "indifferent" to their needs only when what we could do to meet them would interfere with the essential work of therapy. This has to be a judgment we make in each case, and the patient has to concur in it. If he cannot, whether for reasons that are substantially transferential or not, we may have to make compromises to ensure that our neutrality is not perceived as indifference. For I cannot see how therapy can be effective if our patient perceives us as indifferent to him.

Our strongest bulwark against both the substance and appearance of indifference is the intensity with which we listen actively and interpret sensitively. The point I made in our first dialogue—namely, the crucial requirement of restricting our neutrality to the domain of interpretations—is germane here. It justifies the claim that the reason we maintain that neutrality is exactly because we care about our patient's well-being. And construing business broadly and flexibly, exempting matters of business from the strictures of neutrality, and then approaching business issues in a direct, forthright, and considerate way, enables us to approach our patient's narrative with a degree of neutrality that is unique.

Study 4
I Don't Know What to Talk About.

In one or another of its variations—"*I have nothing to say,*" "*There isn't anything to talk about today,*" "*My mind is a blank*"—"*I don't know what to talk about*" is a common way for patients to begin a therapy session, and it isn't restricted to early sessions. So it pays to practice anticipating the variety of contexts and circumstances in which it occurs, becoming familiar with its shades of meanings and reverberations as well as the subtle implications of the different ways we can respond to it. I will discuss a few of these issues in the framework of five main options that students give.

The most popular option is a businesslike reiteration of the Basic Instruction. The advantages are clear enough, but in this circumstance there are also disadvantages. The patient may resent our implying that he had forgotten the instruction. And even if he had forgotten it, the reiteration is likely to be beside the point because it doesn't respond to what he said. (He didn't, after all, say "*I don't know what I should talk about.*") Moreover, the Basic Instruction's directiveness depends on context. In certain contexts it is primarily a notification, but in this particular one it can have the distinct message "Please talk anyway," which is a prodding, an encouragement at best.

Students acknowledge the fact, but claim an advantage to giving a patient encouragement, and I don't dispute that it may be useful in the short run. I do, however, dispute whether it ever "promotes" the therapeutic process. The directive mode, even when used to offer gentle encouragement and support, is so dissonant with the terms and spirit of the Basic Instruction that it should be a recourse of last resort. Moreover, whenever he has the need for encouragement and support, a patient might feel sufficiently gratified when we've understood his need. (Doesn't it bolster one's courage to know that one's intentions, feelings, and experiences, are well grasped?) The appropriate way to give "encouragement" is with simple empathic interpretations. Consider, for instance:

> I gather you are trying to figure out what you want to talk about.

It is supportive enough and also tactful. Even if the patient responded "*No, my mind is just a blank,*" he probably won't have felt prodded or misunderstood, and he might go on to speak about his state of mind.

The second most popular option is the directive itself, which students defend as being helpful in the short run. Here are three succinct examples:

- You don't have to say anything until you are ready to.
- Sometimes it's best not to prepare what to say.
- What were you just thinking about?

They are forthrightly simple—but simply dissonant with the Basic Instruction itself. Moreover, the directive that "*I don't know what to talk about*" can provoke is apt to be more subtle than those. Consider this interpretation: "I take it you are not sure you want to share what you've been thinking." It seems to be an altogether empathic kind of articulation, doesn't it? And even if it turned out to be wrong, it was tactful enough. Yet notice how it conveys the directive "Please share your thoughts," in a subtle way. In fact, because of its subtlety, its directive properties may be insidious, masked as they are behind an empathic attitude.

Next, students include a purely empathic kind of response among their options. Here are two good examples:

I can appreciate that you find yourself in a difficult, and perhaps an awkward, situation, to choose what it is you want to say.

I can understand that it is difficult to decide what to talk about. Perhaps the idea that you can say what you want, that it's up to you, makes you uncomfortable.

These interpretations can be defended on the grounds of being supportive while at the same articulating the patient's experience; and even if they turn out to be inaccurate they are likely to be well-taken because they restrict their focus to the decision process. Compare them, however, with the following example, which focuses instead on the defense, and notice how it takes a significant step away from the patient's statement:

I guess it's hard for you to tell me some of the things you are thinking about.

A speculation like that can easily be taken as a criticism. Even if it turned out to be correct, it might put him on the defensive. (It might even cause him to worry about his suitability for therapy.) And whenever we formulate a supportive remark in a nonempathic kind of way—when we do it didactically, like the following examples do—its understanding component may be washed away and what remains is little more than reassurance: "It is sometimes difficult to decide how to begin"; and "Knowing that you can talk about whatever you like sometimes makes it harder to speak." Being empathic is quite different from being reassuring. Reassurance, unlike empathy, can be unreassuring if its intent is too transparent. (*"Why are you reassuring me? Do you think I'm worried? And if so, should I be?"*) Moreover, reassurance sometimes betrays the reassurer's feelings—and whenever our patient has trouble talking, and especially when therapy (not to mention the therapist) is young, we are prone to experience a sense of worry.

Next, students include a straight interpretation as one of their three options. Their favorite is exemplified by "I take it you are waiting (wishing, or hoping) for me to tell you what you should talk about (help you decide, or suggest a topic)." Next in frequency comes:

> Perhaps it's not that you don't know what to talk about, but rather that you are uncertain whether there are things you should talk about.

> Perhaps thoughts were occurring to you when you were silent, but you weren't sure whether you should tell them.

They also focus on the therapist's reaction:

> Do you have some misgivings about my reaction to some things you want to talk about? Perhaps you were wondering how I would react to your thoughts.

The chief disadvantage to such interpretations (and students acknowledge it) is that they are necessarily too speculative. In practice, of course, the requisite evidence may be gleaned from the previous session in a way that removes the interpretation from the realm of pure speculation and makes a stronger option. In any event, however, our interpretation should address what our patient said rather than his silence. Any attempt to explain the silence is fraught with pitfalls. On the one hand he might resent our having read his silent thoughts; he might even be frightened by it. On the other hand he might wonder why we did and infer that silence was unacceptable. (Consider "Perhaps you believe it is bad to be silent in here." If that turned out to be incorrect, he might respond "*No, I believe no such thing, but I gather you do.*") Yet, even if evidence to support an interpretation were available, I believe it is ill-advised to raise the issue so early. Silence in therapy is likely to be complicated and multi-determined, and shouldn't be dealt with too soon and too superficially; it can wait until both its meanings and its relevancy are especially clear.

But the chief handicap of any interpretation in response to "*I don't know what to talk about*" is that it will inevitably imply a why-question. This amounts to imposing a topic. There is no reason to suppose that the patient was wondering why he didn't know what to talk about, and chances are that any interpretation will be perceived by him as having raised that question;

and then his question becomes *"Why do you raise it? Why do I need to understand why? What's wrong with my not knowing what to talk about?"* To be sure, this is a format issue, so we can justify our having imposed the topic on that basis. But it means we've treated the issue as business—and business isn't the best subject to approach interpretively. We never want our interpretations to impose a topic, especially not a business one.

Moreover, whenever it interprets a format issue, an interpretation runs the risk of becoming a scolding. Consider this flagrant example: "Perhaps you feel it would be easier if I took charge of the session." Even if its thrust is entirely accurate, it readily lends itself to being heard as a scolding. (The patient can complete it with "And you ought not to be feeling that.")

Finally, as one of their five options students suggest a clarification question. But they don't ask it simply and directly—"How do you mean *I don't know what to talk about?*" Instead, they ask a question that enumerates its possible meanings. What thereby remains ambiguous is whether they were referring to the patient's utterance or to his silence. Here are three examples: "—Is that because you have nothing on your mind?" "Is it that what you are thinking seems trivial?" "Are there several things on your mind and you don't know which one to talk about?" Each of them comes too close to asking "Why the silence?" Since that is a piece of interviewing, it calls for a detailed and extended examination of—

The Pitfalls and Perils of Interviewing

I'm sure it's amply clear by now how strongly I believe that our basic and overriding orientation should be one of striving to understand—not only what our patient is experiencing in respect to feelings, intentions, and needs, but his thoughts and ideas as well—and how this orientation requires keeping in mind the question "What does it mean?"

Reader: Yes, it *is* amply clear. Why do you raise it again?

Author: In order to defend two exceptions to our proscription of interviewing questions, and it's one of them. I want to argue that the clarification question is different from a question that asks for new information. Therefore, I need to emphasize that before we say "I don't understand," we must be sure, first of all, that we genuinely didn't, and second of all that we weren't saying "I don't understand *why*—so tell me more about it." The directive should only be: "Help me understand what you mean to be saying; clarify your thinking for me—by saying it another way, perhaps."

Reader: Okay, this means we ask for meaning only when the utterance itself was unclear or ambiguous.

Author: And this study provides a good paradigm of that circumstance, because it isn't clear in what sense our patient meant "*I don't know what to talk about.*" He might be unsure about what would be most beneficial or appropriate to talk about, he might feel the need for direction, his mind might be blank, and the like. So if he responded with a "*Why do you ask?*" we could explain that we weren't sure we understood his meaning, and then enumerate the different possibilities.

Reader: Having a few of them in mind protects us against using the clarification question for directive purposes, I gather.

Author: Yes, I believe it can. If you play the patient to my therapist, I will show you how it might go. I'm not sure I understand how you mean "*I don't know what to talk about.*"

Reader: *How I mean it? What do you mean—isn't it perfectly clear?*

Author: Well, one possibility is that you have several things that you want to talk about but don't know which one to pick.

Reader: *Okay, that makes sense. It happens not to be true, but it fits. But you said it was one possibility, and I can't see what others there are. Did you have anything else in mind?*

Author: Yes, I did. They are more speculative than that one. That's why I mentioned it first. . . .

Reader: *Why did you pause?*

Author: To make sure you wanted to hear my speculations.

Reader: *I am eager to hear them.*

Author: One of them is that you might be expressing some uncertainty about what things would be the most beneficial, or perhaps the most appropriate, to talk about. You may have the conviction that certain topics belong in therapy while others don't.

Reader: What if I disavowed that possibility and asked for more?

Author: I would be loath to comply. After all, my purpose was to show you that I hadn't been disingenuous, and I think I have. Although I could continue listing speculative possibilities, I would now worry that you were stringing me along—and perhaps you were doing it at the outset.

Reader: Would you interpret that?

Author: On no account. It would amount to a flagrant confrontation. But I would think it and wait for a timely opportunity to offer the interpretation in a less diagnostic way.

Reader: Wouldn't the thought distract you?

Author: Not, I would hope, too much. And besides, I'd be "waiting" for the opportunity, not "looking" for it. Now, as I've already told you, I included this study among the Business Studies in order to advocate that it *not* be construed as business, and that when a patient—either at the outset of a session or during the course of it, and even when it's an early session—says "*I don't know what to talk about,*" we needn't initiate an interview. The temptation to do it can be strong, but I believe it should be resisted. And to explain why, I have to examine the interviewing mode in some detail. If you are impatient with this dialogue, you can skip ahead to Chapter 4. We are through with the Business Studies.

Reader: I'll keep you company as long as you stick to the point.

Author: Perhaps the most distinctive aspect of our therapy, and also the most problematic, centers around the proscription against using the interviewing format. This proscription is difficult to defend, because questions for factual information and probes into feelings are natural straightforward ways to facilitate and sharpen a patient's work. But since questions have so many serious drawbacks, so many effects that can impair the therapeutic process and distort the therapy session, I cling to the conviction that we should use them only for matters of business and exceptional circumstances such as impasses and crises.

Reader: And never for narrative. The difference between questions that ask for information and questions that ask for clarification is the difference between asking for something the patient did not say and asking for an explication of what he did say, so the question "What do you mean?" is quite permissible.

It's the first of our two exceptions to the proscription of interviewing questions. What's the second?

Author: It comes up when the patient has been silent but
hasn't commented on it. The question is: "What are you
thinking?"

Reader: That's permissible? It's a bald directive, isn't it?

Author: Yet it's an option that I believe we can keep open.

Reader: Explain!

Author: For one thing, the gap in verbalization that occurs
when a patient was silent isn't the same as a gap in information
when he was speaking, and while there is a surface similarity
between the directives "Tell me the fact you omitted from your
narrative" and "Tell me the thought you had during your
silence," there is also a fundamental difference. The former
runs the risk of imposing a new topic, the latter doesn't. If we
had asked "Why are you silent?"—which isn't the directive I'm
referring to—that could amount to an imposition insofar as it's
quite likely he wasn't thinking about the reason for his silence.
Moreover, even when he answers "*Nothing—I wasn't thinking
of anything,*" we haven't changed the subject or imposed a
topic.

Reader: We have if he feels impelled to consider why.

Author: Yes, but it wasn't really implicit in our question.
And this sometimes has to be made clear. So if he responded as
if I had asked the why-question, I would take pains to make it
clear that I hadn't intended to. Furthermore, asking him to
verbalize his thoughts is significantly different from asking him
to provide an omitted fact or feeling, because we aren't directing
him to speak about anything new and different, something he
wasn't already thinking about.

Reader: But if he was silent because he didn't want to
speak his thoughts, aren't we violating the Basic Instruction by
asking for them? He might respond: "*Look here, you said I was
free to speak about whatever I wanted, and I'm assuming that
included the freedom to remain silent. I was thinking about
something I don't want to talk about. Are you directing me to
speak about it anyway?*"

Author: Whether he articulated the issue as clearly as that
or not, the first thing I'd make clear is that he was free to remain
silent if he wanted to, and I didn't mean to imply that his silence

wasn't all right. Then I'd explain my reasons for having broken his silence as follows:

> I had no way of knowing you were thinking about something you didn't want to talk about. I thought you might have slipped into a reverie, sort of, and perhaps you were having some difficulty overcoming the inertia of the silence itself. So I figured it might be useful to help you overcome that inertia by asking for your thoughts.

Notice, please, how my explanation attempts to avoid the message "I am interested in your unspoken thoughts."

Reader: But it fails to avoid the implication that reverie-like states aren't useful, and raises the question of why it is useful to have the inertia of silence overcome.

Author: My answer is based on the premise that the therapeutic process is enhanced by verbalization, that self-inquiry is facilitated when the patient is not only thinking but also verbalizing his thoughts, mainly because he is then in the position to listen to himself. Other things being equal, self-observation is usually enhanced by observing oneself in action, and for most people, most of the time, verbalizing their thoughts improves their ability to observe those thoughts. So if I judged that my patient was no exception, or that this particular silence wasn't exceptional, I would base my answer on that rationale, saying:

> Overcoming a silence's inertia is useful because speaking your thoughts may help you benefit more from the sessions.

Notice again how the explanation avoids implying that my participation is at issue—namely, I have to know what he's thinking in order to help him understand and discover. To be sure, there's no compelling reason to formulate it that way; we could take the position that the second part of the Basic Instruction required him to speak in order that we could listen. But that point is so self-evident that I'd be inclined to emphasize the first rationale.

Reader: But can't that rationale, with only minor modifications, be adapted to fit a variety of different directives? If we had reason to believe that the therapeutic process could benefit from the exploration of dreams, for instance, the rationale could justify the directive to bring them in. And suppose our patient was speaking about a symptom and focusing only on its current status, and suppose we had reason to believe it might be useful for him to consider its historical origins, why not notify him of that conviction in the form of a directive? Or conversely, if he were speaking only about its genesis, why not "Please talk about the way the symptom happens now, because that might be useful"?

Author: In other words, if promoting the process was our only goal, why should we be prevented from following the most expeditious course of action across a variety of different areas? "WHAT'S WRONG WITH INTERVIEWING?"

Reader: And the Basic Instruction hasn't ruled it out! As far as he is concerned, were we to give any of the directives I mentioned, our patient would have no reason to conclude that we had departed from its conditions—especially since the directives restrict themselves to therapy's procedure. Mind you, I haven't forgotten your mentioning in our initial dialogue that we need to find an appropriate time to amplify on the matter. After we've arrived at the clinical judgment that our patient was a suitable candidate for our form of therapy, we look for an opportunity to notify him that we will "try" not to give him any kind of advice, and we're supposed to clearly specify that this means advice pertaining not only to behavior outside therapy but also in it. He will likely understand why we refrain from advising him on courses of action to follow in his daily life, and the matter is easily explained in terms of our wishing to remain objective and neutral, but he might be puzzled, if not worse, about the restriction on advice as to how he should proceed in the therapy, saying: "*I can see why you wouldn't want to tell me whether I should change my job, or invest in the stock market, or even get married. But that's quite different from telling me what to talk about here, isn't it?*" After all, we have some experience and expertise in this area, we ought to be able to give some useful advice.

Author: Listen, I've already examined the larger answer to this question as well as the specific one—namely, "In my experience, the most useful thing for you to speak about is what you want to speak about." And if you continued to press the question, I could introduce the distinction between short-term and long-term considerations. I could concede that a directive might be useful in the short run but contend that it might impede the long-range goals of therapy.

And there's no need to minimize the potential usefulness of certain directives. If my patient feels at a loss about what to talk about and says it would be *"useful"* for the moment if he got some directive from me, he may be perfectly right; it would be useful. But the question I'd ask myself is whether it would be useful only in the short run, and therefore shortsighted, to fulfill his request, because it would in fact impede the optimal development of the therapeutic process in the long run. This doesn't justify a dogmatic rigidity. It doesn't mean that my sole obligation is to the long-range goal and that under no circumstances can I support short-term benefits. All that's required of me is an awareness of these options, that they can be antithetical to each other, and that it might be more useful to him if I helped him explore why he feels at a loss over what to talk about and feels a need for direction, or why he doesn't bring in his dreams, or why he never speaks about the history of his symptoms. That's the option that has to be kept open, and it requires a readiness on our part to frustrate his need for directives.

But I don't think these considerations apply equally or fully to the silence-breaking directive, "What are you thinking?" Insofar as the short-term benefits don't necessarily conflict with the long-term ones, this may be an exceptional case. Therefore, when our patient falls into a silence and needs our help to end it, I don't recommend frustrating that need—not as a rule, in any case. We can make an effort to distinguish between meditative or reverie-like silences on the one hand, and resistant or defensive silences on the other. We can try to figure out the nature and function of each silence, and depending on our understanding of it choose to interrupt a silence either with the directive or with an interpretation. Or we may decide, of course, not to interrupt it at all.

Reader: So the question "What are you thinking?" is not problematic at all.

Author: I wouldn't put it that strongly. In certain cases and under certain circumstances, I would hesitate to use it. My point is that it isn't necessarily problematic, so the question isn't at issue here.

Reader: And the question that *is* necessarily problematic, and therefore at issue, is the interviewing question proper: a directive to provide information that was not provided. For instance, "How old were you when the incident happened?"

Author: Yes, it equals "Tell me how old you were."

Reader: Similarly, "I'm wondering how come you haven't told me how old you were," equals "Tell me why you left out your age."

Author: And we call it a "probe" when the information solicited is affects and emotions—"How did you feel when it happened?" and "What are your feelings now while you recount it?" Whenever there is a gap in a patient's narrative, a piece of information that he didn't provide, we have four options: direct him to provide it—"I wonder how old you were"; direct him to explain why he failed to provide it—"How come you didn't mention your age?"; guess the information—"I take it you were 6 years old"; speculate on his motive for failing to provide it—"I gather you're ashamed to tell me your age." We can see that the first two are direct questions and the last two are interpretations. My thesis is this: only when an interpretation is at hand, only when it is part of a pending interpretation, is the use of direct questions defensible.

This thesis puts me squarely at odds with practitioners who make active, free, and vital use of direct questions and for whom the probe is practically a stock-in-trade. They would agree that the clarification question, since it conveys interest in the patient's meanings and intentions, is useful. But they would contend that the direct question, and the probe in particular, is equally useful insofar as it shows interest in his facts and feelings. They might also agree that excessive reliance on questions can transform a session into a clinical interview, but would contend that a judicious mix of questions and interpretations can prevent that from happening.

My first response to their argument is to stress the passive position that direct questions and probes cast a patient into, something that needn't be the case for interpretations. I also emphasize that questions and probes cast us into the role of mentor and troubleshooter in a way that interpretations needn't. Moreover, direct questions also exert a subtle but significant influence on the nature of the interpretations that we give, for in the context of interviewing, our interpretations tend to become diagnostic and troubleshooting explanations—explanations that treat the patient more as an object of inquiry than as a subject.

Finally, rarely asking direct questions, and virtually never probing, serves the valuable function of ensuring more active listening on our part and more empathic interpreting. In my experience, the discipline goes far toward guaranteeing that our patient's therapy will achieve the spirit of active and relatively autonomous self-inquiry that reflects the essential character of the therapeutic process.

Reader: But teachers and practitioners disagree with you?

Author: About questions, many don't. However, they draw the line at probes. The exploration of emotions and affects is so vital to therapy, they argue, that the probe must be allowed, if not encouraged. That's the prevailing opinion. And it's based on the observation that factual information may indeed often be therapeutically unimportant, but the same is never true for feelings. Feelings have such intrinsic importance that uncovering them is therapeutically justified across a broad range of circumstances.

Reader: And you disagree?

Author: Not with the observation itself, I don't. I, too, have observed that feelings are never irrelevant. Not only are they a vital aspect of human experience, but they have a special usefulness in therapy as guides and markers to important areas of inner reality. Consequently, they are both intrinsically important and serve an invaluable signaling function. My quarrel is only with the probe as a technique for eliciting and using them. I don't think it's the best way to get at them, and rarely is it the best technique for exploiting their usefulness.

Reader: You will doubtless now tell me why.

Author: My first and foremost objection to the probe is its paradoxical tendency to invoke intellectualization. It often invites the patient to verbalize his feelings and thereby label them.

Reader: And inviting him to do it is never a useful thing to do?

Author: Not never. It can sometimes have the valuable short-term function of helping him gain cognitive control. So if our purpose is to invoke and strengthen certain of his cognitive defenses, then the probe, in encouraging him to put his feelings into commonly understood words, can be a useful technique. But practitioners—and I mean, of course, those who are arguing with me—use it for exactly the opposite purpose. They regard the probe as a technique for circumventing and weakening the defense of intellectualization, and isolation of affect too, thereby getting patients to confront their feelings instead of dealing only with their cognitions. And here is where I disagree, where I regard the technique as antithetical to the purpose, where I believe it can too easily undermine rather than promote.

Consider the reasons a patient might have omitted his feelings and thereby provoked a probe. It might reflect his conviction that we are interested only or mostly in his feelings, so he will frustrate our interest by withholding them. It might reflect the conviction that his feelings are too inarticulate and amorphous to be put into words we can understand. He might be too ashamed of his feelings—or, for that matter, too proud of them—or be convinced they'll incur our contempt or envy. He might hold his feelings in low regard or regard them as irrelevant. And there's also the possibility that he simply doesn't know what his feelings are or were. I needn't belabor the point that such reasons are important to uncover and understand. My point is that the probe isn't the best way to do it.

Reader: Then let's do it with an interpretation—for instance: "I notice you rarely tell me about your feelings, have you been aware of that?" or "Though you usually tell me what your feeling is, you've omitted telling me this time; did you notice that?" These remarks are not probes—unless of course the patient takes them as such and proceeds to tell the feelings, in which case we would make it clear to him that we were asking a different question.

Author: They are, however, confrontations, and the confronting mode is also problematic. I'd rather we formulated the observation more empathically. I'd rather we articulated the feeling, or suggested a reason it was omitted, instead of instructing the patient to. So my guideline comes down to this: we wait until we have some basis on which to make an interpretation; we don't address the matter before then. We don't probe for feelings, we articulate them. Instead of asking "What feeling are you experiencing?" we emphathize or even guess at it; we speculate. And if the time is right, we go ahead and tell him what we've come up with. Similarly, if we have a timely hunch about why the patient has or doesn't have, always has or never has, a certain feeling, we say so with an interpretation.

Reader: But a strong argument can be made for probing first, before interpreting, in order to safeguard against mistaking the patient's feelings. Isn't the probe more prudent in that it takes the precaution of being correct? And isn't the danger of error compounded by the likelihood that a patient won't feel so free to countenance our mistake but instead will fall under the sway of suggestion, "feeling" what we said he was feeling? The issue seems to resolve into the difference between asking after a feeling and guessing it, and the guess is risky because he is apt to be suggestible when it comes to his affects— "*Yes, I suppose you're right, I am feeling angry*," or "*Yes, you must be correct, I did feel happy.*" That risk may not be so great when the guess is about the patient's ideation, because if it's alien to him he can say so, nor so serious when it applies to explanations and integrations, because they have a somewhat theoretical nature to begin with, and all he has to do is judge whether they fit. But when we venture to tell him what he is or was feeling, the influence of suggestion is apt to be pernicious, and the probe is an appropriate way to safeguard against this danger.

Author: That is a strong argument with one weakness; it fails to take account of therapy's extended time frame. Therapy should provide ample time and opportunity for us to assess the role that suggestion may be playing. We can observe the extent to which our interpretations are accepted uncritically, and we can modulate them accordingly. If we want to minimize suggestion, we have to pay careful attention to it—and not only when it comes to affects but in all of our interpretive speculations. To be sure, affects are peculiarly susceptible to suggestion, so a special alertness and caution is called for. But rather than resolve the problem by using probing questions, we have two options: to be especially conservative in our speculations about affect, and to look for opportunities to work interpretively with the problem of suggestion itself. After all, if we have reason to believe the patient is prone to accept our suggestions, working with that therapeutically is bound to benefit him, for we can assume that it's a significant problem outside of therapy as well.

Reader: But isn't it true that therapy, with its manifold potentialities for regression and transference, may accentuate and exaggerate the problem?

Author: Yes, it might even create the problem. But the probe isn't the only way to solve it; a mild confrontation can also do it. If we had a particular reason to be interested in what our patient was feeling but no basis for an inference, or if we judged that the feeling was especially germane to the narrative but hesitated to speculate because he was suggestible, we could draw attention to it with a remark like "I gather you don't know what you're feeling?" In my judgment, it's the lesser of the two evils. But we must be sure our interest isn't idle, or we're interested in the feeling merely for its own sake, so to speak. We are interested not simply because it was omitted, but because we have reason to believe the omission is significant to the ongoing therapeutic process.

Furthermore, whenever we experience the impulse to interrogate, we can take it as a signal. If we are free from misgivings about our position as the listener, and are not being prompted to interrogate out of a sense of wanting to participate more actively in the session, we can then proceed on two assumptions: our impulse was prompted by a significant gap in our patient's narrative, and the gap was determined by a significant reason. Accordingly, we should want to uncover the reason, and the pertinent question to ask is a why-question rather than a what-question.

Reader: What's wrong with the argument that a what-question must precede the why-question, that before we can proceed to explore the reason for an omission we have to know what the omission was?

Author: It overlooks the fact that the former will emerge quite naturally when the latter is being explored. So in practice we can usually avoid the what-question and try to express an interest in the meaning of the omission, rather than a sense of curiosity about what was omitted.

Reader: Won't he simply tell us what was omitted and ignore the why-question?

Author: Yes, and when he does that, we can say something like:

I didn't mean to ask you what it was you left out, or draw
your attention to the fact that it was left out. Rather, I'm
trying to explore the reason you left it out, the meaning of
its having been omitted.

Otherwise, what tends to happen is a division of responsibilities
in which he reports the facts and we inquire after the feelings, or
in which we take responsibility for the gaps by choosing when
to ask about them. And even if he gets the idea that feelings are
important, or that gaps in his narrative are significant, he can
learn to report them routinely, mechanically, and passively.
That, I'm sure you'll agree, would be unfortunate.

Let me now turn to a point I've mentioned in passing: the
special role that affects can play in therapy as guides and
markers to important areas of inner reality. During a session, a
patient's train of thought may be interrupted or diverted because of a feeling he experienced. The probe can then be used
for two purposes: to point out the reason the thought was
interrupted and diverted, and to sensitize him to the ways his
feelings regulate his psychic functioning. Often it's a subtle
feeling, fleeting and difficult to capture, and learning to pay
attention to it can be a useful lesson. The probe is the simplest
and most immediate and direct way to teach that lesson. The
lesson is "Let the feeling be a guide to the fact that something is
up!" By being alerted to pay attention to them, the patient is
taught to use his feelings for the purposes of exploration and
discovery.

So when he asks *"Why do you want to know my feelings?"*
the answer can be: "Because such feelings can give us a
valuable clue to your inner reality—your conflicts, impulses,
and defenses." The mode is didactic; the patient is being
taught how to explore. We play the role of enabler, if not of
teacher, guiding the exploration by using affect as marker and
guidepost. When we say "The fact that you experienced a
twinge of anxiety may mean that a forbidden impulse or
unconscious fantasy or conflict is threatening to emerge," it
isn't an interpretation but a didactic lesson. The fact that the
lesson derives from considerations of theory or out of our
clinical experience, not from evidence the patient is providing,
defines the formulation as didactic. And even if we've put it
more tactfully, saying "Your train of thought was interrupted,

wasn't it? I wonder if that didn't happen because something intruded on your mind, a thought or a feeling, and that might explain the interruption," the extent to which the specific intrusion remains unspecified is the extent to which it remains didactic.

Therefore, while the probe might not be the best technique in these circumstances, it could be the only one available. If there was any basis for inferring a particular affect, then an interpretation can be more effective. When there is no such basis, a probe is our only recourse. So, for the kind of phenomenon I've been describing, its advantages may outweigh its potential disadvantages.

Reader: Are there circumstances in which a question for factual information may have a similar advantage? Is there also an exception to our proscription of that kind of question?

Author: I can think of only one—when we have a timely interpretation in mind and feel the need for a piece of information to validate it.

Reader: Do I hear a touch of asperity in that proviso? Then let's examine the matter by working with a prototypic situation in which I might feel the need for a piece of information in order to validate a timely interpretation. My patient is recounting an event from his childhood and hasn't mentioned how old he was at the time, so the question is: "How old were you?" I want us to assume that it can be asked without any unwanted implications such as "Your account was deficient," or "You should have mentioned your age," and that his not having mentioned it was a simple oversight, or that perhaps he presumed his age wasn't relevant. Therefore, were I to put the question, he'd merely take a moment to add *"Oh, I was 6,"* and then resume his account. Okay?

Author: Okay, so the only question at issue is why the question. What useful function could the information serve? How might it support and improve the therapeutic process?

Reader: I wouldn't have wanted to ask, unless I had reason to believe the information might be important.

Author: But for whom?

Reader: Let's begin with me—to improve my understanding of him.

Author: Then my question to you becomes, "Are you going to share your improved understanding with him?"

Reader: What big difference does that make?

Author: This big difference: if you planned to follow up with an interpretation, saying "That information helps me understand the event, and here's how—" then the question was an integral part of a pending interpretation. Your patient will probably appreciate that you asked it in order to make sure the interpretation had a chance of being correct, that it was more a precaution than anything else. In an important sense, the question was part and parcel of the interpretation. Moreover, if it turned out that the information didn't provide support for the one you had in mind, your having asked can be justified by telling him what the interpretation is, saying "I asked because I had thought to suggest that—." And this, by the way, is something I recommend you do.

Reader: You feel I need to justify the question that much? All right, I will. Then this, I gather, is an exception to our proscription of direct questions; when it is part of a pending interpretation, a question shares the advantages of the interpretive mode and might outweigh the disadvantages of the interviewing mode.

Author: It merely establishes the fact that our understanding and speculation will be tempered and judicious.

Reader: Then what if I didn't intend to explain the event to my patient? What if I had no timely interpretation in mind? In that event, the information will have been useful only to my overall efforts at understanding him.

Author: And that puts a different cast on the matter. Without minimizing this kind of usefulness, and dismissing the likelihood that such understanding can play an important part in your future interpretations, I believe that if you actively gather information that you plan to use only at some future time, you will incur the undesirable side effects of the interviewing format. The main one is your patient's expectation that once you have amassed all the necessary information about him, you will give him useful interpretations. You are defining yourself as a repository of factual information and taking on the interviewer's role of diagnostician and troubleshooter. Consequently, using questions that way, although it differs only in time frame from using them to ensure that an interpretation is valid, can make a significant difference in respect to your role definition.

Reader: Then what about the possibility that the age question, by drawing *his* attention to an important feature of what

he is working on, will have the result of facilitating his therapeutic work? It may well be useful in the sense that it might lead
him to include a valuable feature of the event, thereby in-
creasing the probability of discovery—and for him, not me. All
I conveyed with the question is that it might be helpful to him,
if he took into account what his age was when the event
occurred.

Author: Before I respond, let me point out that a more
direct way to achieve that goal is to treat the matter as business
and put the question in the form of a suggestion—"Let me
suggest to you that it might be helpful if—." In that way you shift
the emphasis from "useful to me" to "useful to you," which in
turn might circumvent some of the role definition problems and
at the same time avoid the implicit promise "If you tell me how
old you were, I will be in a better position to help you understand the event."

Reader: I appreciate your point. The businesslike approach
is certainly more forthright. But suppose the direct question
had that connotation in the first place?

Author: Then two other questions arise. Is it an important
consideration, and what makes you think so? Let's begin with
the second, and put the counter-question in the patient's mouth:
"Why do you think it might be useful to know my age?"

Reader: I can answer it on two grounds: my psychological
theory and my experience as a therapist.

Author: If the choice were mine, I'd choose the second.
Using my theory for a rationale amounts to sharing with him
my belief in a certain conceptual point of view—that develop-
mental stages are important, for instance—and this, in turn,
would raise a number of issues that could have implications.
And that would involve giving him a lesson in psychology.

Reader: I'm not surprised at your not wanting to do that,
but I'll ask you why anyway.

Author: Then let me single out the reason that's bound to
be the most difficult and controversial. Opening a dialogue with
a patient on matters of psychological theory runs the risk of
casting me in the role of an authority on psychology, an expert
on human behavior, and that is a role I'd rather not play.
Psychotherapy rarely requires it of me, and proceeds best when
I don't cover anything other than the conducting of therapy
with the mantle of authority. Now, lest this claim seem implau-

sible to you, I hasten to add that it's not that I pretend to know nothing about psychology or that I have no pragmatic, theoretical, and even scientific knowledge about human behavior. I merely try to avoid the position that I know more than my patient knows. He, too, has a theory of behavior; he, too, has both pragmatic wisdom and an operating theory, and he might also know the science. What I try to do is keep from teaching him mine. The didactic mode has a limited utility in therapy because its main function is usually to provide reassurance and in that respect it overlaps with intellectualization—having the additional disadvantage of being mine instead of his. Therefore, I regard it as generally prudent to avoid any steps that would invoke, or seem to invoke, my knowledge of psychology in general—as distinct from my patient's psychology in particular—and for that reason I wouldn't want to justify a direct question on nomothetic grounds.

Reader: So that leaves me with the second option, my therapy experience, which I'll word this way: "It's been my experience that when patients take into account the age at which events in their past occurred, they can better explore and come to a more complete understanding of them."

Author: Fine! It precludes any possibilities for argument and disputation, something always worth precluding. And while it is clearly both a didactic remark and a normative formulation—insofar as it makes appeal to what is true for other patients—it limits your avowed expertise and defines you only as a therapist.

Reader: I gather we want to avoid normative formulations and never intimate that we were comparing and contrasting our patient with others.

Author: Yes, it's bound to have subtle but significant ramifications for the way he works. Psychotherapy proceeds best when it remains ostensibly ideographic and fully personal, when it restricts itself to evidence and observations that emerge from the patient alone.

Reader: Then let's go back to the key question, the one I raised before your digression. Isn't it true that focusing on his age will help the patient in his explorations of the event?

Author: My temptation is to answer No. That, however, would be an overstatement and only satisfy my need to win the argument. Instead, I can answer "It depends," and concede that if the answer were a "Likely yes" then it could outweigh many of the considerations we've been examining. In other words, if chances were good that the therapeutic process could be significantly improved, then that would tip the balance in favor of the interviewing mode. But my answer, you see, is not a "yes," it's a "generally no"—and that's why I can sustain my fundamental opposition to interviewing. For I do not believe that the level of our patients' work is improved by including factual information of the kind that is typically elicited by our direct questions— especially if we have no ideas, no interpretations in mind, that require the information for their confirmation. Under those circumstances, questioning can amount to little more than a fishing for significance.

Reader: So the critical condition remains—we should have an interpretation in mind before the information can be useful. The point is well taken. But let me mount one final foray. Now, I appreciate that it takes a different perspective from ours; but isn't it easy to suppose that when we actively ask our patient questions we are actively engaged in his therapeutic work? Isn't this the underlying spirit of the interviewing mode?

I will help you uncover and discover; I will participate in your explorations by pointing to areas you are overlooking, by drawing your attention to facts that may seem to you irrelevant, but which may actually turn out to be both relevant and useful.

Moreover, isn't it likely that many of the considerations we examined so far apply mainly to a therapy in which questions are infrequently asked, and that when confronted with a rarely asked question a patient may well wonder why it was asked— what formulation we had in mind for which we needed the information? But if direct questions are often asked him, if they are an integral part of our style and method, then he'd have no reason to wonder why for any particular question.

Author: Yes, that is all quite true—from *that* particular perspective. Ours, however, is predicated on the following observations. The spirit of inquiry that accompanies extensive reliance on interviewing differs fundamentally from the spirit of inquiry that occurs when there is little, if any, reliance on it. It simply makes a profound difference to the way a typical session proceeds, when we rely entirely on what the patient chooses to tell. And the special kind of passivity on our part that is embodied in working only with presented information engenders a special quality of participation on his part.

I don't mean to say that our passivity necessarily causes him to be more active, because it doesn't. He often takes a passive attitude, too. Not a more passive one than ours, of course, because he is speaking and feeling, while we listen and occasionally offer comments. However, the "special quality participation on his part" that I mentioned refers to the fact that a patient who is working within the interviewing format is likely to be less passive, in a certain sense of the term, than one who is not working with it. But his activeness will never lead him into a relatively free kind of mentation, a kind of stream-of-consciousness modality that approximates the underlying spirit of the free-association method. This, however, is not the case when the interviewing format isn't being used. He will often slip quite naturally into that kind of mentation, without having been instructed to, without the disadvantages of taking it as an externally imposed task. This will secure for him the vital benefits of the free-association modality, which include such therapeutically valuable features as a lowered level of self-consciousness and defensiveness, as well as an altered state of consciousness that facilitates an openness to spontaneous and fleeting thoughts and feelings.

Moreover, it also allows, if not encourages, a kind of listening to himself, and of a kind that corresponds to the way we listen to him. And for him to listen to himself, to observe his thoughts and feelings and actions, is most necessary because important discoveries derive from such listening. Interviewing tends to prevent it; interviewing, in certain ways, can obviate the necessity for it. What can happen, paradoxically, is that because we are doing that work for him, the patient doesn't have to observe himself. Interviewing can make him more passive than is optimal—passive and not actively listening to himself.

But discussions of activity-passivity have a way of becoming highly theoretical and getting out of hand. We haven't exhausted the subject, but we may already be exhausted from it. So let me rest with the claim that the best place for our patient

isn't at any of the extremes of activity-passivity's various
dimensions, but fluctuating somewhere in between. And when
we ask questions and put probes, when we use the interviewing
mode for anything other than business matters, we are likely to
push him toward one or the other extreme.

4 _____

INTERPRETATION

The Form and Function of Interpretations

Imagine an 18 year old, in his tenth session, telling us about an episode of hysterical laughter he had while watching his sister doing yoga exercises with her friend Pat. He'd been studying in his room but their music distracted him, so he went to watch, and when Pat *"went into this real far-out position, with her ankles up around the back of her neck,"* he started laughing and couldn't stop. *"I don't know why, because it wasn't all that funny, actually. In fact, you know, it was actually a bit disgusting to see her like that."*

Listening to his account, which is the first of the Interpretation Studies, we are likely to think of an explanation; keeping ourselves from doing it is virtually impossible. But before we offer it, we need a clear sense of purpose. If our intention was to provide him with an intellectual understanding of the episode, then his narrative has given us plenty to work with. It contains enough material to support an explanation of his uncontrolled laughter in terms of anxiety, and that anxiety, in turn, can be formulated as the signal of intrapsychic conflict. Accordingly, his feelings of disgust can be construed as the product of a defensive need to ward off unacceptable ideas (of a sexual nature), and his hysterical laughter the sign of an imminent

119

breakdown in the defense. I composed a narrative with exactly that formulation in mind, thereby inviting an interpretation containing one, several, or all of its elements.

However, even if our sole purpose was to offer an intellectual understanding, we must give serious consideration to the way we structure it. Our understanding has to be cast in the form of an interpretation, after all, and an interpretation has a formal structure—its verbal features, its stylistic inflections, its implicit communicative gestures—and they convey significant information as well. Let's suppose we worded our interpretation this way:

> You were feeling sexually aroused, but the feeling was unacceptable to you because of your sister's presence, so you experienced instead a sense of disgust. But a conflict like that can make a person anxious and tense, which in turn can result in such hysterical reactions as uncontrollable laughter.

Its completeness and explicitness, its certainty of voice, along with the implicit message "I can understand what you cannot" (perhaps also "Look how wise I am in the ways of men! Listen to the fine explanations I have to offer you!") are its salient tone and overtones. And notice also to what extent the interpretation is theoretical and normative. "People like you, in situations like yours, when they behave the way you did, are most likely under the sway of this conflict and that defense—and when the defense breaks down, this is what happens." This is its formal structure, and a formulation of that kind can be considered to be *diagnostic*.

But what alternatives do we have? What formal features are desirable? Our central timing criterion provides a general answer: we formulate our interpretations in such a way, and at such a time, that the patient will explore the episode as fully as possible, and thereby make fresh discoveries for himself. A complete and authoritative explanation, no matter how "true," usually won't serve that purpose. Since, however, we cannot direct him to deliberate and explore (in actuality as well as in the study), we may have to offer some explanatory remarks that the patient will find useful, evocative, and interesting. Therefore, the solutions for the problems posed by these studies—

given also the limitations of the transcripts and the fact that we know so little about our patient—may necessarily be compromises.

Before examining them, let's consider a further possibility: the patient might be speaking disingenuously, he actually isn't so mystified by his behavior. (For one thing, he knows he was sexually aroused—why else did he leave his studying to go and watch?) If that's the case he might be inviting us to say something he already knows, and this basically is a transference issue. So the good interpretation would be something along the lines of "I believe you are not as mystified as you say, but you need me to play the role of explainer."

Another possibility, and potentially a more germane one, is that he is being disingenuous not with us but with himself; he is being naive, or playing dumb, perhaps quite deliberately and purposely. This would signify a defensive process and invite the hypothesis that the same defense that operated during the event was operating during the recounting of it. Just as he defended himself against the recognition of his feelings, impulses, and conflicts then, he is defending against a similar recognition now—including a recognition of the explanation itself. This hypothesis has important ramifications. It means that his work of exploration and self-inquiry is being impaired by an aspect of his personality that stands in the way of self-knowledge. Because this work is the therapeutic process itself, and because our therapy's central timing criterion is satisfied when we supervise the process, our active participation is called for. The question, however, remains. What kind of active participation is most appropriate and useful?

In my opinion the best answer to this question, at the level of practice at least, is to accept the working hypothesis that the patient probably does "know" what he needs to know; most of the useful articulations and valid explanations are already present in his mind—at some level, at least, and in some form. This working hypothesis derives from the psychoanalytic conception of the *system-preconscious* and the proposition that interpretations address preconscious derivatives of unconscious mentation. Their function, accordingly, is to facilitate the emergence of unconscious ideas, memories, and fantasies. From another vantage point, interpretations make contact with the barrier (the censorship, the countercathexis, or the defense), and in one way or another weaken it to permit not only the uncovering of unconscious contents but also their reorganization. But psychoanalysis also has a structural theory that requires our interpretations to address the ego. Insofar as it serves the three masters of id, superego, and reality, the ego must compromise on three fronts, and interpretations appeal to its so-called synthetic function. What complicates matters is that ego is at once the knowing agency and the defending agency, so interpretations have to take account of its conflicting interests—when, of course, they are in conflict.

Whichever way we conceptualize it, this working hypothesis implies that most of our relevant and germane interpretations can be prefaced with "This is what is in your mind; this is your thought / idea / attitude / belief / conflict / feeling / mood." In other words, the most useful interpretations are those that address mental content, so to speak, those that interpret what he already *has in mind*. And such interpretations are, by my definition, *empathic*.

An empathic interpretation needn't reflect an act of empathy on our part. Whether it is or isn't based on the process of with-feeling, or reading-into, is beside the point. The main reason I choose to call it an *empathic interpretation* is that calling it an "interpretation of mental content" is clumsy. Neither does it have to be correct. Just because it happens to be mistaken and misreads a patient's mental content doesn't disqualify it as an empathic interpretation. And neither, by the way, does it vitiate its usefulness; an incorrect interpretation can still have a desirable result. The relevant consideration is that the interpretation speaks to his phenomenal experience—it speaks to what he already *knows*, or nearly knows.

Along with thinking and feeling and wishing, what he already *knows* includes remembering and recalling, believing, judging and conjecturing, whatever the phenomenal experience may be. Moreover, it can also include explanations, but only when they are his own. Only when they are authentically his and we can preface our interpretation with "This is your explanation / theory / hypothesis," do explanations qualify as "empathic." All other kinds of explanations fall into the category of what I call "diagnostic." Simply stated, then, diagnostic formulations are those that cannot be ascribed to the patient's phenomenal experience. ("I believe you're saying how mystified you are in order to get me to explain the event to you" is a diagnostic formulation.)

Can we, in principle at least, do without them? No, because the working hypothesis I stated above has an important corollary that is reflected in the further question: "So how come you aren't aware of what's in your mind? Why or how do you need to defend yourself against the knowledge?" And this relates to the technical guideline that urges us to pay special attention to our patient's defenses. (Sometimes they are broadly construed to include his character traits.) Because they lie somehow outside his mind, we cannot address them with exclusively empathic interpretations. At least it seems intuitively necessary to construe the defense against knowledge at a different level of abstraction than the knowledge itself. Accordingly, the defense cannot be addressed with a "This is what is in your mind," it can only be articulated with an interpretation whose form is "This is how you behave—you obfuscate / forget / overlook / deceive; this is how you relate—you cajole / seduce / bully / submit / dominate," which is clearly diagnostic—unless, of course, the patient had it in mind already.

The same is true for dynamic formulations. "You have this mental content and that phenomenal experience—you are thinking this and feeling that," is empathic, and nondynamic as well, to the extent that the connective "and" is weak. But substitute a "because," and we are deeper into the realm of diagnosis. Insofar as the "because" cannot be taken as an aspect of phenomenal experience, the interpretation, by definition, is diagnostic. Diagnostic interpretations range from the simple "This is connected to that, or this is associated in your mind with that," to complex causal-functional dynamic formulations. But I can now hear a reader objecting—

Reader: Simply substituting a "because" for an "and" transforms an empathic interpretation into a diagnostic one? How come? After all, the two empathic elements—the "this" and the "that"—are still there.

Author: I meant to say it made it "more" diagnostic. What it does, you see, is introduce a stronger diagnostic element, so that the interpretation is now "less" empathic than it was—as well as "more" diagnostic.

Reader: Then the two types of elements are complementary, a more diagnostic interpretation is perforce a less empathic one.

Author: That's my point. An interpretation can be an amalgam of both kinds of elements, and it makes a certain intuitive sense to measure the degree of its empathic-ness and diagnostic-ness by judging their relative preponderance. But of course, simply counting and comparing the components won't do. We have to weigh them on the scales of clinical judgment. And it's on that basis that I characterize certain interpretations in these pages as "mildly / somewhat" diagnostic, and others as "highly / very / flagrantly" so.

Reader: The purest form of empathic interpretation is a simple articulation. It says "This is what is in your mind." What is the purest form of diagnostic interpretation?

Author: A confrontation. The explanatory formulations that we've been examining have some empathic elements—the "this" and the "that"—but a confrontation can have none at all. A confrontation is an observation of a patient's behavior, or action, and it is nonmental in that sense. It takes the following form: "This is how you are / what you do / how you come across—how you act / interact / communicate." By our definition, that's diagnostic, and it's a form of confrontation that addresses the domain of a patient's behavior instead of the domain of his mind.

Reader: Yet aren't there grades of confrontingness as well? Can't we judge a purely diagnostic interpetation "only mildly" confronting when it comes close to what the patient himself was observing about himself?

Author: Yes. In fact, all of these distinctions and dimensions depend a great deal on the patient—who he is, where he is, what's the state of his resistance, his transference, and the like. There is no other way to fully operationalize them.

Reader: All right. So what's our attitude toward diagnostic and confronting interpretations? Apparently, we cannot avoid them entirely and still pay attention to our patient's defenses. Whenever he himself is aware of them, we can formulate our interpretation: "I believe part of you has noticed / glimpsed / suspected that you are (or were) defending / avoiding / forgetting / intellectualizing / displacing," thereby maintaining the empathic position. But surely we cannot restrict ourselves to those moments.

Author: Whenever the fully empathic formulation is not available to us, our defense interpretation will necessarily be diagnostic, and in addition to trying to keep it minimally diagnostic, we have to be alert to its undesired side effects and implications—and take active steps against them as soon as possible.

Reader: But isn't the same true for highly empathic interpretations? Not only do they, too, have undesirable side effects—fostering of a symbiotic transference, for example—but they, too, must be used "sparingly," in the sense that excessive interpreting of any kind can distort the therapeutic process.

Author: So my thesis is that the preponderance of our interpretations should be empathic, because their unwanted side effects and implications can be ameliorated more readily in the course of our work, and they foster our preferred role definition as the one who supervises the therapeutic process. But supervising the process isn't our only role. It is our principal one, to be sure, but not our exclusive one. When circumstances allow and warrant it, we can also venture to participate in the process as a kind of partner. Occasionally, therefore, we can do some noticing for our patient, some diagnosing and confronting—and those participatory functions are examined in the course of the Interpretation Studies. Because of the limitations of the material, and because we assume that an interpretation is timely, the studies often require us to arrive at an understanding of our own, at a discovery that we ourselves make. Our chief technical problem then is to formulate it in a way that can best advance the therapeutic process.

The various aspects of the technical problem are examined in the light of my students' responses in the five studies. I will try to organize my discussion of each study around a particular technical issue, thereby minimizing redundancy, but it won't be possible—as you'll have noticed—to avoid repeating myself, for which I can only apologize.

Instructions for the Interpretation Studies

Each study provides a narrative for which interpretations can be formulated. Your task is to formulate the best one for each. In the interests of making your interpretation a full one, you may want to divide it into parts; if so, you will have to compose more narrative for the patient. (You may assume that therapy is about twelve sessions old.)

Study 1
A Fit of Hysterical Laughter

Yesterday afternoon my sister and her friend Pat got sore at me because I had a fit of hysterical laughter at them. They were in the living room doing their yoga exercises. They've been into yoga for over a month now, so I'm used to seeing them in these weird positions and everything, but I still find it funny . . . I went to my room to study, but they kept distracting me . . . I know what you're thinking; you're thinking why didn't I stay in my room if I wanted to study. But they had the stereo on, one of my sister's Indian ragas, and it disturbed me. I hate that music. I don't know why, but. . . . Anyway, since I couldn't get any work done, I went back into the living room and sat around. . . . Sometimes I'm . . . I get sort of put off by Pat. She's an okay-looking girl but she's too chubby and sweats a lot . . . Anyway, she went into this real far-out position, with her ankles up around the back of her neck, and all. And I just started in laughing hysterically . . . I couldn't stop, I was laughing so hard . . . I don't know why, because it wasn't all that funny, actually . . . In fact, you know, it was actually a bit disgusting to see her like that.

Students infer that this 18-year-old is a naive young man and therefore had to be treated with special tact. The technical problem is how to maintain this tact without at the same time being gingerly. Consider "It seems possible that you have some feelings about Pat that you aren't quite in touch with," and "You seem a little disturbed at your attraction to your sister's friend." They seem to epitomize tactfulness—except they also epitomize gingerliness. Why so vague? Why not say what kind of "feelings" and "attraction" are being alluded to? It's clear enough that sexual ones are meant, and the fact that it wasn't said can convey the message "There is something here to be cautious about, if not apprehensive." In a certain sense, that could amount to tactlessness. (The effort to be tactful, like the effort to be reassuring, can easily backfire.) On the other hand consider this piece of no-beating-around-the-bush: "Maybe you felt as if you were watching Pat masturbate." It epitomizes tactlessness for this study. Our patient is bound to be shocked by the idea when it is put so bluntly, so suddenly.

Tact can often be preserved when we take a gradual or stepwise approach, dividing an interpretation into parts that allow him to move ahead gradually while regulating the speed and direction. A student gives a good illustration of this technique in this continuation:

T1: I wonder if you weren't laughing because you were nervous and frightened.

P2: *But why should I be frightened? I'm not afraid of Pat.*

T2: No, but perhaps you were afraid of your own feelings.

P3: *Well, I was disgusted, seeing her like that—so . . . so exposed.*

T3: It could be that part of you found her attractive, or sexually exciting, and part of you was frightened and disgusted by these feelings.

The technique of gradualness is best used for developing a single idea or theme, rather than for introducing a number of separate ones. If a patient hasn't accepted our part-interpretations, switching over to an altogether different one is risky. When the technique didn't work, we can tell him what our full interpretation was or else drop the matter; offering another interpretation is rarely a good option. Notice how the following continuation runs afoul of this guideline twice, once at T3 and again at T4:

T1: I take it you were both attracted and repelled by Pat.

P2: *Well, yes. As I said, she's not bad looking. But she just looked funny in those positions, that's all.*

T2: Seeing her in those positions made you feel uncomfortable, it seems. I'm wondering whether you felt sexually aroused by her, and part of your discomfort had to do with feeling aroused.

P3: *That seems a little farfetched. I just thought it was hilarious the way they were carrying on. And I also said I wanted to study except for the damn music.*

T3:   I can see why you might find what I said farfetched.
          What do you think of the possibility that you were
          also quite angry at your sister?

P4:   *Angry? Well, the music . . . But I don't know what
          else.*

T4:   Perhaps because you felt she had taken all of Pat's
          attention from you.

And here's a continuation that amplifies only a single issue, the
patient's conflict, but remains quite tactless because it isn't
gradual enough and the therapist is too directive:

T1:   I wonder if part of you didn't find the scene exciting,
          and another part of you was disgusted at your excite-
          ment.

P2:   *I don't know. I had the feeling while I was laughing
          that it was just hysterically funny. But then when I
          stopped laughing, I didn't know why I was laugh-
          ing.*

T2:   Perhaps your laughing was a way of trying to make
          them stop, while at the same time enjoying the
          excitement.

P3:   *I did feel excited. I don't understand that, because I
          really don't find Pat that attractive sexually. But
          the slow, repetitious pulsing of the music and the
          way their bodies were entwined really set me off.*

T3:   Are you saying that you were sexually attracted only
          to Pat?

P4:   *(frightened look) What are you suggesting?*

T4:   Well, although Pat and your sister were there to-
          gether, Pat is the only one you describe yourself
          reacting to. I am suggesting that perhaps some of
          your sexual arousal came from looking at your sister.

P5:   *Wow, that's pretty heavy!*

Instead of that highly diagnostic formulation at T2, I would stay
with the patient's mystification, saying "You had no idea
then—and still have no idea, I gather—what the reason could
have been." If he insisted on his mystification, I would repeat
the contents of T1, emphasizing the unbearable conflict. And
T3 is too confronting; I would want first to clarify what the

patient meant by *"set me off."* Finally, taking my cue from his frightened look at *P4,* I might wonder aloud whether he didn't have an inkling of what I was referring to, and then perhaps give him a chance to say it himself. Of course, if he didn't, I'd be obliged to tell him, but I could keep it minimally diagnostic by formulating it this way: "I take it the possibility that you might be sexually attracted to your sister makes you feel disgusted."

Tact, however, doesn't necessarily call for a gradual approach. If we focus directly on what our patient is seeking to understand, we are also being tactful. Since he isn't wondering why he was distracted and fascinated by the goings-on in the living room, drawing his attention to it runs the risk of changing the subject—and that, aside from other considerations, is potentially tactless. Whenever we change the subject, we run the risk of imposing an idea that might be unsettling, perhaps shocking. Even such relatively empathic interpretations as the following can be considered tactless from this perspective: "Perhaps you were angry because you felt left out," and "I wonder if you weren't contemptuous of Pat." Conversely, even a highly diagnostic formulation can be tactful if it addresses what our patient is concerned about—namely, why he laughed uncontrollably. Here's an interpretation that does this, and offers a diagnostic explanation that is tactful enough:

> I wonder if you were laughing, despite the fact that you found the scene disgusting, to ease your sense of disgust. Feeling disgusted may have made you tense, and perhaps you laughed as a way of releasing the tension.

Nevertheless, diagnostic formulations—especially those that attempt to explain the funtional basis of a patient's behavior, as does the above interpretation—do tend to grow tactless when they implicate impulses and wishes he hadn't mentioned having, and in that sense, change the subject. Here are two extreme examples:

> Your laughter might have been a way of relieving frustration and dissipating your tension. At the same time it was almost like an attack on the girls, too, a way of putting them down.

> When you laughed you may have been expressing your
> tension. You wanted to belong to your sister and her friend,
> but you weren't sure how to be part of their situation—or
> even if you should want to be. Perhaps it was also a partial
> solution to yourdilemma. You drew attention to yourself
> and got them to include you by getting angry with you.

Suggesting that the laughing was an attempt to hide his feelings, or that it was an expression of hostility or defensive in a
particular way, can only be done with a diagnostic formulation
that, among its other drawbacks, is apt to be tactless.

The way a number of the foregoing examples formulate
conflict is worth noting because it reflects a form that can
subserve tact. Instead of saying "you wish," we say "a part of
you wishes," implying that he had conflicting feelings about the
matter. Inasmuch as it allows the patient to acknowledge the
wish without having to fully embrace it, I regard the form as
useful and tactful. To be sure, it also has shortcomings. A sense
of disavowed, or disowned, responsibility is the most serious,
and overtones of a split personality, or divided self, is another.
Yet, when we use it only to articulate conflict, more as a stylistic
device than a theoretical formulation, it can be relatively free of
those implications. At any rate, my experience has been that
patients will usually appreciate its tactfulness and won't misuse
it in the interests of externalization and disavowal.

Perhaps the best way to be tactful, and at the same time
promote exploration and self-inquiry, is to continue the study
exactly where the patient left off. He had just said *"In fact, it
was a bit disgusting to see her like that."* The question I would
raise is whether this was what he felt then or whether it just
now occurred to him for the first time. This could make a
significant difference, because if he was now realizing that he
was disgusted, it would mean the therapeutic process was
already in motion and I could try to get into gear with it, thereby
steering clear of diagnostic as well as tactless remarks.

Since I had an interpretation in mind, I could venture the
direct question "Are you saying you felt disgusted then, or are
you realizing it right now?" If his response was *"I felt disgusted
then—but why do you ask?"* I could reply:

> Because I was wondering if it wasn't your explanation for
> the hysterical laughter. I thought you might be saying that
> it was those feelings that brought it on.

And then it should be relatively easy to find a suitable opportunity to suggest that the disgust stemmed from mixed feelings, and that one of them was sexual arousal. If, however, he answered that it just occurred to him now, and asked why I asked, I could say he was now realizing something in his feelings that he was only dimly aware of then.

> I wonder if you are now realizing that you had conflicting feelings; that part of you found it funny but another part was disgusted. And maybe that's why you lost control of yourself.

It might be only a short step from here to the insight that sex had reared its ugly head.

Study 2
Am I Like Your Other Patients?

The patient is in his mid-thirties.

> *I never told you this, but I've always had a good singing voice. I still do. My mother used to say I should've become a singer. I sang in the school choir in high school, but I quit. It was a big choir, about two hundred kids in it. The reason I quit was it bothered me that I couldn't hear my voice in the choir. I remember telling the music teacher about it, and he told me that always happens. You can't really hear your own voice when you sing in a choir, did you know that? I was surprised to find it out. But I couldn't get used to the idea. I don't really know why. . . . Anyway, it wasn't the reason I quit. I wanted to devote myself to my studies. I was a very good student. I loved history best of all, and always worked on topics that were different from the ones the other kids picked. I remember working extra hard on a paper on Alexander the Great— researching his childhood, describing his education with Aristotle, and things like that. It was a great paper. My history teacher made me submit it to the school literary magazine, and it was published.*

The patient is apparently telling us he needs to feel special, but there's no clue to why he's telling it. However, the transcript as presented isn't complete. The narrative is actually a continuation of *P2* in the following exchange:

> **P1:**   *Am I like your other patients?*
> **T1:**   How do you mean?
> **P2:**   *I don't know. It's a stupid question. I take it back.*

If we ignore the exchange, we are limited to interpretations that articulate his self-image. Our interpretation might focus on his concern about being different or feeling special or worthwhile; it can emphasize his being comfortable with himself only when he stands out or apart; it can infer a need to be different for its own sake, or else conjecture that the need subserves his sense of importance and self-worth, perhaps being essential to his very identity. For example:

> You feel as if you aren't really sure who you are unless you're someone special, apart from all the others.

Such interpretations can be formulated empathically, and they have intrinsic merit. Yet, they may not be the best ones for this study because they fail to regard the exchange as part of the narrative.

The exchange has put us in a good position to understand the purport and meaning of the entire narrative; *P2* can be regarded as an explication of *P1*. We can readily infer that our patient is telling us why he is concerned over being like our other patients. *"I used to be special,"* is the answer, thereby suggesting that the underlying question was *"Am I special to you?"* Accordingly, our interpretation can articulate an important aspect of his self-image while at the same time explicating the meaning of his concern. Furthermore, we can attempt to explain the past in a way that has relevance to the present, and show how the present has connections with the past. The technical problem is how to formulate all of this in a way that can be useful not only for the patient himself, so to speak, but also for his work in therapy.

Students cast their interpretation in the form of "I now understand why you asked the question," and then go on to highlight one or another aspect of his self-image. They do it in these ways:

Perhaps you're worried that I don't perceive you as distinct from my other patients, and this bothers you.

You feel you don't stand out from other people as an individual; you have to work extra hard to ensure being noticed. When you asked if you're like my other patients, you were probably asking me if there's anything about you that is different, anything that marks you as an individual. Here, too, I think you don't want your voice to be lost in a chorus of two hundred voices, you want to stand out here with me as excellent in some way.

By now you've answered that question about whether you are like my other patients, or at least why it concerns you so. You've been telling me how important it is for you to feel special. I think your asking me if you're like my other patients was really asking if I could hear your voice, or if you were a member of a choir here. It's important to you to feel special.

Perhaps you are telling me, in a roundabout way, that you feel I'm not paying enough attention to you, or that I don't recognize your individuality. And unless you can convince me of your special qualities, you'll remain an anonymous member of my "choir" of patients.

The problem with these interpretations, as I see it, lies in their nonempathic character. Basically, they tell the patient that his narrative had a certain purpose—it served the function of making a certain point—and that, strictly speaking, isn't a formulation of "mental content." The interpretations are explanatory in a way that is essentially diagnostic. Not only are we saying "This is *my* explanation of why you reminisced the way you did," we are also suggesting that "It served the function of communicating something to me."

As we have seen, explanations can rarely be formulated empathically. They require a speculation that is imposed from the outside, so to speak, and do not speak to a patient's mental content. "This is *my* explanation," is the characteristic form of a diagnostic interpretation, and though we'd rather not do it that way, it often is quite unavoidable. But that isn't the case here. In this study, we are in an excellent position to maintain a fully empathic position by offering an interpretation whose form is "This is *your* explanation." Instead of saying "Based on your account and your associations, I have come to the following conclusion about what happened and why you behaved the way you did," we can say "Based on your account and associations, I believe the following is the way *you* understand what happened and how *you* explain why you behaved the way you did."

And in addition to articulating the patient's explanation in that way, we might also be able to say something about why he hadn't recognized his explanation, why he needed us to do it. If we were thinking, not only why did the thing happen, but why was he telling it now, we might have noticed that he was inviting us to give an explanation he already knew well enough. Issues of activity and passivity might be entailed, issues of role definition (casting us into the role of parent-teacher who gives explanations, for example), and they may reflect important transference issues. So rather than saying "I think I know why you asked me whether you're like my other patients," I'd be inclined to say:

> I think you may have explained why you are concerned about whether you are like my other patients—and I suspect you also realize it.

If the patient was mystified by my remark, I could no longer maintain a purely empathic position; my remarks would have to become diagnostic. But I would steer clear of addressing the defensive implications of his mystification—because the study provides me with no material on which to base a defense interpretation, and I don't want to indulge in sheer speculation. Instead, I might stay with my original point by spelling out the explanation as he had given it in associational and reminiscence form.

In either event, however, this can be an effective way of providing an explanation without imposing it and / or casting it in diagnostic form, because it remains the patient's and I am doing little more than articulating it. To be sure, if he said he had no idea what I meant, I would have to make it clear that I was speculating. But I would make sure to focus on the fact that the explanation was indeed his, and I was doing little more than articulating it. I could first remind him of his initial question, how he had dismissed it as silly, and then formulate a speculation this way:

> I think you've been explaining to me why it wasn't such a silly question, and I have a hunch that part of you knows it. What I mean is by now you may have caught a glimpse of the fact that what you've told me about your childhood amounts to an explanation of what your question meant to you—it meant you have the need to stand out as someone different, perhaps special.

I might refer to some of the details (quitting choir, doing a special history paper) but my overall emphasis would be on the fact that his reminiscences provided an explanation that threw light on his original question—and "part of him" knew it:

> I believe you are telling me how important it is for you now, and how important it has always been, to see yourself as different and special. And I also believe that part of you knows that it explains why you asked whether you were like my other patients.

To be sure, this approach has ended on a rather confronting and didactic note, but it needn't have. In any event, it can be justified on the grounds that two purposes were served: an aspect of his personality was explored, and an aspect of our therapy was explicated.

In the next study, our patient again begins with a question and follows it up with relevant associations. This time, however, there are additional considerations that militate against the approach I've recommended. The relevant interpretation cannot address itself only to the initial question and the consequent reminiscences. It has to take into account the fact that the patient was experiencing anxiety.

Study 3
Why Do You Sit So Far from Me?

This patient is in his mid-twenties. The session is drawing to a close, and it has been a good one.

*Why do you sit so far from me? Your chair could be closer,
you know. Somehow, the distance between us seems
greater now than it usually is. That's crazy . . . Sometimes I feel like speaking softly here, but I can't because
then you wouldn't hear me . . . My kid brother always
yells. It used to be funny when he was little, and my
parents would tease him about it. He just couldn't say
anything in a normal voice, always at the top of his
lungs. He was a cuddly little butterball of a kid, always
smooching up to people. But the minute he opened his
mouth. . . . It was hilarious. My mother is sort of a yeller
too, always at the top of her lungs. But not my father; he
never ever spoke loud. He was always sort of calm and
. . . you know, sort of removed from people. He loved to sit
off by himself and read or watch TV. He liked to be left
alone. When my brother or I hurt ourselves or something
like that, we never went to him, only to my mother. She
just loved to cuddle us. A lot of times we'd both climb on
her together. . . . I don't know why I'm thinking about all
this now . . . . You know, I'm feeling a bit anxious—sort of
funny, in a way. . . . I don't like the feeling one bit.*

An impulse threatening to breach defenses against its conscious recognition and expression, that's the formulation I had
in mind when I composed this study. I tried to depict a patient
wishing for physical intimacy with his therapist, but instead of
acknowledging it, he conveys the wish through association and
reminiscence—and then, when it comes too close to awareness,
he experiences anxiety. My chief purpose was to exemplify a
situation where a brief, pointed interpretation focused on an
impulse can be the most efficacious kind of interpretation to
make. Though the widely accepted rule "Defenses Before Impulses" is generally a useful one, there are occasions when the
impulse can be interpreted first, because anything else could
amount to either an evasion of the issue or an invitation to
intellectualization.

Our technical problem is whether to make the empathic
interpretation "I believe you have the wish to be cuddled by
me," or the more diagnostic "I believe you are feeling anxious
because you have the wish to be cuddled by me, and that wish
is unacceptable to you." To be sure, it might make no practical

difference, because were we to choose the latter our patient might hear the former; all that would matter to him is the articulation of the wish. But would he hear it better when it isunencumbered with explanation? Since I think he will, I would articulate his wish as succinctly as possible, and save the defense for later.

A student starts out by saying "Do you think that this feeling may have something to do with the wish to be cuddled again?" which is fine—but then has the patient respond *"How so? I don't see that,"* which invites the elaboration:

> Well, that was the last thing you were speaking about when you started to feel that way, anxious and sort of funny. Maybe you'd like me to be more nurturant with you, less distant, so that you could feel free to express those needs to be cuddled here.

Notice how intellectual, and even tangential, the explanation is, so that the impact of the articulation is weakened. Here are two examples that are more direct, but notice the temptation to bury the point of the interpretation in side issues:

> Perhaps you want me to comfort you. You'd like to sit closer to me, maybe even climb into my lap. But you feel anxious because you think I'd react as your father did, and prefer to be left alone.

> I think you're feeling anxious because the thoughts you had about my sitting so far from you reminded you of the feelings you had as a child. Perhaps you'd like to climb into my lap now and be cuddled, but that feeling makes you anxious.

The following interpretation should come to a full stop after "cuddled":

> I think I know part of the reason for your anxiety. You feel a wish to be cuddled and dependent, and a contrary wish to be independent. And you fear that either or both of your wishes may be granted.

Interestingly, the student has the patient respond: *"I don't think I understand all that. I can see how I want to be cuddled,* taken care of. After all, doesn't everybody? But what about the rest of it?" The affective situation has now changed markedly and what ensues is an intellectual discussion whose usefulness is dubious.

We tend to fall into a stilted intellectuality when we give in to the temptation to elaborate. This will hardly promote deeper insight in our patients. Here's another example of an initially insightful interpretation that loses force as it goes on:

> I think you're uncomfortable because a part of you would like to ask me to draw closer to you. You spoke of this on a physical level—moving the chairs closer—but I think you'd also like an emotional closeness, the kind your mother shared with you when she cuddled you. But another part of you is unwilling to acknowledge this desire for more closeness with me, and so you're feeling anxious because of this conflict between the two parts of yourself.

What, beyond a *"Yes, you're right—and so perceptive!"* can the patient say now?

Whenever a patient experiences a distressing affect, like anxiety, we are subject to the impulse to make it go away, to comfort him and make it better. Yet clinical experience suggests that affects, like anxiety—and especially anxiety—can serve a valuable signaling function. Anxiety may signal the activation of a conflict based on a burgeoning wish or fantasy that cannot be safely countenanced. Consequently, addressing the patient's anxiety, by exploring the conflict that generated it, can be useful. A student does it by:

> Could it be that the anxiety you're feeling stems from your wish that I were like your mother, loud and cuddling, but you fear instead that I will be more like your father, and I won't be there when you hurt?

I don't mean to suggest that the signal theory of anxiety is our only option; consider this student's way of formulating the anxiety:

> Maybe you're anxious because you miss that, being able to climb into your mother's lap and be comforted, and that upsets you.

—and when the patient responded "*Yes, I guess so. I just can't have that anymore, I guess, that kind of closeness and support,*" she articulated the impulse clearly and sensitively with:

> But you'd like to have it still. That's perhaps why you feel the distance between us is greater today, because you are feeling that need to be held and comforted, to be close.

Here's a continuation that offers a well-articulated alternative to the signal theory:

> **T1:** It seems you see me as being quiet and removed like your father. I wonder if you wish I were closer and more affectionate with you, as your mother was, and this wish makes you feel anxious.
> **P2:** *Why should it make me feel anxious?*
> **T2:** Perhaps you had a similar wish about your father.
> **P3:** *I guess I had. But he never paid any attention to what I wished.*
> **T3:** I guess that made you angry.
> **P4:** *Yes, it did. But I never could do anything about it. I felt so frustrated by him! I just couldn't reach him.*
> **T4:** And when I remind you of him in that way, it makes you anxious, because you still don't know what to do with that frustration and anger.

And yet another interesting alternative is:

> It must have hurt you not to be able to get close to your father. I wonder if you're feeling close to me now, and you're conflicted over how to get me to respond. And that's what you're anxious about.

—although it makes the error of introducing a new topic: our responsiveness.

Finally, the ubiquitous question "Why now?" may be asked. The introduction revealed that today's session was a good one, and thereby provided a basis for answering the question. Students include that answer in their interpretations. The following is a sensitive piece of work:

T1: I have an idea why you may be feeling anxious. Your earlier comment about my sitting so far away from you sounds similar to your description of how your father loved to sit off by himself. He was distant from people. He liked to be left alone.

P2: *Yes, I can see that. But why would that make me anxious?*

T2: Perhaps you're feeling that you've been "cuddling up" to me today. But instead of reacting with warmth, as your mother would have, I chose to remain distant and aloof, like your father.

Study 4
You Have a Supervisor, Don't You?

This 20-year-old patient has never expressed any hostility toward you—nor toward anyone else, as far as you know—but he does have a big tendency to tease, which he chalks up to a good sense of humor.

> *You have a supervisor, don't you? I know you must, so you don't have to answer the question. Yes, I'm sure you have a supervisor and you discuss these sessions with him. And he tells you what you did wrong, eh!* (broad smile) *That's cool! . . . Sometimes I have the impulse to fool around here, maybe make things up—like tell you something that happened to Peter as if it had happened to me. Or tell you one of his dreams.* (impish smile) *Give you and your supervisor a run for your money. . . . I wonder how much he criticizes you, like tells you you shouldn't have said something you said to me. That must feel crummy when he does that. . . . Hey, you know what? Let me talk to him. Yes, and I'll tell him how great you really are.* (warm smile) *Don't worry, I'll do right by you!*

Our patient likes to tease, and he is probably unaware of any hostile intent. The narrative consists of a piece of good-natured teasing, and the study invites us to interpret its underlying hostility. Our chief problem is to find a way to do it tactfully and empathically. We might have to throw some cold water on his teasing, but we will have to avoid any hint of chastising him.

First, a word about responding with some good-natured teasing of our own: I don't think it's a good idea. In a situation like this, where the humor is of a teasing kind, any attempt to respond with humor is also likely to have a teasing component. I'm sure an inventive therapist could come up with a humorous response that highlights the intent of our patient's teasing without itself being a tease, but that takes a special knack and skill—and anyway it's risky. To retort "So will I," to his "*Don't worry, I'll do right by you!*" is perhaps safe enough, but what purpose would it serve? And "Thanks! I won't worry," and "I'll make sure to tell him," are little more than sarcasms that could amount to a put-down. So I would respond in my regular way and not try to compete with his humor. At the same time, however, I would try to respond to the form of his narrative, not only to its content.

Yet the opposite temptation is equally strong; students not only steer completely clear of the teasing, making no mention of the humor, but they also steer clear of the hostile implications. Instead, they offer sober interpretations that focus on the possible meanings of the patient's thoughts and impulses. They construe the narrative as reflecting a concern over their competency:

I'm wondering if perhaps you are having some doubts about whether I will do right by you.

They focus on the need for control and power:

Perhaps you're enjoying the thought that you have power over me via my supervisor.

They infer that he is feeling critical:

I'm wondering whether it isn't easier for you to think of my supervisor being critical of me than to consider the possibility that you might have criticisms of your own.

Here's one that is interesting, if farfetched, but at least it makes allusion to the teasing:

> I wonder if your impulse to fool around here might be due
> to your fear that if you really told me how you were feeling,
> I would criticize you and then you'd feel crummy.

They speculate that he is retaliating out of some perceived
criticisms:

> Yes, but maybe you also have some critical feelings toward
> me, some feelings that I've said or done something wrong.
> And perhaps your impulse to fool around expresses a wish
> to get back at me for it.

> Could it be you sometimes don't like the things I say to
> you, that you take my remarks as criticisms, and therefore
> the idea of someone criticizing me, as well as your *putting
> me on*, is a way of getting even?

And they infer that he is angry:

> I wonder if your kidding around isn't a way of expressing
> anger toward me.

Incidentally, the implied criticism and put-down of such a
diagnostic interpretation will not be attenuated by adding an
explanation of his anger:

> Perhaps you are angry because you feel mistreated and
> used. You may believe my performance here is more
> important to me than my understanding what you say.

Now, all of those interpretations, especially the more empathic
ones, are good and well-intended—only this isn't the right
moment for them. Their usefulness is apt to be limited because
they fail to take account of context. I find it difficult to imagine
that such interpretations would evoke a useful response from
the patient; I can only picture him insisting that he was just
teasing, that's all—so why was I being so uptight?

Few students infer hostility in the narrative (despite the
introduction) and those who do don't find a way of interpreting
it empathically. Instead, they retreat to the didactic mode. For
example:

> **T1:** You seem to be teasing me.
> **P2:** *I hope I haven't made you angry.*

T2: Whether I'm angry or not is not at issue here. I would like you to understand that a lot of hostility can be expressed through humor.
(P3: You must be kidding!)

A student winds up a continuation with: "Nevertheless, humor does frequently have an element of hostility, and words have effects as well as causes." *(PT: No fooling!)*

But interpreting hostility without being confronting or didactic isn't easy. Several students try to solve the problem by construing the narrative as indicating the patient's concern that we will judge him as hostile. An interesting example of this is:

Do you think I feel you're being hostile when you're amused at the thought of my being criticized and made to feel crummy? What do you think of the possibility that your joking offer of a testimonial on my behalf is a way of making amends for your thoughts?

Unfortunately, however, it is too diagnostic a formulation—what can the patient say except *"Interesting!"*? Similarly, the following continuation focuses well on this theme, but only by resorting to diagnosis:

T1: You seem to feel the need to stay on my good side, while at the same time poking a little fun at me.
P2: *I do like you, you know, even if you do make a lot of mistakes.*
T2: I think there's another reason why you feel the need to stay on my good side: you're afraid I may become angry at your kidding.
P3: *Some people do become angry. And besides, if my therapist were to become angry then I'd be stuck— she couldn't help.*
T3: I think another reason for your fear of making me angry is that it would lead you to feel the hostility implicit in your comments, and perhaps become aware of hostile feelings.

Drawing a patient's attention to the hostility behind his teasing, while at the same time remaining sufficiently empathic, tactful, and neutral, isn't easy. Perhaps it is impossible. Even an interpretation as good as this one doesn't solve the problem, although it may be a good compromise:

> I know this seems like good-natured teasing to you, but I wonder whether you also feel some of the hostility in it. I think you may have the impulse to hurt me, but that is dangerous for you. So instead, you tease.

In my experience the best way to deal with the problem is to wait—to wait and listen—for something the patient may say that could provide a basis for suggesting that he himself suspected his hostility. Since, however, the study doesn't allow me to wait, I might start with a remark that acknowledged his teasing: "I appreciate that you are teasing and fooling around." Then I would look for something he had said that could suggest his having a glimmer of some hostile feelings or intentions. It might be:

> I wonder if you yourself suspect something about the way you're teasing me. What you said about my supervisor's criticisms suggests to me that you may sense a streak of hostility there.

This approach may be too indirect. The patient could readily recognize that I had something in mind but was hesitant to say it. He might even think I was grasping at straws. Still, I remained quite empathic insofar as I alluded to what *he* was experiencing rather than to the impact or intent that I experienced. A student captures the spirit of this approach in the following continuation:

T1: For a moment it seemed you were seriously trying to imagine being in my position, and then you continued joking. I wonder if perhaps you needed to get away from your feelings of identifying with me, because it made you feel too close to me.

P2: *Yeah, that sure didn't last long. It didn't feel too good. But too close? I don't know what you mean—at least, I don't think I do.* (He has a glimmer!)

T2: Perhaps you wanted to get away from your feeling of identifying with me, because it gave you a different

perspective on your joking here. From your point of
view it seemed more hostile to you than it usually
does.

That was a bit fancy for my tastes, but I like the inventive way
it stayed empathic. (And my solution was a bit fancy, too.)

Study 5
The Critic—or *What's Wrong with You?*

This patient has described himself as a critical person but has
never been critical of you. At the beginning of the previous
session, you notified him of a pending cancellation. He showed
no significant reaction at the time. The narrative came at the
beginning of this session and was preceded by a silence.

*I've been meaning to tell you this for a long time but
somehow I haven't. This isn't the first time I thought it,
but your clothes . . . the clothes you wear are awful.
Don't you know anything about how to dress? I can't
understand how you could choose that shirt, it doesn't fit
with anything else you're wearing. Not that anything else
you've got on really matches, but you must be color-blind
or something. . . . And the way you speak, in that slow
and halting way. I meant to mention it before, because it
bugs me sometimes. You never say a whole sentence
right out straight. You always always have to stop and
find the right word, and that makes it so god-awful
slow. . . . And another thing while I'm at it, you always
speak so softly and so damned seriously.*

This study is expressly designed to afford me the opportunity to
examine—and fault—what is arguably Number 1 on the all-time
Hit Parade of Popular Interpretations: namely, "You are feeling
angry." I depend on students to presume that the patient is
expressing and experiencing anger. I count on their deeming it
appropriate to tell him so, thereby giving me the chance to
persuade them that there are occasions when the interpretation
of anger may go too deep, too fast. I point out that I composed
the study with a patient in mind who is feeling nothing but the

need to criticize, and perhaps also the intent to hurt; he is giving in to the impulse to insult but has no phenomenal experience of any anger. (Not that this is a persuasive argument. "How should we have known *that*?" protest my students.) In fact, I imagined someone for whom anger was an unacceptable feeling, and what allowed him to give expression to such criticalness was the defense mechanism of isolation of affect. Therefore, to say to him "You are feeling angry," would be wrong not only because he isn't feeling angry, but because it flies in the teeth of his defense.

His criticalness can be viewed as defensive in three ways. It is a derivative of the anger, or a transformed expression of it; it's a displacement of another impulse altogether; it's a tamed or socialized rendition of a primitive, perhaps unconscious, wish. Construing it as defensive in these ways has several implications, but none of them requires us to assume that his criticisms were necessarily poorly founded. In fact, I would rather presume that they were completely accurate—because I believe it's quite beside the point. In any case, however, he is free to criticize as well as verbally attack us, and we have to protect that freedom. (The question of limits here—to what extent ought we allow ourselves to be verbally abused by patients—is an interesting one, and I'm tempted to answer it with an "as much as we can bear." But there are diagnostic considerations that have to be taken into account.)

Why is he attacking us? Consider this answer:

I can understand your criticisms of my manner of dress and speech. But since you said you've been meaning to tell me this for a long time, I wonder if your reason for criticizing me now may perhaps be due to your feeling angry at me.

There are at least two problems with this interpretation. One is specific to the patient; it fails to construe his behavior as defensive. The other is specific to the psychology of affects; it construes the anger as an instigator of his attacking behavior. The former raises the question of how best to work with a patient's defenses, how to interpret them in a way that doesn't breach or circumvent them. The latter raises the theoretical question: "What role do affects play in behavior? Are they motivators, or is that the privilege of drives and impulses (experienced as wishes and fantasies), whereas affects serve the function of mobilizing /preparing /expressing /signaling?" Happily, we needn't take a position on this question of theory in order to take a stand in our practice; clinical utility and clinical experience have something to say about it, too. And this experience has shown (at least, mine has) that the drive/impulse formulation is likely to be the more efficacious one. It merits a brief digression on—

Interpreting Affects

Imagine a patient thinking about succulent foods and appetizing dishes, reminiscing about meals he's eaten and fantasizing about meals he's going to eat. Which interpretation is better, "You are feeling hungry" or "You have a wish to eat"?

Reader: The difference seems trivial.

Author: But the reason is worth considering. It seems trivial because the formulations are functionally identical, and the patient will intuitively make the necessary translation from the one into the other. English makes it easy to translate affect language into impulse language. "I *feel* happy" is equivalent to "I *feel* like rejoicing or laughing." "I *feel* sad" is equivalent to "I *feel* like despairing or weeping." "I *feel* angry" is equivalent to "I *feel* like attacking or retaliating." And "I *feel* hungry" is equivalent to "I *feel* like eating."

Reader: What about anxiety and guilt? Why do you leave them out?

Author: They may be exceptional cases—although anxiety can be translated into "fear," in which case the impulse is to flee, while guilt can be translated into a wish to atone and make amends by self-punishment. Both in principle and in practice, however, every affect statement can be transmuted into a statement of an impulse or wish, or a conflict thereof. So instead of telling a patient he is *feeling* angry, we can tell him he *feels* like striking out. Instead of saying he is hostile, we can say he wishes to annihilate. And we can also interpret most affects for their communication or signaling properties. For instance, to weep may be to communicate helplessness and not intent to fight. Furthermore, and more germane to the study, if he is actually engaged in eating food, it will seem pointless to offer the interpretation "You are feeling hungry," and that may be no different, I submit, from saying to a patient who is engaged in the act of attacking us: "You are feeling angry."

Reader: Yes, but it would only *seem* pointless. I gather you are bent on persuading me that interpreting in conative and cognitive terms is better than doing it in affect terms. You must tell me why.

Author: For one thing, affect language tends to be diagnostic. Affect words are themselves diagnostic labels that generally serve the same intellectual and conceptual functions that diagnostic formulations serve; they are abstractions that categorize and organize experience into intellectually comprehensible forms.

Reader: I hope you aren't referring to the affective experiences themselves.

Author: Of course not. They aren't diagnostic and abstract; only their verbal expressions are—in contrast to ideas, thoughts, and wishes, which can readily be verbalized in unequivocal and noninferential terms, insofar as they are directly utterable. Our feelings and affects, however, can only be verbalized through a process of interpretation. In order to say what we feel, and say it in such a way that our utterance carries an emotional message, we must formulate and express it in a unique way. Feelings and moods can be expressed by a wide variety of motor and action terms; they are communicated through a process like empathy, and this has important ramifications for any therapy that relies principally on verbalization. In such a modality, affective experiences—no matter what their ontological nature may be, no matter what biological functions they serve, no matter what psychological role they play in the determination of behavior and experience—can only be approached in conative and cognitive terms—

Reader: short of inviting the patient to introspect on his feelings and moods. And even if we wanted to do that, we would have to take account of the fact that whenever one introspects reflectively on an affect state, it diminishes in its intensity. In fact, for our structuralist forebears it disappeared so completely that they had no choice but to conclude that affect wasn't a basic element of consciousness.

Author: Whatever the truth may be, it's a phenomenon with ramifications. It means that our work can diminish the affect we're working with. Perhaps this is only another way of saying that intellectual control over feelings occurs in such a way as to diminish their intensity and vividness, and the implication for therapy is that we must be on guard so as not to promote intellectualization as a defense against affect. Therefore, saying to a patient "You are feeling angry at me," could have the effect of attenuating the anger by bringing it under cognitive control. Verbalizing the anger might encourage him to experience it cognitively instead of only affectively, which could result in a lessening of the anger itself.

Reader: But that is very different, isn't it, from telling him "I can feel the anger you are feeling"? Now he is invited to notice the feeling and experience it affectively, which might have the short-term effect of enhancing it.

Author: Yes, but it isn't often that we can expect such an "empathic" response to have that effect. Moreover, it opens the door to telling the patient how *we* feel—and that is fraught with implications. For one thing, it makes him responsible for our feelings, something that can become a burden for him. So it's a technique we must use with utmost judiciousness, and I don't think our patient in Study 5 is ready for it.

We can assume that he is quite unaware of feeling angry—else why interpret it to him, except to make him stop feeling it?—and we can also assume that he is quite unaware of a wish to hurt us. Based on this pair of assumptions my thesis is: we should aim at uncovering and exploring the wish, and if we try to deal with the affect as well, better to suggest to him "You are angry at me because you wish to hurt me," than to suggest "You wish to hurt me because you are angry at me." Bear in mind that his intent to be hurtful is apt to be closer to awareness than his feeling of anger, and therefore requires less of an inference. It is certainly closer to the narrative, and perhaps also more available to us in terms of a countertransference reaction.

A similar argument can be made in respect to his motivation for choosing this time. ("Why today?") The study gives us a piece of information that could be relevant: the fact that a pending session was cancelled during the previous session. Our interpretation might therefore take one of two forms: (1) "The cancellation made you angry and you are now expressing that anger in the form of criticalness"—for example:

> Perhaps another thing that bugs you, that's been on your mind for some time, is the fact that last time I told you I would have to cancel a session.

(2) "The cancellation hurt you, and you are now expressing that hurt by retaliating in kind"—for example:

> I think I understand why you are being so critical of me today. You felt I didn't care about you when I canceled the session, and by criticizing me you are saying you have reasons not to care about me either.

The thrust of my argument is that the second interpretation, although diagnostic, is the better one to work with. It avoids the pitfalls of working with the affect itself, and it makes more psychological sense.

We are in a better position to offer an empathic interpretation if we explain the patient's behavior in terms of a felt need to retaliate out of feelings of rejection, or else a sense of hurt or a feeling that we don't care. But when we try to address the defense itself—by focusing on the fact that he expressed his reaction indirectly, for instance—we have little choice but to resort to diagnostic interpretations. Consider this example:

> **T1:** It seems to me that your criticisms may mask your anger at me for canceling your next session.
> **P2:** *But why wasn't I angry last time after you told me?*
> **T2:** I would guess you were. But to show it then would have been to indicate more directly that you need me.

Moreover, an attempt to interpret a defense head-on often runs head-on into the defense itself. We can expect that to happen, and it should keep us from that kind of persistent approach (or attack) exemplifed in the following continuation:

T1: I wonder why you chose this particular time to find so many things wrong with me. Last time I did tell you I wouldn't be able to see you next session.

P2: *So what?*

T2: Well, you didn't seem to care one way or another. So I wonder if your criticisms today could be a disguised way of expressing anger toward me for the hurt you experienced but couldn't admit to me and maybe even to yourself.

P3: *I didn't feel hurt. It didn't bother me at all.*

T3: And your finding fault with me would make the separation easier to bear; it might help you to feel that you were doing the rejecting.

Admittedly, I am giving an unusually extreme example that caricatures the problem. But my point is this: the least we could have done after *P3*'s disavowal is suggest that he was now doing the same thing again—namely, defending himself exactly the way T2 suggested he was. And we have to avoid being defensive ourselves. Students give way to the same kind of defensiveness as the patient does. An example:

T1: I'm wondering why you choose this particular time to tell me all these things, since, as you say, you've been meaning to tell them for a long time.

P2: *I really don't know. You said I could talk about whatever I wished to. I wanted to bring it up now.*

T2: Could it be that you feel hurt by something other than my clothes or my style?

Whenever we develop an interpretation gradually, we should try to avoid both a sparring interchange and a dialogue in which we remain coyly allusive (as in "something other than," above). When a patient is critical and disgruntled, as he is in this study, the risks of engaging him in argument are particularly great. We have to be especially alert to the possibilities both of defusing his criticalness and of intensifying it. Notice how the following example succeeds in avoiding these pitfalls, and how well the student takes advantage of the technique of gradualness:

T1: You seem annoyed with me today.

P2 *There you go again, with your serious remarks. Sure, I'm annoyed, but it's not just today. Like I said, I've been meaning to say this for a while. You just kind of bug me sometimes.*

T2: And you decided to tell me today, because you've been annoyed with me?

P3: *I don't know. Actually, I wasn't thinking much about you since last time, and I usually think of things I'll be wanting to tell you. But I do remember feeling sort of pissed-off at how slowly you talked last session.*

T3: It was during that session that I told you we wouldn't be meeting next Friday.

P4: *Yeah, but that's really okay, because I can always use the extra time. But . . . but I guess maybe it does bother me that you can sort of dismiss me so easily.*

T4: Then you were feeling sort of dismissed last time, and today you're sort of dismissing me with your critical remarks.

But I wouldn't have expected a patient to introspect at *P3*. This kind of obliging response will occur at certain stages of therapy or with certain patients, but not all. "*Yeah? So what? What are you trying to tell me?*" is my best guess for our patient's response to T2.

Finally, the study offers a potentially relevant piece of information in the fact that we know our patient to be a critical person. A student makes use of that in the following interpretation (which would clearly benefit from being divided into its parts):

I wonder if your criticisms of me now are related to the fact that I told you I'm canceling a session, and you are angry with me for that. And instead of telling me you're angry, you criticize me for something else. And since you've told me several times that you consider yourself a critical person, I wonder if this isn't what's happening when you are critical of people—that is, you are angry at them for something. But instead of experiencing the anger directly, you become critical of them.

It is a good illustration of how an interpretation can address itself to an aspect of character without at the same time being too confronting. I would delete the final sentence; it was gratuitously diagnostic. Of course, the first part of the interpretation was rather diagnostic too—how could it have been otherwise?— but it was sufficiently "personal." The patient might resent the fact that we were trying to take the heat off by implying that the criticisms themselves are unwarranted, so I might preface the interpretation with: "I don't mean to be saying that what you're criticizing me for isn't valid. Instead, what I'm thinking about is why you haven't voiced the criticisms until today and therefore what they might mean now." As I indicated, such a remark might preface any kind of interpretation we make to this study.

Study 6
The Power behind the Throne

This is the same patient as in Study 4. He is an only child, and his father is a successful lawyer who apparently doted on him. In the following narrative he is revealing something about an underlying fantasy he has long had.

I can make you laugh whenever I want to. I like that. Peter has a stoneface for a shrink, who never even cracks a smile. Poor Peter! Remember a couple of weeks ago when I was kidding you about you and your supervisor? Well, I was lying in bed one night, having my usual trouble falling asleep, and I was thinking about that. I was thinking that you're a student, so you're being evaluated on how you perform as my therapist. . . . If I was your supervisor, I'd give you an A. I really mean it, you know—no kidding. At first I thought you were too inexperienced and young to be much good, but then I saw that wasn't true. Hey, I hope it doesn't embarrass you, but I think you're terrific! . . . Anyway, while I was trying to fall asleep I was thinking that how I do here as your patient makes a big difference in how your supervisor evaluates you. I mean, if I get better, then you get your A. (broad smile) I know that's not really true. It's a crazy idea. But it helped me fall asleep.

The introduction suggests that his predormal dream will have reflected a favorite fantasy of his. The study's title also tips off the nature of the fantasy. However, the title was not in place when the study was given. (In fact, none of the study titles were given; they were added for the purposes of clarity and indexing.) It also suggests a historical basis for the fantasy. But our problems aren't solved by figuring out the fantasy; we have to figure out what to do with it, too. Consider this solution:

> Maybe what helped you fall asleep was the idea that you could have such power over me. For instance, you mentioned your power to make me laugh, and then you had the fantasy of being able to control the kind of evaluation I'll get from my supervisor by determining whether you'll get better or not, and thinking that that would influence how successful I seemed as your therapist. Maybe this is a fantasy you also had about your father—that however successful his career might be, you had the power to control his success, or even his appearance of success, according to how well you turned out as his only son.

What more could one ask for?—only that it enlist the patient's participation in the process of explanation, not to mention exploration. Yes, he'd probably find it an intellectually interesting and personally illuminating explanation—but from the passive position of audience. The interpretation's form, so thorough, so thoroughly reasoned, implies that he was wholly unaware of what the fantasy was about and therefore incapable of exploring it himself.

The student who wrote the interpretation seems not to have asked herself what purpose she wanted to achieve with it. Either that, or the answer didn't take account of the fact that the therapeutic process appeared to be in good shape in the narrative. Our patient was showing no signs of blocking or of resistance. In fact, there was no reason for us to feel called upon to offer any interpretation at all. But since the study requires us to participate at the end of the transcript, and it's one of the "Interpretation Studies," we are obliged to formulate an interpretation (or a line of interpretation), and not only its content, but its form and function, must carefully be considered. With that in mind, let's begin by examining the student's formulations. First and foremost, they focus on the patient's need for control and power:

> The fantasy that you can help me get an A evidently pleases you. Feeling I am dependent on you for a good grade is a little like being able to make me laugh: it gives you a sense of power and control.

> Perhaps your believing you have some control over my fate makes you feel less vulnerable to what I say to you here.

They extend it to his problem with falling asleep:

> I think I understand why you often have difficulty falling asleep. Could it be you're hesitant to give up conscious control to sleep, just as you wish to feel totally in control here in therapy?

They generalize it to all of his interpersonal relationships:

> It seems you need to feel you have great control over people and situations. Perhaps this helps you maintain control over yourself.

They make reference to his father:

> I think you want to be as important to me as you are to your father. You seem to feel my success depends on you. Perhaps you feel that way about your father.

> You think your behavior here would affect my supervisor's evaluation of me as you used to think your behavior would affect other people's evaluation of your father.

> I think a part of you would like to see me as similar to your father, someone who is really terrific and whom you can help by performing well—in this case by "getting better."

And this continuation puts it all together:

> **T1:** That would make you powerful in a way. By getting better or not you would have great control over me, and, in a sense, by feeling good or bad you could control me.
>
> **P2:** *I know it's a crazy idea. I said that. But the thought of having such power over you is really pretty neat.*

T2:   Falling asleep is a kind of losing control. So I wonder
if the need to have control is not a major issue with
you.

P3:   *I always just sort of thought of myself as an insom-
niac, one that good old Sominex didn't help. But it is
possible. I just never thought of it that way.*

T3:   It's a specific kind of fantasy of power and control,
isn't it? It's the kind that a child might have to
control a father. And knowing you're an only child,
and that you've said your father always doted on
you, I wonder if you might not have done something
similar with your father. And it worked to a degree.
And if all that is true, then it might very well be
frightening to a child to have such power.

By taking a speculative step away from the material, as T3 in
the foregoing example does, and by falling into the category of
plausible but unfounded (as T3 does, too), an interpretation
runs a number of risks. The main one, of course, is that a
patient will be puzzled. But a concomitant implication, and one
that pertains most directly to our patient, is that he will feel
squelched. Consider this interesting example:

> It seems hard for you to believe that anyone would be
> interested in you for any other reason than to enhance his
> prestige.

If it happened to be invalid, it would be quite an insult, wouldn't
it? But even if it was altogether accurate, notice how it could be
a subtle put-down. It has an evaluative edge that is sharpened
by its speculativeness. The same is true for this interesting one:

> I think that a part of you still wants an A from your father,
> in the same way that you want me to get an A from my
> supervisor. Perhaps thinking of yourself as so inexperi-
> enced and young in relation to your father made you feel as
> if you were no good.

Since the patient had said none of those things, he might
wonder why we did, and this could lead him to infer that we

were criticizing him. And students do give him a verbal rap on the knuckles—for example:

> It seems to me as though your being able to please me, and give me an A as a therapist, is more important to you than how *you* are doing and what *you* may be getting as a patient.

An interpretation like that can be justified on the basis that it focused attention on the way a patient was viewing therapy—and whenever we see the opportunity to do this we should take it. But I am faulting the form of the interpretation, not its content. Compare the following example, and notice how it manages to strike a much less critical tone:

> You seem to be implying that we can make a deal, an A for me and getting better for you. I wonder if you're assuming that you'll get better because it will be I who'll work hard—because an A is important to me.

This kind of interpretation has intrinsic value because it draws attention to a potentially significant way the patient regards his therapy. We could argue, in fact, that it had priority over his need for control, his attitude toward his father, or the new version of his old fantasy.

Lest I seem to be discouraging speculation, let me return to the point about enlisting a patient's active participation. A few pages ago, when I faulted "plausible but unfounded," I questioned the merits of plausibility as a basis for speculation. But I didn't mean to be questioning the merits of speculation itself. (I am referring to formulations that say "It seems likely—" meaning "I believe it's altogether plausible that—" meaning they are based on probability, or common experience, or common sense, or on theory.) Observe how the following continuation centers around a highly speculative interpretation but stays grounded in further material that the patient provides, and thereby sidesteps the pitfalls I've been alluding to:

T1: So it was your pleasure at my success—won with your help—that helped you fall asleep?

P2: *Yeah. You know . . . it's sort of like when my father would come in at night and tuck me in. He always said "we," you know—"we" did this today at the office, and "we" did that. It always felt good, and I'd go to sleep.*

T2: So your feeling of togetherness and friendship with your father was very pleasurable.

P3: *Uh-huh. In fact, I sometimes wondered if maybe I wasn't a little weird for feeling that way. I mean, he's my father! I don't know . . .*

T3: I wonder if you had a fantasy of sexual relations with him, which you found very pleasurable, too.

P4: *(taken aback) I think I did! You know, I sometimes would masturbate after he left the room and then fall asleep.*

That, of course, wasn't quite gradual enough! That T3 can await further developments, and we could instead inquire into what the patient meant by *"a little weird"* and *"for feeling that way."* Whenever an interpretation is met by surprise, we can infer that it was tactless and therefore premature. Not that his experience of being taken aback by an insight, perhaps even awed by it, isn't a vital ingredient in therapy. Far from it. But ideally it will have been an insight or revelation that he himself arrived at, or that we have helped him arrive at, instead of one he passively received. I can imagine achieving this by substituting the following T3 and composing further narrative for the patient, as follows:

T3: Do you mean you sometimes wondered if it was a little weird for you to have such feelings for your father?

P4: *Well, sure . . . because . . .*

T4: They were weird feelings.

P5: *Yeah. Maybe kind of unnatural. He wouldn't touch me or hug me, but the way he talked . . .*

T5: Was the way he was touching and hugging you unnatural?

P6: *Sexual, for christsakes! There was something sexual about it. I mean, I'd feel something . . .*

>*something come over me . . . like he was in bed with me, or something.*

T6: I know this feels weird because it was a fantasy of having sex with him, wasn't it? And it was so pleasurable!

P7: *I think so! You know, I sometimes would masturbate after he left the room, and then fall asleep. Wow!*

He is probably having what I call an "analytic experience."

An analytic experience is one of revelation—of awesome insight, we may say—that occasionally happens during the therapeutic process. It may, but need not, be accompanied by a change in state of consciousness, perhaps a reverie-like or deeply contemplative state of mind. In any event, the patient is now talking "from the gut" and with feelings that are rare and different. It may be an altogether new feeling for him or it may be a long unexperienced old feeling, but it feels rare and profound, even shaking. He may be having a new insight into himself, or into what he was talking about when it came on, but it's the sense of revelation that really counts—the sense of something deeply valid and authentic for him. It doesn't have to be so new or so startling, yet it does feel rare and revelatory, and the feelings that accompany it are likely to be uncanny, ineffable ones, whatever its manifest content may be.

Now, if our patient *was* having such an experience, I *did* play an active role in it. But more as facilitator than instigator. I doubt whether he's going to feel that I did it to him. (Not any more than he felt his father did it to him! Nevertheless, this transference issue will probably develop and burgeon as this therapy progresses.) Bear in mind that the therapeutic process was in good condition in this study. The narrative therefore lent itself to a gradual form of interpretation in which we worked with parts of a complete formulation and structured each part in a way that invited the patient's active participation. We could try for interpretations that were simple and open-ended, more evocative than explanatory, beginning with an observation like:

>I think you understand why the fantasy helped you get to sleep. It's a comforting and reassuring one, isn't it?

He would probably dwell a moment on the idea, and we might then be able to suggest that the fantasy of his father's success as a lawyer being dependent on him was also "comforting and reassuring." And we could speculate that it probably had its origins in his childhood when his father was a powerful man in his eyes:

What do you think of the possibility that you used to have this kind of fantasy about your father?

We might want to hold back the key interpretation—namely, "Your fantasy is that you have a lot of power over him, that you are the power behind the throne; and now, with me as well, you have this fantasy"—until we were sure he needed the help. The transference motif can be kept in the foreground, where it will have served two purposes: bringing to the surface and clarifying an important way he was viewing therapy (as well as us); and exposing for exploration an important fantasy about himself that he has probably long nurtured. The therapeutic process, not to overlook the patient himself, will have been well served by this use of the interpretive mode.

5

TIMING

Instructions for the Timing Studies

Each study gives a running transcript of the beginning of a therapy session. Each transcript is constructed in a way that makes it possible for the therapist to have said nothing. Your task is to speak for the therapist, to say where you would intervene and exactly what you would say. Try for a minimum of four separate and independent interventions for each study, and try to base them on what has gone before, not on what you see coming.

Study 1
The Pseudosickness

The patient is an inhibited and detached 25 year old who speaks slowly, in an apparent effort to maintain his composure. This is his fifth session. It started with a one-minute silence.

This morning I was thinking about something I should tell you. It's something I've thought about a lot, and whenever I do it always mystifies me because I don't understand why I did it, what it was all about. And it's something I am very ashamed of. . . .

161

During this pause we may want to let the patient know we are interested to hear what he has to tell; we might also want to say something to help him get started on the narrative. No interpretation, at this juncture, is likely to do any more than that. An articulation of his reluctance to tell whatever it is he feels he *should* tell will only convey the message "Yes, I understand, but please go ahead anyway." A more diagnostic interpretation, such as "Perhaps because it evokes such shame you mustn't allow yourself to understand it," would probably amount to little more than a supportive gesture. Moreover, when we refrain from making any sort of gesture at times like this, we make a significant contribution to the quality and texture of a therapy session; we define it as a self-directed monologue and distinguish it from a clinical interview.

> *But I guess I should tell you about it. . . .*

At this repetition, students choose to intervene with an interpretation connecting his sense of *should* with the fact that the event was shameful. The patient might also be saying he'd rather not have to recount the event, but feels compelled out of a conviction that it will be important for therapy. Drawing his attention to that—by raising the question "In what sense do you mean *should?*"—could have value, especially if there was reason to suspect he'd forgotten or misconstrued the Basic Instruction. Otherwise, however, it runs the risk of conveying the paradoxical message "You ought not to feel *you should.*" So I would rather make no comment now and keep the matter in mind. Chances are good that later on I will be able to return to the *should* and use it in a meaningful way, saying "I think I now understand why you said at the beginning that this was something you felt you *should* tell me."

> *It happened when I was about 11 years old, going on 12, I believe. What I did was fake an illness. And I spent almost a whole year—a full school year, I mean—in bed, pretending I was sick when I really wasn't. . . .*

This pause is where therapists would tend to ask a question. It would have to be an interviewing question, and at best could serve the function of facilitating the narrative. Instead of offering that kind of help, I'd rather wait, thereby showing confidence that the patient, at his own pace, will recount the event to his satisfaction.

It was a terrible thing to do . . . uh . . . to my parents.

The speech disruption is noteworthy, and if we thought he had intended to say *"to my parents"* and caught himself starting to say *"to myself,"* we might ask "Were you going to say *to myself?"* But not only is this a confronting remark, it also smacks of reading his mind—which is subtly but significantly different from understanding his mind. So it's better to wait until the relevance and meaning of the speech disruption is clearer. We are assuming, of course, that nothing he talked about during the previous sessions had any bearing on it.

Timing is normally based on the background of the entire course of therapy, and a great deal depends on the session that preceded. Given that the transcript, along with its brief introduction, provides our only context, our considerations of timing must be limited to it. And my commentaries, too, are going to be selective; by no means will I attempt an exhaustive consideration of interventional possibilities. My chief purpose in these studies is to illustrate and defend our central timing criterion, which can be formulated quite simply according to the concept of the therapeutic process—namely, we speak when we judge that the process might benefit from something we say. At the same time, however, we have to decide what kind of intervention will best serve this purpose, and in the majority of instances it will turn out be an empathic interpretation. But I want to emphasize that although interpretations can be construed as bearers (and barers) of insight, attainment of insight is not synonymous with the therapeutic process. Insightful discovery might be a result or outcome of the process, but the process itself denotes the patient's principal way of working. Thus, the fundamental timing question (of how interpreting relates to the therapeutic process) is "How does our principal way of working relate to his?" The Timing Studies were designed to help answer this question, and Study 1 was designed to pose it in this form: "How do we work with a therapeutic process that is engaged in the work of reminiscence?"

*They were very worried, because I was supposedly sick
and yet the doctor didn't know what was wrong with
me. . . .*

During this pause many of us would be thinking: "I am the
doctor also, and he is referring to therapy too." Few of us,
however, would venture to say as much to the patient. It would
stop the narrative in midstream and introduce the transference
prematurely; it would be going too far too fast. But the thought
could influence the way we listened and heard the ensuing
narrative, and that would be useful so long as it didn't cause us
to listen too selectively. It isn't easy to pay full attention with a
hypothesis in mind, but it's one of the skills we acquire.

*It was an easy thing to do, too. It was really quite easy. All
I had to do was say I didn't feel well. And the only
symptom I had . . . I mean, I showed, was a low-grade
fever, and I found a way to fake that. What I did was put
the thermometer under my body, under the blankets,
when no one was looking, and it was enough to make it
go up to around ninety-nine* (takes a cigarette, but doesn't
light it).

Students choose this break in the narrative for the first of their
four interventions. They comment on the ease with which the
patient was able to fool his parents, and draw speculative
inferences from it:

So you found that it was very easy to fool your parents, and
the doctor as well. They weren't as sharp as you thought
they were. An 11 year old like you could fool them.

They also infer feelings of guilt over it, and wonder whether the
experience wasn't also frightening. I see no useful purpose in
such speculations at this point. The patient hasn't yet alluded
to any thoughts or feelings, and we want to avoid speculations
that are based on theoretical considerations alone. (Or even, for
that matter, those based on common sense alone.) His taking a
cigarette at this juncture can be taken as a sign of anxiety, but
is it appropriate to suggest so? A student says:

Your taking a cigarette now might mean you are feeling
anxious about the event, or about telling it to me, don't you
think?

In addition to considerations I've already mentioned, this interpretation tells him how he feels, which is very different from
helping him articulate his feelings.

However, in view of the fact that the narrative was interrupted, the moment may be right for an intervention. But what
kind should it be? Whenever we sense that the therapeutic
process requires us to say "something," we have two options:
one is an interpretation, the other is a gratuity. With no good
interpretation in mind, we are limited to a simple paraphrasing
of what the patient had said. Yet, this might be better than
nothing, and chances are often good that we can add something
significant to our gratuitous remark, something that might turn
out to be useful. For instance, if we said "I gather you discovered a way to appear sick when you didn't feel it," the idea of
"appear" versus "feel" might turn out to have some significant
reverberations both for his reconstruction of the past, as well as
his construction of the present (the current "sickness" for
which he is consulting us). A student gives this variation, which
might have similar reverberations: "I gather you discovered an
easy way to fool your parents and the doctor, too."

However, students also give voice to surprise, and to disbelief
as well, that it could have been possible to fake an illness for
such a long time. One puts it this way:

I fail to see how a temperature of ninety-nine degrees could
have been considered serious enough to keep you at home
for a year.

Another challenges with:

I wonder if you truly did not feel well, if not physically then
psychologically.

And I regard such remarks, even when their skepticism is more
muted, as serious technical errors. Now, it frequently happens
in therapy that incredible things are recounted and we experience a sense of disbelief, but to express such reactions to the

patient introduces a fresh element into the situation. It implicates our personal beliefs and experiences, and can stir up
doubt in his mind, doubt which at the moment may serve no
useful purpose. I think it's important that we keep from defining
ourselves as the doubter or even as the skeptic. Taking at face
value what our patient is taking at face value is altogether
prudent, and good timing requires a sensitivity to those moments when he is ready to experience some doubt, when he is
prepared to reconsider the condition of his memory. Notice that
our patient hasn't hinted at any doubts. And bear in mind that
this early in therapy it may be impossible for us to know
whether he was truly pretending the illness or whether he was
the one who was fooled. We also don't know to what extent his
memory of the event may be faulty.

> *The way it all started was that when we got back from
> our summer vacation. . . . No, I was at camp that sum-
> mer, I think. . . . Yes, at camp. Anyway, I got sick, truly
> sick, with a sore throat and fever and . . . and I had to
> stay in bed for over two weeks. Then I got better. And it
> was the middle of September already, and I had to go to
> school, into a new grade. It was the seventh grade, I
> think. Yes, the seventh. And I guess I wasn't happy in
> school—though I don't remember that part of it too well.*

He has already given several indications that his memory of the
event is shaky, so a student chooses this moment to speculate:

> I wonder if the reason you don't remember it too well is
> that it's painful to recall how it felt not to be happy in
> school.

Inasmuch as the patient might be showing the defense of
repression, and defenses have priority with respect to timing,
this kind of interpretation can be useful. If we wanted to initiate
an exploration of the defense, we could try this:

> Do you notice how uncertain you are of several aspects of
> the event? You're uncertain whether you were at camp
> that summer, whether it was the seventh grade, whether
> you were unhappy in school.

It might, however, be too confronting. To be sure, if he responded with "*Yes, but why do you want me to notice the fact?*" we could say: "Because I'm wondering whether this kind of uncertainty is typical for your memory of your childhood or whether it is associated specifically with the incident you're telling me about." And if he persisted with a "*So what if it is?*" we could suggest that he might be applying the defense of repression to this particular event because it was associated with profound feelings of shame. But that's a highly diagnostic formulation—and confronting interventions have a tendency to wind up in such interpretations.

> *And so one morning I decided I wanted to stay home. So I told my mother I wasn't feeling well again, and . . . she let me stay in bed. . . . And that's when it all started, when I got the idea of faking being sick. I remember she decided to take my temperature, and she left the room while the thermometer was in my mouth. And I just took it out and put it under my body so it would show a fever* (lights the cigarette). *I couldn't have been sure it would work, but it did. I don't know where I got the idea to do it. I just . . . I just did it. . . . My mother never suspected anything, and neither did the doctor. And once it began, once I was into it, I just kept right on doing it. . . . And the longer it went on, the more impossible, you know, it was to stop.*

Students introduce the theme of guilt at this point, and suggest to the patient that he must have felt frightened. For example:

> And I wonder if perhaps that wasn't frightening, to have started something and then find there was no turning back.

Aside from prompting the question "*Why should that be frightening?*" this interpretation comes too close to being reassuring and supportive and nothing more. Even a confrontation—such as "I notice you lit the cigarette right after you spoke about putting the thermometer under your body. I wonder if there is something about this detail that makes you nervous"—could serve no more than a supportive function because it neglects to provide a specific explanation—namely, what is the "something about this detail" that makes him "nervous."

> *So I just stayed in bed and played sick. . . . I can re-*
> *member times when I felt awful about it, mostly because*
> *my parents were so worried—and so needlessly, too. . . .*
> *But my mother was really wonderful about it. She was*
> *always good when any of us were sick, thinking up all*
> *kinds of projects to keep us occupied. She taught me*
> *things, and she was always buying me new books. She*
> *used to play cards and chess with me; and she even made*
> *me do exercises so I wouldn't get too weak, and she'd do*
> *them with me. She tried to keep my spirits up, even*
> *though . . . even though my spirits were actually quite*
> *high anyway. . . . I wasn't unhappy about staying in bed.*
> *Actually, I was . . . very happy.*

He is describing his mother as a willing, if not eager, accomplice. I might consider underscoring the fact with "I gather you remember your mother as a sort of accomplice in your deception." Even so, I would probably not interject the remark at this point in the narrative, despite the fact that it could lead to a better understanding of the episode and also resonate with an important transference theme. (The current accomplice is, after all, who?) For one thing, it undercuts the patient's mystification and presumes that he doesn't recognize the import of what he is recounting. Staying home and being sick was altogether pleasant, and for his mother, too, yet he remains mystified by his motivation. Unless I assumed he hasn't recognized the significance of what he was recounting, I wouldn't expect to get very far with a line of inquiry that sought to uncover the reason for the event. That's my main criticism of the following interpretation:

> Are you saying you're not sure whether it was something
> distressing about school that made you stay away, or
> something very appealing about staying home that deter-
> mined your behavior?

He wasn't wondering what "determined" his behavior, he was reminiscing. The intervention shifts gears out of the mnemonic

mode into an explanatory one. I don't think that's ever a good
idea. So the only remark I would now make is one that draws
attention to the tentative manner in which he said he was
happy. I might say: "I take it you're not really sure whether you
were happy." It stays in the narrative mode, it speaks to his
memory, and it is only mildly confronting. Consider, however,
this example:

I have the impression that she almost encouraged you to
be sick.

The only point of doing it now would be to help him explain the
event, if not also to exonerate him from culpability, and this
raises a fundamental question that I have been skirting. Should
we be wondering why the incident occurred at all? More precisely: In what way and for what reasons should we be wondering why it occurred?

Now, expecting us to listen to the account of an event like this
without wondering why it happened, is expecting too much.
But keeping a certain perspective on that mental activity is
actually quite easy. The temptation to play the role of sage, or
detective, to help solve a mystery for the patient, is always
there—and it is likely, of course, to be what he hopes for and
expects, if not sometimes also fears. But that isn't the reason for
resisting the temptation. The role is usually dissonant with the
timing criteria of facilitating and promoting the therapeutic
process.

Offering interpretations can be construed as our way of
participating in the therapeutic process. But insofar as it por-
trays us as providing understanding or information about the
patient's inner and outer realities, and doing it for his benefit, or
if it is taken to imply that we help him make discoveries by
making interpretations in order to maximize the occurrence of
such discoveries, even that formulation is potentially misleading. Therefore, I prefer to regard interpretations as our way of
"supervising" the therapeutic process; it emphasizes that our
chief purpose in offering them is to promote the ongoing process
itself. Since the process is conceptualized as intrapsychic, as
entailing autonomous action on the patient's part, and since the
overriding goal is for him to be active—to actively strive for
understanding, actively exercise and strengthen his synthetic

function, and thereby maximize his control and freedom—it
follows that our chief goal is not to impart information and
explanations, nor to give understanding and insight, but rather
to provide the optimal conditions under which he can openly
and freely examine his life and achieve as full and authentic an
understanding of himself as possible.

If he's engaged, as our patient is, in exploring an event out of
his past, and wants to figure it out, then our useful role is
mainly to help clear the way by pointing out the road blocks.
And the major ones will lie in the present, not in the past—
although they may well have originated from there. At any rate,
my point is this: we shouldn't be trying very hard to figure out
the reason our patient feigned the illness when he was 11, or
even what it meant to him at the time. What we might try to
figure out is what the event means to him now, why he is
recounting it this way, why he is having such trouble remembering and understanding it, the relevance it might have
in respect to his attitude towards us and therapy. To be sure, in
order to arrive at these reasons, figuring out why it happened
in the first place could be helpful. But if we play too active a
role in that achievement, it will be seriously compromised.

> There was plenty to do, and I was never bored. . . . I kept
> up my schoolwork; my teacher would send me work-
> books, and my parents would help me with my les-
> sons. . . . And my father would come home from work
> and spend time with me. He would even read the news-
> paper to me—The New York Times. And that's when I
> started being such a devoted newspaper reader; I have to
> read the Times every day or else my day isn't com-
> plete. . . .

I inserted this piece of material deliberately (and maliciously) in
order to lure my students into a neat interpretation of the *New
York Times* habit. Patients do that, too, by providing us with
the grounds for an interpretation they already know full well.
(They enjoy setting us up, so to speak, and watching us do our
stuff.) At any rate, my students are unable to resist the temptation. Their interpretations are varied and not uninteresting,
but I won't examine them here. Suffice it to say, they could only
spoil our patient's bad habit—and alas, they're not likely to be

sufficient to the task. But let me repeat: in a sense, the entire study is an exercise in restraint, for just as we don't want to explain his *New York Times* habit, we don't want to explain the event he is reminiscing about.

> *So it was really very nice staying home all that time. . . . Except for the fact that I was pretending and making them worry for nothing. That used to make me feel bad.*

The experience of having pretended to be sick and feeling bad about it—conceivably it can be bereft of any significance for his being in therapy. Few therapists, however, would seriously entertain that possibility. Yet many would agree that it was premature to introduce a transference theme at this point. They would concur with my criticism of the following example:

> The thought occurs to me that in telling me how easy it was for you to fool your parents, you are expressing some concern that you may be able to fool me.

For one thing, it comes straight out of the blue. The patient is likely to be taken aback and find the idea farfetched. For another, he might arrive at the realization himself if we give him time as well as some helpful kinds of interpretations formulated to be congruent with the transference theme. We can be guided by the transference theme, making interpretations that are either preliminary to it or can later be translated into its terms— interpretations that lay the groundwork, in a sense. A good possibility is conveyed by this example:

> Perhaps you felt that only by pretending to be sick could you get the help and attention you wanted and needed.

Another good possibility is:

> Perhaps on some level you enjoyed being able to assert yourself, even indirectly, and control the situation—to manipulate their actions and even their feelings. That's a kind of power you might have enjoyed, even though you felt bad about it at times.

And here's one that articulates the conflict in a way that is most congruent with the transference theme:

> Do you think it possible that part of you wanted your parents to help you go back to school? Perhaps feeling bad had more to do with the fact that you felt they allowed you to fool them, than with playing sick.

Out of context, these interpretations can be faulted for aiming at an explanation of the event in purely historical terms; but the fact that they are likely to have significant implications for the present—we have a transference interpretation in mind, and it's a transference issue that is bound to have a profound effect on the way the patient construes therapy and relates to us—more than compensates for that defect.

On Transference

Let's take a brief time-out for a discussion of transference. There's a prevalent point of view among practitioners and teachers that transference must have the highest priority with respect to timing, that manifestations of transference require our most diligent attention. Some qualify the point this way: transference requires attention only when it also functions as a resistance—otherwise, "Keep the Transference in the Background!" As resistance can readily be formulated in terms of the therapeutic process, I am tempted to take the position that "true" transference is a fortiori resistance—and if it isn't a resistance it doesn't deserve to be called Transference. But I believe transference phenomena cannot routinely be regarded and treated as forms of resistance against the essential work of therapy; sometimes they are resistance and sometimes they aren't. When they are, whether by cause or by effect, we can satisfy our central timing criterion by formulating the transference in a way that highlights its resistive function, and our decision to make the transference interpretation will be based on the goal of restoring the therapeutic process. Whether we construe the transference as intrinsic to the naturally functioning therapeutic process or as based on our impersonality and neutrality makes little difference; the fact that it served to impede the process is what counts. But when a transference phenomenon wasn't serving as a resistance, another rationale for making the interpretation must be chosen.

Moreover, even if we accepted the point of view that all transference is resistance, there's the patient's point of view to consider. In order for theoretical formulations to be clinically useful, they have to be translated into the terms of his experience. The critical test, after all, is how meaningful and valid they are to him. And transference experiences frequently have a special quality that sets them apart from resistance. A patient will usually experience them as if they were integral to therapy and in no way an impediment. For instance, if it's a so-called "positive" transference (he regards us as a nurturing, loving, and perhaps all-powerful figure), then the possibility that it could be serving a defensive or resistive function may strike him as farfetched. And even "negative" transference can have a facilitating effect on therapeutic movement. Viewing us as a demanding, even critical, figure, for instance, could spur him on in the work of therapy. So it's quite possible, and also quite common, to encounter a fullblown transference that can be understood technically as a resistance but not interpreted as such to the patient because he doesn't feel that he is resisting.

Faced with this situation, we have to judge whether our central timing criterion should maintain its priority or whether interpreting the transference—"because it is there"—has an overriding benefit. If we preferred to keep the transference in the background, we would pay attention to the therapeutic process and leave the patient's transference alone, so to speak— and that is my general preference. I don't believe, not as a general rule at least, that transference must be given a special priority. When my patient is "working well," I don't think I need to "work with" him on transference issues; I can allow them to "work themselves out" the same way other issues do. For one thing, I want to avoid teaching him that the way to elicit more active participation on my part is by focusing on feelings and fantasies about me and / or therapy. For another, I don't want to foster the transference and cause it to assume an artificially exaggerated significance.

Reader: But isn't transference the key process in psycho-therapy? Don't you believe that it plays a central role in the dynamics of therapeutic movement and efficacy? How can it be artificial and exaggerated, if it has such importance?

Author: Precisely because I believe it *can* have such great importance do I emphasize that it mustn't be actively imposed by us in a way that could be artificial and exaggerated. For I believe that transference stands the chance of playing a central role in the dynamics of therapeutic movement only if we allow it to evolve naturally. This means we show no special interest nor give it special priority in our interpretations. If there is an equally valid formulation that doesn't implicate transference, we should be inclined to give it and save the transference for issues where it might have the greatest validity. In other words, we should be especially loath to speculate on the transference. That, in my opinion, can exaggerate it and make it artificial.

Reader: But aren't there certain diagnostic considerations that militate against keeping the transference in the back-ground? I am referring principally to narcissism and the clinical observation that patients with significant narcissistic features tend to form a transference that assumes a special significance of its own, rather than serving its traditional functions—namely, transference in the service of recall and reintegration. These patients typically use us as "objects" with whom they play out a variety of intrapsychic processes, such as incorpora-tion and projection; we become, in a certain way, an actual part of their intrapsychic structure. Moreover, that a resistive func-tion is thereby being served is by no means evident. Rather, the so-called narcissistic transference tends to become the arena within which the crucial therapeutic issues take place. And when that's the case, doesn't it become necessary for us to take exception to our fundamental timing criterion? Doesn't it be-come necessary, in other words, to work with the patient's narcissistic transference for its own sake?

Author: Yes—when that is the case. And a substantial body of opinion among analysts holds that this is equally true for every genuine transference-neurosis—as distinct from transference-reaction. Moreover, there are certain clinical situ-ations and circumstances in which the transference must have a special priority, and Study 1 might be one of them. The particular form of our patient's transference, the way it pertains to his underlying attitude toward treatment in general and doctors in particular, happens to be especially pertinent to the way the therapy is likely to unfold. And to the extent that it is pertinent, we may have to take active measures to uncover it as early as possible in order to ensure that therapy will proceed. But we mustn't rush the matter, because if there is a danger in not uncovering it early enough, there is also the danger of uncovering it too early. We want to make sure that our patient is ready for the idea and won't seal it off. His role in the work of uncovering it mustn't be too passive. Therefore, as I've mentioned, to do anything more than lay groundwork at this point in the narrative is likely to be premature.

Meanwhile, back at the study—

> *I was able to fool them so easily. It was really such a simple thing to do. And sometimes I would worry that they would find out what I was doing. I also thought I would have to tell them sooner or later—that I would just have to, you know. . . .*

A student takes note of his repeated "*sometimes*" by questioning with a succinct "sometimes?" The patient seems to be suggesting there were times he enjoyed worrying his parents for nothing, and times he wished they would find out what he was doing. This might be useful to explore. But "Sometimes?" is more of a directive to elaborate rather than clarify, so I would put it into the form of an interpretation: "I take it (I wonder if)—"

A student takes this opportunity to draw an interesting connection with the way our narrative began:

> I'm wondering why you're telling this secret to me, and I remember your saying before that you felt you "should" tell it to me, as if something or someone were forcing you.

This suggests that the present recounting is meant somehow to undo the fact that he *never* told his parents. As it stands, however, without the fuller interpretation, it is too diagnostic. The following interpretation makes the same point and gives it a more explicit transference significance:

Perhaps you feel that in telling me, you have satisfied the sense of obligation you felt then—that you would have to tell them sooner or later—and that maybe in some way I am taking the place of your parents.

That's an appealing and sensitive way to introduce the transference theme because it fits the context so nicely, and the patient is likely to find it congenial. Yet, although I don't expect him to react defensively to that interpretation, it is still too diagnostic for my taste. Therefore, I would forgo that opportunity and wait for one that allowed me to make the point in a more empathic way. (At the very least, I would omit the last phrase.)

I remember even thinking that they must really know I was pretending. . . . You know, that they did know it . . . after a while, anyway, but they decided for some reason or other not to say anything to me about it . . . to go along with it. I don't know why I thought that. . . .

A student tells him why:

Perhaps your feeling that they really knew you were pretending was a way of easing your guilt about fooling them. By thinking they weren't fooled, you could be sure of not being blamed for fooling them.

An intelligent speculation it is, and satisfy the patient intellectually it might, but a good use of speculation it isn't. Speculating on a patient's thoughts and feelings (his mental content) is one thing, speculating on his dynamics is quite another. And notice how diagnostic the interpretation is; there isn't much alternative when we make a dynamic formulation. In fact, it is so diagnostic that I wouldn't even have it in mind. To be sure, he may be thinking that I know he's fooling me and that I'm going along with it, but to say so would run the risk of creating what I imagine I'm discovering. Consider the following example:

Perhaps you also think that I see through you, and that I realize you are not telling me things you feel you should, but I am going along with it and not saying anything about it for my own reasons.

Haven't we thereby "seen through" him? Moreover, to introduce the transference at this juncture smacks of opportunism. The patient wasn't thinking about therapy; he was wondering why he used to think he wasn't really fooling anybody. Inserting a transference motif into his deliberations is bound to be an intrusion, if not also a shocking one. Even this tactful rendition might take him aback:

Perhaps you are wondering the same thing about therapy? This might seem like another situation in which you have the same kind of control, and that may be worrying you.

I think we should wait. After all, the narrative may almost be finished.

But then, there's so much about the whole thing that I don't know. Why did I do it in the first place? Why did I keep it up so long? What was really going on? (puts out the cigarette and falls silent)

The narrative now seems finished—the transcript, in any case, is—and the patient has again expressed his mystification. The moment is right for an intervention that will lead to fresh avenues of exploration. Our timing criterion is well satisfied; now we have only to find the intervention. Will it be an attempt to answer his questions, or will it focus on the questions themselves? Will it address his sense of expectancy or the fact that he seems more mystified than he "needs" to be? He has, after all, given some substantial reasons why he feigned the illness, as well as why he kept it up, and we might wonder why his sense of mystification remains so great. Students don't, but I believe practitioners would—and with an observation such as:

You know, you've spelled out some cogent reasons, and yet you feel mystified. I wonder if you sense that you've left something out, something possibly important, something perhaps so painful and forbidden that it has to remain a secret.

I would do that only if I could specify what the "something" might be.

What students do is answer the patient's questions with an unspeculative interpretation that spells out the cogent reasons that he has already given us—and I see little point in it. Even an interpretation that added a significant dimension, as the following one does, is not worth making so long as it only aims to explain the event:

> I wonder if you and your parents still had a need to have you be a little boy again at that time, a time in most boys' lives when they are becoming men.

Not only does this interpretation stay focused on the past, it makes the error of interpreting the parents' behavior.

Students tend to offer a lengthy, summary-like interpretation. Here's an example that ends with a remark attributing some contemporary significance to the event:

> Here's the way I understand what happened. Perhaps you initially started feigning illness because you were angry at them for sending you off to camp. (And why that made you angry we will obviously have to explore later on!) It was your way of refusing to be sent off again (that's my diagnosis!), this time to school. At first the attention and concern pleased you, it pleased you to worry them (retaliation, you see!), but then there was no turning back, you had created a monster. And I think it frightened you that nobody understood you enough to know that you were fooling, and nobody would stop you. And you couldn't stop your self-created game either because you began to fear what they would do—you probably felt grownups would be angry at being fooled by a little boy. (Don't all little boys feel that?) I wonder if you still feel that you still successfully fool people today, that they too won't understand or know you enough, and that they, too, would be angry when they realized you had fooled them.

Such detailed summaries can only be defended on the grounds that they provide a patient with a variety of possibilities to consider, and offer him the choice of what to pursue and explore. ("Here are the different possibilities, as I see them," is the message, "You may choose what is most meaningful and important in your judgment.") Aside from the fact that they often close things off, rather than open them up for further exploration (and rarely do they lead to important insights), they run the risk of fostering an intellectualized approach to experience. Moreover, its final section, which could stand as a separate interpretation, raises another problem; it may deflect attention from what the patient himself was considering, thereby changing the subject.

At any rate, the moment may be right for the transference interpretation itself, and the question is how far it should go—further than laying more groundwork? In my opinion, it shouldn't. The transference theme is still premature. Consider this example:

> I wonder if what you've just told me is somehow analogous to what you are feeling about therapy. As a child you found you could command a lot of love and attention by faking an illness. Perhaps you are feeling that the problem which brought you here is also somehow a fake, a bid for attention. And perhaps you are afraid that I'm on to you, but I am pretending to go along with it, as your parents did.

I think it goes much too far. I picture our patient startled by it. To be sure, there are hints in the material that it might not be so far from his awareness. His repetition of *"I should tell you"* can be taken as such a hint, particularly since it matches his remark that he thought he would have to tell his parents. (*"That I would just have to, you know."*) Nevertheless, there remains the risk of his being taken aback, perhaps shocked, and if that happened he might fall back on his defenses and the issue would be sealed off. The risk, in my estimation, is not worth it. So important to therapy is the issue that we must be confident of its reception when we introduce it.

Therefore, my preferred response to the patient's questions would be silence. Other things being equal, that would be my candidate for Best Intervention. And it would be an active intervention too, to the degree that it conveyed the message "I do not know why you did it in the first place, why you kept it up so long, and what was really going on." Alas, however, *that* isn't the only message it could convey—and other things are *not* equal. For one thing, our timing criterion calls for an explicit intervention. For another, silence could convey an uncaring detachment. So I would opt for a response that addressed his sense of expectancy and touched lightly on the transference, saying:

> You've told me about an important event in your life, and raised questions about it, and you did it because you felt you should. Now you may be feeling that I *should* answer these questions. And when you asked what was *really* going on, I thought you might be thinking that I knew— just like your parents and the doctor knew what was really going on—namely, that you were faking the illness.

Aside from introducing our transference theme, the interpretation bears on the phenomenon of multiple messages and several-layered meanings. If, for instance, the patient responded in shame over having been "devious" and "found out," we would have the opportunity to do two things: relate that feeling to the narrative itself, and draw attention to the processes of over-determination and multiple messages. When we do this, however, we must be careful to avoid suggesting that the underlying message was the "real" one—as if conscious meanings and intentions were somehow less meaningful than those that lie at or beyond the boundaries of consciousness. And in addition to avoiding the implication that unconscious events are the ones that really count, we have to avoid giving the impression that we will be the one who uncovers them. There is, after all, a mutuality between conscious and unconscious mental events; and psychotherapy works best when our role and the patient's are mutual as well.

Study 2
Should I Go into Business with Harvey?

Lizzy is a girlfriend of about two months' standing; Harvey is an old friend. The patient has been enthusiastic about therapy, and involved. This is his twentieth session. He begins speaking right away. Ordinarily he doesn't begin quite as fast.

> *Lizzy sends her love.* (grins broadly and a bit foolishly) *I was over at her place just before, and when I split she said, "Give your shrink my love."* (loosens collar) *She said that once last week, too, but I didn't tell you. She's been bugging me lately about what goes on in here—asking me what you tell me, and things like that. But she says therapy is not her bag. Her mother wants her to see a shrink, and she's been hassling her about it for over a year. I think she can use it, too. I told you about these downs of hers; they can last for weeks at a time. But she says she can handle her own problems herself.* (slouches down)

"Perhaps you're wondering about that yourself now—whether you can, or should be able to, handle your problems yourself." This is an interpretation many practitioners would give, and its timeliness lies in the fact that it articulates a feeling about therapy that contains the seeds of a resistance. My preference would be the remark "And you can't?" It succinctly makes the point and conveys that I wasn't sure it was what he had in mind to say.

What about the slouching down? Should we use it as evidence for an interpretation, and say so? ("The way you slouched down suggests to me that—") The same question arose in Study 1 when our patient lit the cigarette. We took it as evidence of anxiety, but should we have said so? Most practitioners and teachers would disagree with my answer, which is No. For I believe in the rule of thumb that abjures us from commenting on a patient's actions, gestures, or appearance, and even when they have contributed to the formulation of an interpretation. Drawing attention to his behavior can make a patient self-conscious (as distinct from reflective) and cause him to worry about (as distinct from reflect upon) the signals he is sending unwittingly (or even wittingly, for that matter). But I will avoid the digression that this subject deserves, and restrict myself to two points: (1) Verbal utterance is likely to be in more active control than nonverbal behavior, and therefore a patient can experience a greater sense of command over what he says than over how he says it; (2) The Basic Instruction promises that he will be listened to, not watched. Not that we aren't observant as we listen, or that our interpretations won't be significantly influenced by what we see and hear, but we can easily limit our remarks to the verbal content and keep everything else in the background—and to do anything more is usually unnecessary. In any event, this restriction makes a rather profound difference; it fosters a sense of freedom from scrutiny, from a kind of self-consciousness, that can distort the therapeutic process.

> *A couple of days ago she asked me what you thought about my going into business with Harvey, into the shop he wants us to set up. And she didn't believe me when I told her you didn't say one way or the other. I explained how you don't ever tell me what to do, or anything like that. I don't even know whether you think the scheme is okay or not. . . . She doesn't buy that. Her friend Amy's shrink is always telling Amy what to do. . . .*

> Perhaps a part of you wishes that I would tell you exactly what to do.

This qualifies as a timely interpretation for reasons I've already given. Students also focus on the indirect way he expressed his wish. One suggests:

> You prefer me to do the same thing, tell you what to do, although you don't feel you can ask directly.

Another puts it more strongly:

> I wonder if by telling me what Lizzy thinks, you're not telling me indirectly how you feel about it. Perhaps you resent the fact that I won't tell you what I think of the scheme, and I wonder if you don't find it easier to tell me that Lizzy *doesn't buy that* than to say that you don't.

That, of course, was very diagnostic, so I wouldn't venture it. But if I did, I'd go easier and not suggest anything more than embarrassment, saying:

I think you're finding it difficult, embarrassing perhaps, to say you wish I'd tell you what I think of the scheme. I wonder if you're aware of having expressed that wish in an indirect way.

This reduces the risk of my playing the role of detective, the one who looks beneath or behind the manifest content for hidden meanings and implications. I don't mean to say that I will never try to understand the different meanings and implications of his utterances, including the hidden ones; but when he isn't concerned with them, when he isn't actively trying to discover them, I'll keep my efforts in the background.

I spoke to Harvey on the phone last night. He needs to know this week whether I'm in or not. He wants to get the shop started already. I told him I still wasn't sure, I need more time. . . . My father is still dead set against the idea. He thinks it's harebrained and I'll get stung. Harvey's going to go ahead with it no matter what, and he said he'll get someone else if I cop out. Lizzy thinks it's a bad scene, too. But she gets all the money she wants from her father, so she doesn't see what's in it for me. All she's hung up about is the time, the evenings and Saturdays I'll have to be at the shop. . . . You know, that part of it is really cool. It's something I've never done before. I guess it's like my father, working late at the store and then coming home all filled with it. You know, my old man never rapped about the store. He just never talked about his work at all. All he ever said was he didn't want for me to work like he had to. I would have a profession and keep decent hours and make lots of dough. I guess I must've resented that, you know. I remember playing store a lot when I was a kid, pretending I was a storekeeper like my father. One time, it was a rainy day, a Sunday. I set up a play store in my room. Boy, I remember how hard I worked setting it up, all elaborate and everything! I must've worked for two hours getting it all set up. Then I called my father and asked him to come and be the customer, and—typical!—he refused. Wouldn't tear his ass away from the fucking TV.

Will we take this opportunity to suggest that he wanted to be like his father and his father didn't let him? I don't think we should. There is no reason to suppose he isn't perfectly aware of it, so the only nongratuitous function of such an interpretation is to show some understanding. In my opinion, even an interpretation like this one is gratuitous:

> Maybe one reason the business with Harvey is appealing to you is that you think it might be a way of communicating with, or getting closer to your father—by being like him, just as you played being him as a child.

It has the further disadvantage of coming close to being an explaining-away of the wish to go into business (even though we were careful to say "one reason" instead of leaving the impression it could be the whole reason). Moreover, for reasons I've amply discussed, I would avoid trying to explain the wish to go into business with Harvey; that particular piece of therapeutic work can be left to him.

Students draw transference implications at this point. Two examples:

> Perhaps your telling me about this possible business venture is similar to your asking your father to play store with you. If I don't show interest or encourage you, I'll be like your father.

> Perhaps you feel that if you asked me to give you advice about it I also—*typically!*—would refuse.

Such interpretations could be useful—but not now. They would probably be more timely later on in the session when they didn't interrupt any reminiscences, and when we don't interject ourselves into his narrative so abruptly.

> *And my mother got into a big hassle with him about it. "Alex, why don't you go and play with him? You never play with him anymore!" And then they were off into one of their regular yelling bouts. I hated it when they hassled each other. Before you knew it, she would drag in the kitchen sink—every fucking complaint in the book. Like how he never took her anyplace, never talked to her,*

*never bought her anything—the whole fucking shmeer.
And then he'd sink into one of his slow burns. "Leave me
alone, for godsakes! I'm tired! I work hard all week. Get
off my back!" . . . What an awful scene!*

If it was clear that we weren't interpreting the mother's behavior, this succinct formulation might be useful: "Your mother was using you to get back at your father?" If it found a way to articulate his *"upset,"* or simply repeated his *"I hated it,"* this one is good, too:

> I take it you were upset because you had wanted to please
> your father by being like him, but instead you felt responsible for a fight in which he expressed dissatisfaction with
> his work, which was what you were imitating.

My preference would be to underscore that his mother began by fighting his fight but soon was fighting her own, because it suggests her having encouraged a kind of identification with him, an alliance against the father. But I would do two things: carefully avoid the implication that that was, in fact, her intention, and save the formulation for a more timely moment. The first would ensure that I wasn't interpreting his mother's behavior; the second would let me wait and see whether he already noticed it, and if so, what he made of it. And I wouldn't worry about having missed an opportunity, because if he changed the subject (or returned to the original one) it might entail nothing more than a postponement. Such a central issue—if that's what it is—is unlikely never to be repeated, and whenever it makes its reappearance I can say "What I'm thinking is how you once recounted the way your parents would argue—"

Now, in view of the fact that my commentaries are growing repetitious, inasmuch as I steadily criticize the timeliness of interpretations and recommend a wait-and-see position, I want to emphasize that we aren't overly constrained by the timing criterion of promoting the therapeutic process. It is our principal timing criterion, but it isn't our only one. And this merits a brief digression—

On Timing

Imagine a patient dealing with his relationship to his brother and talking about his long-standing hostility, and imagine him doing it well—speaking openly, expressing feelings, reminiscing and reconstructing, sticking to the subject. Suppose I have an idea about why he is hostile toward his brother, or I spot something he was overlooking. Suppose even further that I have reason to believe that were I to share my idea with him, his hostility might diminish and the relationship with his brother might improve. Am I going to offer the interpretation or draw his attention to what he overlooked?

Reader: Apparently not! How come?

Author: Because I don't have the requisite reason to. The therapeutic process is proceeding optimally, and *it* has no need for an intervention. Are you familiar with the principal criterion of timing in psychoanalytic therapy?

Reader: It centers on the patient's readiness to comprehend and apprehend. The critical consideration is his state of mind as reflected in the condition of his transference and resistance; when they are right, the time is right.

Author: Accordingly, a therapist might in practice draw no distinction between whether the patient can use the interpretation and whether he needs it. The latter often gets more-or-less taken for granted; if he can use it, he needs it. But that's the criterion to which I give priority. Whether the patient can use and assimilate the interpretation becomes the secondary consideration.

Reader: Isn't the efficacy of that criterion open to question? And isn't it a position that might look all right on paper but won't work well in practice?

Author: Yes, but my clinical experience has convinced me that it can have a great efficacy and contribute substantially to the patient's well-being.

Reader: Okay, then how *do* you proceed? What are you going to do with your insight and observation?

Author: I'm going to say to myself: "Let him arrive at it himself; let him discover what it was he overlooked." After all, if he's actually working so well, I can reasonably expect him to achieve this insight, or arrive at others of equal value, perhaps insights that haven't occurred to me. And if my expectation is realized, then his achievement would be all the more meaningful and effective. His relationship with his brother may benefit more substantially from an insight arrived at by himself rather than receiving one passively from me. That, you see, is my working hypothesis.

And I base it on the conviction that changes in our patients' behavior, in their attitudes and their phenomenal experience, are a natural consequence of the naturally functioning therapeutic process. The process is what commands our attention. When *it* falters or breaks down, it's *then* that our insights and observations and formulations can be maximally useful. So if my patient experiences an impasse—he blocks, becomes defensive, feels a pang of anxiety—it is then that I can "do something" with my insight. Then I could usefully intervene with an interpretation of this form: "I think I know why you blocked, or why your thoughts drifted away from what you were talking about or why you feel defensive or anxious. It's because you came face to face with a painful thought about your hostility toward your brother, or you might have caught a glimpse of something you've been overlooking." I might even pause to ask him whether he knew what the "painful thought" was, or whether he spotted what he'd been "overlooking."

Reader: That sounds like you're asking him to read your mind. How come you're willing to do it?

Author: As with most pieces of poor technique, I never intend to avoid them entirely. Calling them "bad" in these pages usually implies only that we should use them rarely. "Do you know what I'm thinking, or referring to?" needn't be too different from "Do you understand what I'm saying?" In any case, however, if he said he didn't, I'd go on to tell him. An interpretation of that form is likely to be more effective than one that says "I think I know why you are hostile" or "I see something you've been overlooking," because the patient can learn something about himself that will not only benefit his relationship with his brother but will also enhance his work in therapy.

Reader: That's all well and good, but I see two problems with your main criterion. One has to do with the fact that it is always possible to improve on the therapeutic process, in principle at least, and therefore always possible to justify an interpretation on these grounds.

Author: Yes, that is a difficulty. In practice, whenever we feel the impulse to offer an interpretation, we can usually persuade ourselves that it might improve the patient's level of work—and that judgment can be awfully difficult to prevail against. What's the second problem with our main criterion?

Reader: It has to do with the potential reinforcement effects of applying it stringently. There's a good probability that the patient will notice how we offer him substantive help only when he isn't speaking freely and openly. It doesn't take much acumen to learn that one has only to falter and grope, or slip into a defensive posture, and "useful" things will be heard. So if we speak only when he isn't working well, he has an additional incentive to avoid working well.

Author: Moreover, interpretations are likely to have a limited effect against that kind of reinforcement. It therefore becomes yet another timing consideration, and could be formulated in the terms of our criterion in the following way: "I offered the interpretation because the therapeutic process needed it, in the sense that it would have been negatively reinforcing to withhold it." But that makes matters so elastic as to be useless in practice. Consequently, in view of the two difficulties you raised, I see no way of avoiding the conclusion that our central timing criterion can only be regarded as the principal one, it cannot be the exclusive one. Others have to be included.

Reader: Such as?

Author: An additional criterion, which is relevant to Study 2 and the interpretation that provoked this discussion, relates to the stage of therapy. Interpretations gradually change their function as therapy develops. During the beginning phases they can serve purposes that become quite unnecessary and even gratuitous during the later phases. For instance, at the beginning, my patient has to learn the way I participate—the way I listen empathically but dispassionately, and formulate understanding without judgment and criticism—and I will offer interpretations in order to show him that. Another "lesson" he might have to learn is that there is going to be relatively little real conversation or dialogue between us. So I will time my interpretations in such a way that he does learn it, and it will also actualize my freedom of choice.

Reader: How is that really done in practice?

Author: By calling attention to his efforts to solicit remarks from me and by interpreting his reactions to my nonresponsiveness.

Reader: But what about taking some steps to keep the reinforcement effects to a minimum, if not also to attenuate the sheer monotony and tiresomeness of only interpreting the therapeutic process? Isn't there any value in variety, especially in the use of interpretations? Surely, we don't want our rigor with respect to timing to shade into rigidity. Can't an occasional "lapse" or deviation from the principal criteria have some positive value?

Author: Sure. So I will occasionally allow myself to offer an insight or discovery "for its own sake." I will sometimes participate in the therapeutic process as a kind of partner, the one who can also make discoveries. And I do this not so much to show my patient how it's done, nor to lead him to discoveries, but more in the spirit of active participation. So I might say something like "Look, I've noticed something about the argument! Your mother begins by fighting for you and right away she's fighting for herself," and say it in the spirit of "That's intriguing! It could help us understand some things about you." But this kind of participation can have undesirable implications and consequences—fostering a symbiotic transference, for instance—and therefore has to be kept in balance. To be sure, as the therapy progresses our direct participation can increase; more of our interpretations can be made for their own sake. But the ubiquitous transference and role definition implications have to borne in mind throughout.

Reader: I will. But now I'd rather get back to the study.

Author: After describing his parents' argument the patient says:

You know, sometimes when Lizzy hassles me I feel just like my old man. I even tell her to get off my back, like he tells my mother. And that time two weeks ago when I hit her . . . I mean, I hit Lizzy. (shoulders jerk up)

This speech disruption (and startle reaction) might be a kind of slip of thought. He was probably going to say *"When I hit my mother."* If I thought so, I'd find it difficult to keep from wondering aloud "Did you suppose I would think you hit your mother?" However, my rule of thumb against interpreting involuntary actions extends to slips of the tongue, and this might be included. (It also runs the risk of fostering a kind of quasi-therapy game-playing—*"Wow, just like the movies—and the textbooks!"*)

I told you about that, didn't I?

Simply answering "Yes," or "No, I don't recall it," is better than "Perhaps you can't remember whether you told me about it, because you were feeling embarrassed by it." This kind of speculation is justified only in the case of a patient who regularly resorts to repressive defenses.

> *Well, she was hassling me about the time I spend rapping with the guys at the students' lounge. I told her what I do with my time is my business and she can split if she doesn't like it, and she said I was a selfish bastard and started yelling. And without really meaning to, or realizing what I was doing, I hauled off and slapped her—pretty damned hard, too. . . .*

The argument with Lizzy is not unlike his parents', and his striking her was what he may wish his father had done to his mother. Students spell it out. For example:

> Perhaps the reason why Lizzy's actions got you so angry is that they set off the anger you felt towards your mother for interfering in something that was primarily between your father and you.

Students also suggest that he identifies with his father, and Lizzy may be a displacement for his mother. But those interpretations are likely to be premature if they don't allude to, or lay the groundwork for, a transference implication—namely, that it is now Lizzy interfering between us. The important consideration is whether he was now thinking about why he had struck Lizzy, because if he wasn't, then offering him an explanation will be beside the point.

I wish I could make up my mind whether to go in with Harvey or not. He says all I have to do is commit for a month, and then if I don't like it I can get out. Just a month, so what've I got to lose? I'm in good shape in school; the term paper is almost half done, and I can finish it in a day if I really work at it. (sighs and falls silent)

The problem is stated; relevant aspects of the conflict, along with relevant historical antecedents, have been articulated. The question is now: What, if anything, should we say? Should we say something about his expectation of us? Should we say something about why the decision itself remains such a difficult one? Should we try to be of some help in resolving his conflict and facilitating a decision? Let's consider these three examples:

Perhaps it's so difficult to make a decision because the situation contains so many elements of past family conflicts. You are still trying to set up shop like your father. He is still withholding his approval. And the woman—this time Lizzy—is the complainer about how your desire to earn money is depriving her of your attention.

It sounds like you're following in your father's footsteps. Like him, you'll manage to be so busy between school and work that you won't have any time to deal with Lizzy.

Perhaps your problem is not so much deciding if you want a job like your father's, but if you really want to be like him or not.

For reasons that need no repetition here, I regard them as ill-advised. They define us as the problem solver, the one who figures out what the patient's problem "really" is. He'll be better served by our focusing on those elements of his conflict that contribute to his difficulty in exploring the problem and / or by our focusing on the transference-resistance issues that might be involved. If we hadn't already done it, we could now address the transference:

It seems to me you feel pressured by Harvey and Lizzy and your father, telling you what to do. And along with that, I wonder if you don't also have a wish that I would tell you what to do—as I promised I wouldn't, and as Amy's therapist does.

But I don't see what other transference issue is at hand that could outweigh the advantages of simply remaining silent, which is the course of action I would take.

Consider the advantages. He is apparently waiting for some help from me to help him decide what to do. Silence conveys the message "I will not help you make that decision, excepting insofar as I can help elucidate the reasons for your difficulty making it." Would it be better to convey that message explicitly? Not necessarily. For one thing, insofar as he already knows it, the explicit message might convey the additional message "So please stop wanting my help with the decision itself"—and there's the risk of its being taken as a piece of scolding or of defensiveness, or both. The most judicious way to convey the message is by actualizing it. And if he broke the silence with a show of resentment or disappointment, it would provide the occasion for a useful interpretation. But there's the chance that he won't, that he will return to his deliberations and explore his problem further and deeper. If that happened, it will have been my silence that permitted it. The silence will have promoted the therapeutic process.

Study 3
The Learner's Permit

Since the beginning of therapy over four months ago, this 20 year old has been a "model patient"—never late, never impertinent, always the good boy. Today he is ten minutes late, and he is flustered and flushed.

I'm sorry . . . I'm sorry for coming late. . . . I'm very upset. I'm sorry. . . .

Are we going to comment on the apology? Two students do; one with a clarification question "Are you apologizing for being late or for being upset?"; the other with an articulation: "I take it you feel being late is some kind of transgression against me."

While the matter is undoubtedly important—an apology is inappropriate and might reflect an underlying attitude worth uncovering (especially in the case of a "model patient")—this is the wrong time to explore it. The lateness, after all, was unusual, and he will most likely talk about it. So the clarification question is unnecessary. Furthermore, his reply would probably be that he was apologizing for being late (and later it becomes clear that he regarded being upset as an equivalent offense because, like coming late, it interfered with the session)—what would we *do* with that reply? Bear in mind that it will have been us who imposed the topic (he was obviously not planning to discuss his apology), and it is an untimely thing to do when he had something else on his mind, when he was about to recount what caused him to be upset. So let's store the apology and keep it in mind.

> *I just had a terrible experience, and I feel . . . (averts gaze)*
> *I'm very upset. . . .*

What feeling is he having such trouble articulating? We cannot probe for it, the most we could do is make a supportive remark such as "I gather you're having difficulty expressing the way you are feeling." But that would probably amount to an indirect probe. So let's wait and see whether he continues to need help articulating the feeling—and why.

> *I came late because I was at the Motor Vehicles Bureau*
> *trying to get my learner's permit. There was a long line at*
> *the window, so it took forever. And then, when I finally*
> *got to the window, the man told me I filled out the form*
> *wrong and I have to do it all over again. I tried to correct*
> *it, but he wouldn't let me. He gave me a lecture and said*
> *I had to go fill out a new one and then get back in line*
> *again. And . . . and I was so . . . so upset, I felt like*
> *throwing the damn application form right in his face.*

The problem of articulating the feeling is now repeated, and since the event that provoked it has been described, it may no longer be premature to comment. But what sort of comment is appropriate? It is clear enough that the unexpressible feeling is anger—rage, in fact—and students simply say so. Few of them, however, wonder aloud what prevented him from saying he was (and perhaps still is) angry.

Now, if there's a distinction between articulating an affect and naming it, and I believe there is, it can only be a fine one. In the case of our patient, however, it might be an especially significant one, and I don't see what we can do beyond naming the feeling. I think we therefore shouldn't try. Moreover, we have good reason to suspect ("always the good boy") that he might be quite accurate when he says he feels *upset*. Perhaps he actually doesn't experience anger because it is too dangerous a feeling. If that happened to be the case, then exploring the reasons why anger was so unacceptable, and examining the ways he defended against its recognition, is bound to be more therapeutic. How to help him begin this exploration and examination is the technical problem. Simply naming the feeling for him won't do.

It sounds as if you were very angry with him, yet you say you were "upset." Perhaps you didn't describe yourself as angry, because you feel that being angry is unacceptable.

The trouble with this approach is its failure to invite an exploration. It offers the explanation and invites the patient to concur. (And we can easily imagine his accepting the idea and proceeding to substitute *angry* for *upset*.) Another way to approach the problem might be:

I'm wondering what else you feel. Whenever you try to tell me, you pause and fall back on the description "upset."

My main quarrel with this approach is the implication that anger is "something else." He did, after all, feel "something else"—"*I felt like throwing the damn application form right in his face.*" He might not want to call it "anger," but his cognitive experience was fully appropriate. In fact, if he had been retreating to "*I felt angry,*" I might well have chosen to offer the interpretation "I take it you felt like throwing it in his face," and perhaps followed it up with "You felt like hurting the man." Isn't that what it ordinarily means to be angry?

Students assume "anger" and offer explanations. For example:

He made you feel like an incompetent child—you felt
powerless—and that made you very angry.

If he had been wondering why he was so *upset,* such explanations might be helpful. But more importantly, he hadn't said
"angry." Throughout this study students speak about his anger
and rage, and do it without seeming to notice that he never used
such terms; they simply assume he knows he was (and still may
be) furious. Now, I composed the transcript with a patient in
mind for whom the recognition of anger is so dangerous, so
dissonant with his self-image, that he is self-deprecatory, inhibited, and always the "good boy." Moreover, he could also be a
person who provokes others to anger, judging from the fact that
students express a good deal of anger at him in their interventions. They make interpretations that are critical, scolding,
lecture-ish, and confronting (something they do far less in the
other three studies). Such countertransference feelings are
instructive and can be useful signals to us. In this case, they
remind us that "passive" and "incompetent" can provoke
anger, and an angry response is often rewarding for them.

> *So I had to fill out another application, and when I got
> back to the line it was even longer than before. It was
> obviously going to take at least a half hour to get to the
> window, and I saw I was going to be late here if I waited
> that long. And I just didn't know what to do. I began to
> shake . . . my legs began to shake, like sometimes when
> I'm practicing the piano. I kept looking at the clock and
> trying to figure out whether I should wait and get the
> damn thing finished with, or whether I should leave it for
> next week and come here on time. I didn't know what to
> do. I knew I'd be late if I waited any longer, and . . .
> and . . . and typically, I . . . what I did was wait in line for
> another fifteen minutes, until I knew I was going to be
> late here anyway, and then I left without getting the
> application in. So look what I did! I screwed myself up
> both ways. I'll have to go back next week and start all
> over again, and I came here late.*

Throughout the study, students look for an opportunity to
suggest to our patient that he chose to do what he did, and came
late because he wanted to. One does it here with:

I wonder what you think of the possibility that part of you wanted to come to therapy on time, and thereby be a good boy, and part of you wanted to be late and be a bad boy.

Since the evidence is shaky, the student seeks justification in this charge, which preceded the good boy/bad boy interpretation:

It does seem to me that you behaved, as you said, typically. You set the situation up in such a way that you did not have to take responsibility for the choices. You waited until it was too late to decide.

I doubt whether our patient would find this a convincing proof—though being such a good boy he would probably acquiesce and use it as further ammunition for his self-deprecations.

And I'm so upset now, feeling so shaky and everything, that . . . that I don't know what good this session is going to do me. If I'm feeling so upset, what good is . . .

Is the elided word "*therapy?*" If it is, he has made a startling statement. Students therefore speak up:

You don't believe anything can be accomplished here if you are not calm and in control of your feelings?

It's frightening for you to be here when you are feeling so upset? Perhaps you're afraid of what you'll do or say when you feel so shaky.

I'm unclear why you feel that your being upset would lead you to question the good of the session. Are you feeling like a bad patient due to your lateness, and perhaps feel that I have the same opinion?

These are timely interventions, although they tend to go too far and too fast. My inclination would be to ascertain first whether the unspoken word was "therapy" (or perhaps it's the phrase "talking about it here") and then allow him to elaborate on the thought. If he didn't, I'd postpone speculation and ask him to explain: "It's not clear to me what you meant when you said 'If I'm feeling so upset, what good is therapy' "—or I might say: "I take it you mean to say that talking about your feelings will do you no good when you are so upset."

The issue at hand, his attitude toward therapy, has a high priority in timing, calling for steps on our part to explore his beliefs, and hopefully also his underlying fantasies and fears, now that they have surfaced. In view of the fact that he is such a "model patient," the opportunities are likely to be limited. A possible approach is drawing attention to the apparent equivalency of his having missed fifteen minutes of the session and his having to return to the bureau to repeat the time-consuming procedure—both *screw me up.* How are they the same? In what way is coming late an equivalent inconvenience? Is it perhaps I who was inconvenienced and therefore angry? Does he believe his having come late and being so upset has affected my feeling for him? The answer might emerge when I say something like:

> I see how it screws you up to have to go back to the bureau and repeat the unpleasant procedure, but I don't see how it screws you up the same way to come late here.

Referring to the apology that began the session and putting it like this, is another possibility:

> I think I understand now why you apologized at the beginning. It may be that you believe your coming late has screwed me up in the same way.

It might emerge spontaneously when he was exploring his attitude toward therapy, but I may have to take some initiative in promoting that work.

> (In a whining tone of voice and close to tears) *What a stupid mess! . . . On the subway I felt like pushing people out of my way. And I felt like crying, too. . . .*

In describing his impulse to push people out of his way, he shows us the ideational content of his rage; but instead of experiencing the affect, he felt like crying. Explaining this to him is likely to be both didactic and gratuitous. Moreover, he is too likely to take our explanation as an exoneration and / or a scolding. Yet there can be some value in articulating the affect in its current form, in the way it might be alive right now, and it could also be supportive. A student observes:

> You were very angry. Maybe crying would have partially hidden that from you, because a part of you feels very uncomfortable about being angry.

She doesn't stop with that diagnostic formulation, however, but continues rather importantly with:

> I think you're still feeling angry right now, and you are trying to keep it from yourself in a similar way.

This can be a good interpretation at this time, though for my tastes it is too didactic and its overall tone is highly diagnostic.

> *This only proves that I can't do anything right. Just like my father has always said: I can't do anything right. . . .*

> You mentioned that you felt like crying and also like pushing people out of your way, and I wonder if these are the two feelings you are expressing now, a feeling of despair and helplessness—as if your father is correct in saying you can't do anything right—and also a feeling of rage at this helplessness.

That's a good interpretation and well timed. My inclination would be to prune it. I would want to focus more on the impulse to push people out of his way, on the concrete ideation, in order to explore its substitute function and perhaps also the underlying conflict. Consider this example, however, and notice how it berates the patient in the guise of "understanding" him:

> I think I understand why you waited in line for fifteen minutes when you knew it would screw you up both ways. It provides you with a way to not be the good boy, which you have consistently been in therapy, and it gives you a

reason to be upset and to tell yourself that it's no use trying.

Only a highly diagnostic interpretation could do that.

So what's the use of even trying if . . . if . . . So what can I do? So I come here and tell you how I'm all screwed up, and you . . . you . . . You just want me to talk about it. What's the good of that? I just can't do anything right, and that's all there is to it. I prove it all the time—the simplest things . . .

He is apparently saying *"What good is therapy?"*—a sentiment that easily arouses our defensiveness. So it's no surprise that students intervene here with remarks that apparently betray their indignation. They deliver a little scolding. Some do it in the form of a didactic, school-teacherish lecture:

It might be that one of the reasons you always seem to set yourself up in a situation in which you fail is because then you don't have to take the responsibility for your actions. As if you say to yourself, "I always screw things up, therefore I don't have to try."

—others with a simpler diagnostic formulation. And here's an interpretation that avoids those implications and pitfalls, mainly because it's quite empathic:

I think you're trying to convince me that you are incompetent. Perhaps one part of you wants me to agree with your father and prove you totally inept, while another part of you wants me to reassure and comfort you.

But my inclination would be to make no remark at all, not yet, because it isn't sufficiently clear what's up. Is he saying that therapy is ineffective for someone so inept as he? Is he struggling with feelings of disappointment at me? Is he angry? A good way to find out is to wait—a moment or two at least.

You don't even seem to care that I came late. But maybe that's only because you won't say. You're probably saying to yourself that I shouldn't have screwed up the application in the first place—such a simple thing and I can't do it right. And when I saw the time was getting

close, I should have . . . I should not have gotten back in
line and waited another fifteen minutes, I should've left
and gotten here on time.

Now we have something of vital importance: how the patient
construes our basic attitude toward him and his problems—
namely, do we care? An opportunity like this shouldn't be
passed up, and students don't. They emphasize that he is
expecting us to be angry:

Perhaps you expected to be scolded for being late—and
since you weren't, you're doing it yourself.

I wonder if on some level you want me to be critical of what
you've done. You want to prove that you're incompetent,
and that I, as an authority figure, should confirm that
proof, saying "Yes, you really are incompetent."

Only their failure to address the issue of caring keeps them from
being excellent interpretations. This succinct example comes
closer:

You seem to expect me to view you as your father did.
Perhaps you wish I would.

This one gets the closest:

I think you're assuming that I am as critical of you as you
feel your father is. And on the other hand, if I am not
critical, then I don't care about you.

There is more at issue here than the equating of caring with
scolding and criticizing. He is probably also saying that if we
cared, as his father does, we would tell him what he should have
done. A student captures this point well with:

I think you're annoyed that I took no steps to help you out
of your predicament, and now you wonder if I even care
about you. Perhaps you think that if people care about you
they ought to step in and get you out of frustrating
situations.

In order to attenuate the criticism inherent in this interpretation, I would divide it into several parts (although, of course, the study doesn't permit it). I would begin with:

> I take it you assume that I do care; I care that you came late, but I simply choose not to tell you. And that must mean that I feel like scolding you, but I'm keeping myself from doing it.

—and be ready to follow it with:

> And you assume that I'm thinking to myself the same things you are thinking, and it is what your father has always said to you: namely, you shouldn't have been so incompetent.

After he had concurred, and perhaps explored the idea, I would offer this speculation:

> Telling you what to do, and scolding you for being inept: *that* means caring for you, doesn't it?

Finally, I would seek the opportunity to add:

> And as your father shows his caring by telling you what you should do, so you believe I must show my caring by telling you how you should be competent.

This would show caring on my part—and not attenuate my neutrality.

> *God, I hated that stupid man! What a mean old bastard! Making me fill out another application form instead of making a few corrections. He did it on purpose, the son-of-a-bitch! The bureaucratic mentality is horrible. That's what we deserve for electing Reagan.*

Careful now! This is a trap. (Mine, not the patient's.) Our political sentiments must play no part in psychotherapy. My students, though they share his convictions about Reagan and government bureaucracy, try to steer clear of the issue. But

they are struck by the illogic of his statement, and especially by
the aura of externalization-of-blame (although "internalization-
of-blame" might be more accurate), so they comment on it. I see
no useful purpose in drawing a patient's attention to the illogic
of his remark; it runs the risk of being a criticism, partly
because it can be cast only in purely diagnostic terms. Even this
one, which is not so diagnostic, is not worth making:

> It sounds as if one reason you are so upset is because you
> felt helpless and impotent against the man and the bureau-
> cracy—as if you were up against Reagan and his entire
> administration.

> *You know something, I feel like just dropping the whole
> thing, just forgetting it. So I won't learn how to drive! I
> probably won't be able to learn to anyhow. And Peter will
> just have to do all the driving this summer on our trip out
> West—that's all. . . .*

In the final pause, is he thinking about his problem or is he
sulking? Is he deliberating silently about his resolution of the
problem or is he experiencing a break in the therapeutic
process? If I judged it to be a contemplative silence, then I would
remain contemplatively silent as well. Except it happens also to
be the end of transcript, therefore students assume that an
intervention is called for. They interpret his passive resignation:

> I can appreciate how annoying this incident is for you. But
> at the same time it seems to have provided you with a
> convenient way of avoiding the responsibility of having to
> learn to drive.

(It really *is* difficult to make a diagnostic interpretation without
putting him down, isn't it!) Still, we can address his feelings if
we take the trouble to formulate our interpretation carefully, as
this one does:

> I can understand your feelings of rage and helplessness,
> and I wonder what you think of this possibility—that your
> sense of it's no use trying, either in the session or in
> learning to drive, is a reaction to these feelings.

It does more than simply articulate the defense, more than simply say his passive resignation is a cop out; it offers an explanation in terms of his affects. The explanation itself is open to criticism, but the interpretation's form goes far toward precluding valuation.

What about the transference implications in letting Peter do all the driving? They are probably there, but not in readily interpretable form. If I suspected that he was trying to get me to demonstrate my competency at interpreting—at doing the driving, so to speak—I would be in a paradoxical position. When I spoke the interpretation, I'd be fulfilling the expectation and satisfying the need. To say, as a student curtly puts it, "Perhaps you'd like me to do all the driving here," is to have taken the wheel. This could be another reason for choosing silence—or more precisely, choosing the option of making no remark.

If his silence became prolonged and I felt that mine was too cold and ungiving, I might ask "What are you thinking?" This, as I've already discussed, is a directive I use with few misgivings. And this is an occasion in which it might do more than help break the inertia of his silence. For one thing, it might convey my interest in learning whether he was dwelling on his passive resignation, or whether he was experiencing any transference feelings. Perhaps he is simply waiting for me to say something.

Study 4
The Disgusting Dream

This patient, who entered therapy mainly because he fears becoming like his alcoholic father, is in his mid-thirties. Therapy is in its sixth month.

I had another great dream last night. You know, I never dreamed as much as I've been dreaming, since I started seeing you. I used to have a dream, oh, once a month on the average, if not less, but now I have one at least every week. I'm not complaining, mind you, but I do . . . I wonder why I'm dreaming so much. I guess it must have a lot to do with coming here. Your interpretations are very interesting. And I find them very helpful. Like what you said last week that my father looked so big in the

*dream because I was seeing him from the perspective of
a child. I guess I've always seen him as being bigger than
he really is. Anyway, here's the dream I had last night. I
was in a very large room, and . . . Hey! I guess that means
I was a child again. That's interesting! The room was like
a gymnasium or an auditorium. There were lots of rows
of wooden chairs that faced a sort of a stage. It wasn't a
real stage, just a raised platform of some kind. Anyway,
I was looking for something—*

Interrupting a dream narrative—or any narrative, for that
matter—with an interpretation is rarely a good idea. Yet a
student chooses this moment to observe:

Perhaps you feel somewhat as if you're on stage here. But
here if you look for signs of approval from the audience
there aren't any.

Why not wait until the dream is recounted and the patient is
engaged in trying to understand its meaning?

*—or maybe I was looking for someone. I don't remember
that part of it too well. And there was nobody there except
for this one man who was walking around the place,
maybe also looking for something. And he was walking
funny, as if he were sick or something. I kept thinking he
was going to fall down.*

Students don't fail to notice that the man behaved as if he were
drunk, but they fail to resist the temptation of telling it to the
patient. For example:

The man might represent your father, since you've described him as walking around funny and stumbling,
which may be similar to the way someone on alcohol
behaves.

This isn't the best time for such a speculation; better to wait
until the dream is finished. (After the dream has been recounted, and he puts the question "So what do you think?" a
student responds: "I'm wondering if your father didn't often
walk funny when he was drunk.") Among the purposes in

waiting is to see whether the *patient* has already noticed the fact, and, if not, whether he will, if we gave him the chance. (Some therapists would then encourage him by asking whether the way the man walked brought anything to mind, which is the free-association method. The patient is instructed to slip into that mode at this moment, for the purpose of uncovering the meaning of that dream element.)

> *Then he walked up to this raised platform and started to do some kind of a strange dance. And I couldn't figure out what it was or anything. The next part I don't remember so well. He might have motioned me to come up on the platform with him. Maybe he didn't, I'm not sure. But the next thing I remember, I was standing on the platform with him, and . . . No! Now I remember. He was gone, and I was alone up there. Yes. And I started to take my clothes off, as if I was doing a striptease. And then . . . and then I did the . . . the weirdest thing. It embarrasses me to have to tell you. Boy! I knew it was going to be hard for me to tell you this part, but . . . But I didn't expect to find it this hard. I'm feeling funny about . . . embarrassed, actually. That's weird! Here I tell you everything, the most embarrassing things too, and I'm feeling ashamed to tell you this.*

Perhaps you are feeling very exposed here, right now, like when you had your clothes off in the dream. The part of the dream just before this part seemed to express the opposite of shameful feelings, the part where you were taking off your clothes. Maybe a part of you is not ashamed, and wants to expose yourself.

These interventions can be justified on the grounds that our patient was experiencing difficulty proceeding with the dream and an interpretation might help. In that case, the first example is apt to be quite sufficient; the second introduces a fresh topic that might deflect his attention away from the dream. But my inclination, once again, would be to offer no help at this juncture.

> *Anyway, what I did in the dream was urinate. Yes, I started to piss. And then I woke up and went to the bathroom, because I actually had to piss. . . . So what do you think? . . . .*

To argue, as I intend to argue, that we should maintain our silence, is to court a host of questions and qualms. Isn't it tactless, if not harsh? Isn't it pointless, if not provocative? Doesn't it make a parody of autonomy, a game of technique, and won't our patient have the right to be outraged? Not necessarily, is my rejoinder. Bear in mind that therapy is six months old. We've had that much time to establish its nondirective format. Also bear in mind the apparently "positive" transference—in fact, the intimations of an idealized one. (Not that I'd therefore take steps to try and change it, but I'd take it into account.) These considerations can mitigate the potential tactlessness and provocativeness of our remaining silent in the face of his direct question.

What is he asking? For us to take an active role, to tell him what the dream means and thereby rescue him from his embarrassment? If so, the optimal way to meet this request is to remain passive—"actively passive," we might say. Notice, moreover, that even a good interpretation to that effect, such as "—so you can be the embarrassed little boy and I can be the all-knowing (perhaps nonalcoholic) father," could have the paradoxical effect of my assuming the transference position in the very act of interpreting it. This kind of dilemma is not uncommon in our work, and neither is it restricted to transference issues. In fact, since our silence is a form of response, it makes no psychological sense to maintain that it was ever nonresponsive. I have little doubt that at this moment in the session it will amount to a significant response, but I believe it is both the technically correct and therapeutically responsible one.

Few students opt for silence. Instead they tend to deflect the patient's question with remarks like "I wonder what thoughts you have about it," or else offer an interpretation that implicates his father. Here are two good examples:

Perhaps the dream has to do with your fear of becoming like your father, taking his place as a man who sometimes loses control of himself or acts incomprehensibly.

Perhaps the man on the stage represents your father. As you said, it may have been an incident in your childhood, and children sometimes believe that drunk people are sick, because of their gait and manners. And it's possible that though you didn't know why your father was different than other fathers, you were embarrassed that he was.

Students also implicate the transference:

I think it's possible that what you did in the dream represents on some level your wish to expose yourself and let yourself go here.

I wonder if the shame and embarrassment you mention about disclosing yourself to me aren't partly a reaction to the pleasurable excitement of being looked at while you strip and show yourself to me.

And here's a strong defense interpretation:

You had a great deal of difficulty telling me that part of your dream, and I have a thought about why. My thought is that urinating in your dream represents a loss of control; and I think you fear that you might lose control of yourself here and would feel terrible about it.

I don't know who the man in the dream was, but he looked kind of familiar. . . . Hey, you know something! I think he could've been the patient who comes here before me on Wednesdays. I always see him when he leaves, and I guess I watch him . . . watch him walk out. He does have a funny walk, you know, and . . . Yes, come to think of it, it could have been him. And that's weird! Why would I dream about him?

Again a question (though this one could well be rhetorical) and again students answer it. Naturally, they speak of jealousy, rivalry, and competitive feelings. A typical example:

Could it be true that you are jealous that I have other patients, with whom you share the stage, so to speak?

An interesting variation:

Perhaps you see him as having something wrong with him, his strange walk. And since you both come here, perhaps you wonder how you appear, how you perform on the stage.

The following one takes things a step further, quite cleverly:

> When you told the part of the dream where you get up on
> the platform, I had the feeling you were very glad to take
> the other man's place on the stage. Maybe that's a feeling
> you have toward some man, like the patient who comes
> before you on Wednesday, or your father.

In practice, I would probably not answer his direct questions
until the idealized transference had been analyzed; I wouldn't
want to reinforce it with shows of cleverness and wisdom. I
might also want to reserve my interpretative work for the
underlying homosexual theme that appears to be surfacing.

> *I think the gymnasium was the one we had in school. We
> had assemblies there. It had wooden chairs like in the
> dream. But why would I be dreaming now about that
> place? It's strange, isn't it?*

"Perhaps it's not so strange if we compare the situation in your
dream with the one right here in therapy." This intervention
has substantial merit; it strikes a good compromise with the
considerations we've been examining. (If the patient says
"*What do you have in mind?*" we'll have to spell it out.)

> *I guess taking off my clothes represents what I do here,
> doesn't it? I certainly tell you all my secrets. That's
> interesting. But . . . but why would I do a thing like
> urinate? That doesn't figure at all. Maybe I wasn't going
> to do that. You know something, I'm not actually sure
> whether it was that or whether I was going to . . . uh . . .
> to shit. You see, I failed to mention that I squatted down,
> and maybe that's because I was going to make a bm.
> Now, that's really embarrassing! . . . I'm waiting for you
> to say something, and . . . and I'm feeling . . . I'm feeling
> a bit tense. . . . More than a bit. Shit!*

He is feeling acutely embarrassed, and by "*tense*" he probably
means anxious. The dream is finished and the therapeutic
process is interrupted, perhaps arrested, so an intervention is
now timely—and up until now I don't think it was.

Once again we face the technical problem of finding the most useful intervention. In my opinion it will have to be an interpretation that focuses on his feelings and simply articulates them. Anything else is likely to be a short-term palliation of his need to intellectualize, and it might also bolster his idealized transference image. Offering him a dream interpretation, instead of articulating the feelings, may collude with his defenses in that it acquiesces to his request for help. (*"I'm waiting for you to say something* because *I'm feeling tense."*) Yet students restrict themselves to interpretations that address the various wishes, conflicts, and feelings that are reflected in the dream. For example:

— Loss of Control: Urinating and defecating might stand for a loss of control that part of you desires and another part fears.

— Exhibitionism: You feel you're exposing yourself to me, and this both excites and embarrasses you.

— Hostility: Urinating and defecating may be ways you can express some of your hostile feelings.

— Shame: You feel there's a hidden or dark side of yourself that is shameful to expose here.

— Transference: You perform for me by producing dreams, as you used to please your parents by producing a bm when you were a little boy.

Those are the culminations of dream interpretations, and fine dream interpretations they are—only this happens not to be the time for them. While the patient may "need" one, the therapeutic process "needs" something different. What it doesn't need is a Band-Aid (for example, an intellectualization); it needs the kind of attention that will revive the work he has to do now—and this is best done by staying with the feelings he is currently experiencing. (If he were experiencing intense anxiety, or were in crisis, then an intellectualization might indeed be helpful and necessary. I don't mean to denigrate short-term goals, and neither do I mean to denigrate intellectualization; it certainly has its useful place both in therapy and outside of it.)

Students do focus on his feelings, but tend to assume that he knows well enough what they are, and therefore what he needs is an explanation. For example:

> Perhaps you are feeling tense because you are uncertain if
> I will accept the parts of you that you consider repulsive
> and embarrassing. I wonder if you are afraid that by
> showing those parts you will become like your father.

That would be a good interpretation to give after his feelings
had been articulated. Admittedly, the distinction between articulating and explaining a patient's feelings isn't a sharp one, and
our interpretations can try for both, but the effort usually isn't
worth it. Consider these two attempts:

> Perhaps you feel compelled to take your clothes off in here
> and tell me everything, however embarrassing. But after
> you do, you resent it—because you feel you were forced—
> and you get an urge to express your resentment, which is
> represented in your dream by urinating and making a bm.

> The defecation might be an act of defiance, as though
> you'd decided not to "walk funny" like the other man—my
> patient, your rival—but to express a less cooperative atti-
> tude toward therapy instead. Maybe that's why you were
> embarrassed to tell me about it, and why you're feeling
> tense now: because you are waiting to see how I'll react
> now that you've revealed the defiant, childlike part of
> yourself to me.

Notice how complicated they are. To be sure, this is partly due
to the fact that the study doesn't permit us to divide our
interpretation into parts. But the interpretation should be a
simple articulation of the feelings that the larger interpretation
would comprise—in the above examples, the feelings are resentment and defiance—and this can be achieved quite simply:
"Are you aware of feeling some resentment (or defiance) toward
me?"
   But are "resentment and defiance" the best feelings to suggest? They come straight out of the dream, not from his
narrative per se. And hasn't he already told us, as best he can,
what he is now feeling? Most practitioners would infer that it
was anxiety, that he was feeling afraid, and many would say so.
We might not want to say "I think you are feeling anxious,"
because that could amount to little more than renaming his

"*tense.*" But we might not hesitate to say "I think you are feeling afraid." This stands the better chance of promoting the therapeutic process, because the question then becomes, "*What am I afraid of?*" and the answer could be an important discovery.

Since I subscribe to the signal theory of anxiety, I would proceed on the assumption that his anxiety was signaling a burgeoning complex of ideas (thoughts/fantasies/memories) that were struggling for awareness. But even if I didn't subscribe to the theory, I'd be willing to accept it as a working hypothesis for now, because it offers me a way to work with the patient's anxiety without defusing it. As I mentioned, to suggest that he was experiencing fear is to invite the question "*What am I afraid of?*" Let's suppose the patient accepted the invitation; I would answer it this way:

> I don't know. But I think you might be afraid of a thought— or perhaps it's a memory—that you aren't fully aware of. It might be something that the dream has brought to mind, and you wish it didn't.

The formulation is clear enough, but it left "something" dangling. Ordinarily, this isn't a good technique; it can amount to an indirect directive for the patient to go search for the thing we left unspecified. At most, therefore, I'd use it sparingly. And if the patient went ahead to search for it with no success, I wouldn't want to leave the "something" dangling any longer. Not only was it my interpretation that raised the issue and sent him on his search, but without something concrete it becomes little more than a didactic formulation. I would therefore feel obliged to offer him some possibilities in the form of a speculative interpretation. For that purpose I could choose from among the various possibilities that my students have given. (I might even think of one or two more—like the homosexual idea I alluded to earlier.) But I'd make sure to be tentative; to stress the speculative nature of my suggestions; to convey that I wasn't looking for confirmation-disconfirmation. And above all, I would try to maintain a sense of unworried expectancy that reflected my abiding faith in the therapeutic power of the therapeutic process.

6 _____

WHAT TO INTERPRET WHEN

Choice of Interpretations

Reader: In the Timing Studies you repeatedly raised the question, "Does the therapeutic process need an interpretation?" And it was often the form of a patient's narrative, more than its content, that commanded your attention. But in practice, won't the content often be compelling, too?

Author: It must of course command our full attention. We are listening, after all, to understand. And as we listen to the content, we interpret it silently. Our decision to break the silence is what timing is all about.

Reader: What do we do with the temptation to speak out whenever we have the conviction that we've understood a bit more than the patient has?

Author: Resist it. We need more reasons to break our silence than simply having understood well; that's what I've been emphasizing a lot. But in this chapter I want to examine a further criterion for offering interpretations, and it has to do with their form and content. For in addition to asking ourselves "Does the therapeutic process need an interpretation now?" we also ask "Is the interpretation I could now give a good one? Maybe it's valid, but is it good?"

You see, we often refrain from speaking out because the interpretation we could give isn't going to be sufficiently succinct, for instance, or it's too diagnostic or speculative. Of course, what's the point in thinking about such formulations, you might ask; if it wasn't something we were prepared to say aloud, why have it in mind in the first place? But that's a pretty unrealistic position to take. Anyhow, the formal features of the particular interpretation we have in mind will often determine whether we keep it there.

Reader: What about the decision as to what to interpret?

Author: Are you referring to the truism that a patient's narrative, like all narrative, is open to varying interpretations?

Reader: No, to the truism that a patient's narrative is multi-faceted and we usually have to select which aspect, or part, of it to interpret. "What should I interpret?" is a timing question too, after all.

Author: In a sense it is. And the answer has to be based on a variety of clinical considerations that require clinical judgment. In respect to a transference theme, for instance, we have to judge whether it is sufficiently in the foreground. If a defense was showing, we have to judge whether it's close enough to awareness. When we listen to a patient talking about his self-image or his interpersonal relations, his conflicting wishes or his fantasies, our decision to address them will be based on considerations that fall within the purview of clinical judgment and therefore outside the scope of this book.

Reader: I appreciate that the studies are written so as to limit us to technical considerations. Therefore, I gather we're going to look to the formal features of our interpretations for an answer to the timing question, by examining the role they play in choosing which aspect of a patient's narrative to address.

Author: Yes. Their role can, and should, be a significant one, because our interpretations tend to require distinctive formulations. Transference interpretations work best when they are fully articulated but divided into graded parts. Defense interpretations work best when their dynamic component has an empathic anchor. Self-image interpretations are best if succinct and unencumbered with explanation. And interpersonal interpretations have to be expressed in a fully impartial way. Our decision with respect to choice of content will sometimes be made on the basis of how readily we are able to formulate the appropriate interpretation. The timing question can therefore be further refined as: Does the content lend itself to an interpretation that I could now give in its optimal way?

Reader: But do we always have to choose? What's wrong with trying to integrate the different themes into a coherent and multi-dimensional formulation?

Author: On the one hand it takes a special effort, and in my opinion the effort is rarely worth it. Whether a succinct and focused interpretation will be better than a richer and more variegated one depends largely on context, but my favorite guideline is to keep interpretations as succinct and as focused as possible. It's the best way to guard against wrapping things up too neatly and getting too intellectual.

Reader: On the other hand, however, don't fuller and richer interpretations have the important advantage of being less confronting and more tactful? Insofar as they offer him a many-sided explanation, isn't the patient likely to feel more understood and not judged?

Author: That's quite true. If we draw his attention to the fact that he was disavowing, for instance, and not offer a reason why he needed to do it, he can hear our remark as both a criticism and a directive to cut it out. Even though giving a reason will tend to be diagnostic, our intervention will not have been so confronting. Similarly, simply pointing out that he was over-idealizing us, without at the same time offering a motivation for it—and perhaps also suggesting a historical basis for the motivation—can be taken as a simple admonition. These are important considerations, especially if those issues of neutrality haven't yet been resolved—and that, I'm afraid, usually means the therapy is still in progress.

And my experience has been that transference interpretations, to be most effective, must be formulated around the patient's wishes and needs; articulating the distortion, or the defense, will often be insufficient. It helps to offer some genetic and dynamic reasons, because that usually makes the wish more plausible to him. But this needn't be done all at once. Usually the articulation can be offered and the rest deferred— for the moment at least—because his reaction to the articulation itself may be strong. Or he may want to complete it himself and perhaps explore its basis. Or indeed he may reject it altogether. And if that's what he did, or if his reaction was one of shame or resentment or perplexity, then we would have to work with that reaction. This is another reason I favor making so-called part-interpretations rather than "complete" ones.

Reader: But his reaction might have been based on the incompleteness of the interpretation itself. Isn't there a school of thought that advocates complete interpretations in order to attenuate such reactions?

Author: And I take exception to it. It sometimes smacks of sweetening the bitter pill, if not sidestepping the issue. Enriching an interpretation in order to make it more plausible is quite different from doing it to make it more palatable. Nevertheless, having the full interpretation in mind, and ready to give, can often be useful.

Reader: But we administer it in doses?

Author: Gradually, or graded, is a more accurate description. Let's take, for example, transference-reactions, and take into consideration the deep emotions that usually accompany them. Because they entail distortions based on unconscious images, they evoke profound feelings of awe as well as apprehension, perhaps a sense of the uncanny as well as of revelation. For those reasons, they have to be approached with special care and understanding. If the therapy is young, I believe we should preface our transference interpretations with a statement indicating that we appreciate what the patient is experiencing and how powerful and awesome his feelings are. Then we might look for the opportunity to express an empathic understanding of how frightening the intensity of his reaction may be, especially since he may be aware of how irrational it is. After all, a genuine transference reaction is intrinsically a deep distortion of reality, and he might sense it. Moreover, when we sense it, too, we won't be prone to take it "personally."

Reader: Yes, but that's a digression. I gather you wanted to remind me that I become prone to some reactions of my own whenever I become the object of a transference.

Author: If it's an idealized transference, for instance, you might want to shake it off, inasmuch as it makes you guilty or embarrassed, perhaps evoking narcissistic fantasies and conflicts of your own. Furthermore, when the idealization is accompanied by feelings of dependency on the therapy—which is often the case—we are prone to additional misgivings and guilt. Not only must we take special pains to keep such feelings well under control, we have to be especially diligent against conveying a sense of defensiveness, a wish to push the patient away, to disavow and disclaim responsibility for his dependency, and to try to dissipate the transference.

Let's work with a narrative. It's the first of my Choice of Interpretation Studies. Imagine a patient, who leans heavily on intellectualization, talking about a pending two-week vacation from therapy and dreading it because his wife doesn't understand his great need for independence. In fact, she doesn't understand him at all—in sharp contrast to us: *"I have you pegged as someone who knows who he is, so you don't have to step on people and smother them."* Can you guess what kinds of interpretations it provokes from my students?

Reader: "Perhaps if I were as understanding as you suggest, I wouldn't be so inconsiderate as to take a vacation."

Author: That's one of them. And what's wrong with it?

Reader: It is a sharp intervention, and it may be dramatic and incisive, but a curt and sarcastic remark like that is likely to embarrass the patient and make him defensive.

Author: A simple interpretation can be either succinct or curt; its context determines which it is. In the context of our patient's anguished intellectualizations, the simple and direct "I'm wondering if you'd really like to go on vacation with me instead of with her," is apt to be curt, and therefore harsh, because it cuts beneath his defense and lays bare what he "really" wants. Telling a patient what he "really" feels is always risky, and an interpretation whose form is succinct usually implies the word. Notice how clearly it is implied in this one—and not just once: "I wonder if you are feeling that if I knew how much you needed me, I wouldn't abandon you for those two weeks."

This, despite his strenuous efforts to stress his need for freedom and independence, not to mention his self-image as the independent one!

Reader: Do you think a gentler, more modulated rendition such as: "I'm not sure, but I think you are flattering me today because part of you wishes you could come with me on vacation," is also curt?

Author: Yes, I do. But perhaps I am confounding curtness with insensitivity. Your formulation interprets the patient's remarks as "flattery," which will probably offend him so much that he won't hear the rest. It certainly dismisses his idealization by chalking it up to a circumscribed wish. And doesn't it say "The *real* reason you are doing it is—"?

Reader: Okay, then what about this formulation of the transference: "I wonder if in ascribing special powers of understanding to me you aren't viewing me as someone special on whom it's all right to allow yourself to become dependent." It is relatively succinct and not insensitive, and doesn't imply any "really."

Author: But it's a potentially ambiguous and misleading formulation, insofar as it speaks of "special powers of understanding." After all, psychotherapy *does* entail a unique relationship with the patient and a unique role definition for you, so you *are* indeed "special"—you *do* show "special understanding." Therefore, his regarding you as the one who understands him in a special way is based on an important piece of reality, and so is his claim that you don't step on people or smother them. These facts mustn't be overlooked. They pose certain technical problems in any attempt to interpret a transference, and not only an idealized one.

Reader: Then what's my best way to approach the problem?

Author: Try centering on the act of generalization and drawing a distinction between your specialness as a therapist and your specialness as a person. Our patient provided for this distinction by picturing you as perfect in your personal relationships. So you might say: "I gather you picture me not only as a special therapist but also a special person—someone completely sure of himself, who treats his family and friends well." And soon you could perhaps offer an interpretation that began with: "I think I understand why you wish, or need, to see me that way." You might mention that he had, of course, no way of knowing what your mundane behavior was like, and therefore the generalization he drew was not irrational, but you could point out that he might have inferred that only your behavior in therapy was "special."

My chief purpose in this discussion was to point out that an interpretation's context and content has an important bearing on its optimal form. And the chief purpose of these studies is to find the optimal form in the light of specific contexts and concrete contents. Each of the narratives was composed so as to permit three types of interpretation, and the instructions are the same as those in Chapter 4 except that they call for three separate interpretations: a transference interpretation (to therapist and / or therapy), a defense interpretation (against impulse and / or affect), and a self-image interpretation.

Study 1
Going on Vacation

The patient is in his late twenties; therapy is in its second year.

I was thinking about the vacation. I'm not exactly sure when we're going to resume here. You said it would be two weeks, didn't you? (Yes, that's right.) So it means we resume on Tuesday the fifth? (Yes.) You said it clearly, but I never remember dates and figures. I'm one of those people who rely on intuition more than on calculation. . . . Vacations are a drag. Most people don't know what to do with them. Like Veblen said—was it Veblen?— leisure is a privilege of the idle rich because they're the only ones who study it. People get conditioned by our society into their daily routines. That's because our society regiments us, makes us dependent on its institutions. But I guess I'm doing what you once pointed out to me, intellectualizing. (small smile) My plans for the two weeks off are still up in the air. Joan wants us to go camping, but I dread being stuck with her all the time. I need to be alone a lot; Joan doesn't understand that. And I'm a terrible camper. She's very good at it, so everything will be up to her. She's a fusspot, too, and that drives me crazy. She doesn't understand why. She doesn't understand me. . . (smile) I was going to say "like you do." But women are biologically incapable of understanding men. I really believe that. The hardest thing for them to understand is our need for independence. Actually, come to think of it, a lot of men don't understand men, either. I

mean, you're practically the only person I know who
does, and I don't know how you do it. I think it's because
you are independent and sure of yourself. I have you
pegged as someone who knows who he is, who doesn't
have to step on people and smother them. Freedom is as
vital as air. You can smother if you don't have enough of
either. I can't stand being smothered. (fidgets and frowns)
That's because I am an existential being. I need to be in
the world and not of it.

Many of us would choose disavowal, not intellectualization, as
the defense of choice. It fits the material and may pose fewer
technical problems. But no matter which defense we choose,
we will want to describe it clearly and show how the patient is
using it. Simply naming it won't suffice. Students tend to name
the defense, and pay most of their attention to its motivational
basis. They come up with astute formulations and strong
interpretations—whose focus, however, is on feelings and mo-
tivations, not the defense. The defense tends to be treated in a
cursory and diagnostic way. Here is an example:

I think part of you feels frightened of the vacation separation, frightened of how dependent you feel on the therapy,
and you are disavowing both of these feelings.

Notice how it articulates a feeling that the patient hadn't
mentioned ("frightened") and speculates that it was this feeling
that provoked the defense—and then formulates the defense in
a curt and diagnostic way. Here's one that shows some interest
in the defense by describing it concretely, but it remains too
diagnostic:

I wonder if the vacation hasn't aroused feelings of dependency and helplessness that you are trying to deal with by
disavowing that they exist. Instead, you are insisting on
your need for freedom and your fear of being smothered.

Here's how I would reformulate this interpretation:

I think the vacation has stirred up feelings you are uncomfortable with—feelings of dependency and helplessness—

and they are feelings you wish you didn't have, feelings you want to disown. You know, I wonder if perhaps you believe, deep down, that if you kept thinking about your need for independence and control—if you could keep your thoughts focused on those traits of yours—then the feelings of dependency will get weaker and perhaps even go away.

Notice how I made no effort to be succinct (I wanted to make sure I wasn't curt), and how hard I tried to stay anchored in the empathic position (and perhaps the strain showed). My main goal was to describe the defense and how it operated, and do it as undiagnostically as I could. That required a speculation, but it was a speculation in the realm of mental content, not affect. Whenever we choose to interpret a defense, a speculation of this kind is quite unavoidable. But it is preferable to a confronting diagnosis. My intuition tells me that our patient would find it preferable as well; he's not going to be as embarrassed and provoked by my formulation as he would have been by the student's.

Students also construe the transference reaction as a vehicle for the defense:

By seeing me as perfect, you don't have to look at how my going on vacation hurts you; you don't have to acknowledge the rejection you feel over my going way.

My reformulation:

If you see me as perfect, it means I never hurt anyone. But I think you are feeling hurt by my going on vacation—you feel it as a rejection. And not only doesn't it fit your picture of me, it makes no sense either. So you want to squash that feeling, you want to get rid of the thought that my going away means I am rejecting you. It feels childish to you, doesn't it?

Here's one that comes close to my model:

I believe you are beginning to feel dependent on therapy and on me, and these feelings seem irrational, frightening,

and unacceptable to you. To cope with them and protect
yourself, you speak rationally and abstractly about independence and freedom, as if to convince yourself that the
more mundane human needs don't apply to you.

All it needs is for "To cope with them and protect yourself," to be
replaced by "I wonder if you don't also believe that if," and for
"as if" to be replaced by "you might be able."

When we choose intellectualization as the defense, we face an
interesting technical problem: whether to regard the intellectual content of the material as a reflection of the patient's beliefs
and opinions, or whether to construe it merely as his attempts
to use intellectualization defensively. It seems to me we have to
make a choice between the two and not try to have it both ways.
Consider this interesting example: "I agree that you're intellectualizing, but I think it would be useful to look at the content of
it"—and when the patient responds "*I don't know what you
have in mind,*" the student explains:

Well, I think you see me as one of society's institutions that
has conditioned you into a routine of dependency on me
and on therapy.

The interpretation is fine, but the patient may be left in some
doubt about whether he was intellectualizing or not. The following example makes things clearer:

It seems more acceptable for you to speak in general terms
of how society conditions people—regiments them and
makes them dependent on institutions—rather than accept your own dependency on the therapy institution and
the feelings that the pending vacation may engender in
you.

But it is diagnostic and therefore critical in tone. And notice also
its intellectuality; it could actually bolster the defense.

The optimal way of formulating a defense is to try and frame
it in the patient's awareness. ("Part of you suspects that what
you're doing may be a defense.") It isn't often that we can frame
it that way, but our patient has provided us with the opportunity; he said he was intellectualizing. However, we must then
limit ourselves to a formulation that explains the defense

without undue speculation, because his being aware of a defense doesn't mean he was no longer under its sway. Consider this interpretation:

> You say you are intellectualizing. I wonder if you're doing it to avoid the anger you feel at me for leaving you.

It makes the mistake of inferring a specific feeling for which there isn't any evidence. ("*What anger?*" could be the response.) In a sense, it can be regarded as tactless. Still, it's not as tactless as:

> It seems to me that your awareness of the fact that you intellectualize gives you a label to rely on in order to explain away your feelings of uneasiness.

That may be quite valid, but so lacking in empathy is it that the patient could experience it as little more than a rap on the knuckles. (Or else, of course, he might welcome its intellectual elegance and include it in his intellectual vocabulary.) Similarly, notice the intellectual (and lofty) stance we seem to be taking with:

> It strikes me that your confusion about the dates and your independent stance today may be a reaction to feelings of loss and disappointment about my going away. Perhaps even your impatience with Joan is a reflection of some anger at me for putting you in that predicament.

Better, therefore, to refer to the pending interruption in therapy and allow the patient to speculate about the feelings; that's likely to be sufficiently simple and direct.

A useful way to interpret a defense is to articulate the way it is currently in operation. A student attempts it with an interpretation whose form is good but whose content is puzzling:

> It seems you were about to say you preferred me to Joan when you began talking about freedom again. So I wonder if perhaps your praise of me makes you uncomfortable, makes you feel smothered, because you suspect it's preventing you from thinking about yourself.

Another student has the idea that what the patient intended with his intellectualization was to confirm the interpretation he alluded to:

Perhaps your use of intellectualization today may in part
be serving to confirm what I pointed out to you last week.
And it may further confirm the idealized picture you have
of me.

I find it rather farfetched, and I suspect our patient would find it
"very interesting." So I would try for something simpler,
perhaps beginning with the suggestion that he was about to say
he preferred to be with me rather than with Joan, and I'd be
ready to continue with:

I think you felt uncomfortable with that idea, because
that's when you began talking about intellectualizing and
about freedom, wasn't it?

Another possibility is to point out that the idealization, both of
me and of freedom, occurred immediately after he experienced
the impulse to express his dependency need (which conflicted
with his self-image).

Finally, what about our self-image interpretation? The study
allows us to articulate it within the framework of a defense
interpretation. But I would want to avoid suggesting that the
self-image itself was a defense or that it subserves a defensive
function, and that's what students tend to do:

Your need to see yourself as free and independent may be
an effort to fend off your fears of both aloneness and
relationships.

Perhaps your image of yourself as an independent, existential being helps you to cope with feelings of dependency
and helplessness.

Not only do they challenge the integrity of his self-image, but
they are highly diagnostic formulations that will back the
patient into a corner. I think the following interpretation is less
likely to have these effects, although it might result in further
intellectualizing: "You see yourself as a person who smothers
easily from overprotection and who needs more freedom than
many others do. I think this might be a reason you're so

sensitive to dependent feelings and why you find it intolerable to experience any helplessness."

He can be given some room, some paths to consider and explore, when the interpretation has stressed his current dilemma—for example:

> It seems that being independent is very important for you now. I wonder if perhaps you must see yourself that way now in order to protect yourself from feelings that have arisen as we are nearing my vacation, feelings of dependency and vulnerablity.

Unfortunately, that formulation seems to cast doubt on the validity of his self-image. At best, it suggests that he was using his self-image to "protect," which implies that he and his self-image were quite separate. Not that we cannot speak of a conflict within his self-image, or of a contradiction in its basic structure, but we have to keep from encumbering it with explanations. Here's one that does it quite successfully:

> So you are clearly letting me know that you see yourself as a person who wants to be free and needs to be independent. But at the same time you describe yourself as in fact being controlled by various external forces—biological rhythms, Joan. Aren't you sort of viewing yourself in two ways: as you feel you need to be—free and independent—and as you feel you are—externally controlled?

It's an interesting formulation and could pique the patient's interest—although he might still press it into the service of further intellectualization. ("*Yes, I guess I am complicated and perhaps also a bit mixed up,*" is easy to imagine for a response.) Similarly, here's one that is incisive and provocative:

> I hear you saying that you are dependent on others to allow you to be free, that there's nothing you yourself can do to be free. You depend on others even for your independence.

But what will it provoke—further intellectualization in order to defend against criticism? I believe we should keep the self-image formulation very simple. Our patient can be counted on to complicate it by himself, and his intellectualizing needs little support from us. Therefore, the remark, "You see yourself as a person who can't be easily understood," is apt to be quite sufficient. Its form takes full account of its content.

Study 2
The Fiasco

The patient is in his late thirties. Jimmy is his roommate and also his lover.

Jimmy is a bitch! The dinner party last night was a fiasco—a big fiasco! Nothing went right, nothing! And it was his fault. I told you how we planned it, we'd do everything together this time. I guess that was a mistake. He's so damned unreliable! We shopped in the afternoon, and he chose the vegetables. Well, the lettuce was limp and the tomatoes tasteless, so the salad was awful. And the roast I prepared the evening before wasn't heated through enough, because he didn't turn the oven on high enough. And the souffle, it never rose! I did it the same way I always do, and I don't know why it didn't rise. I think he must have slammed the oven door, he's so fucking careless! Thoughtless! And of course I was a nervous wreck during the dinner, but not him. He couldn't have cared less. All chirpy and gay as if everything was okay. . . . I broke one of our best glasses. . . . And then the after-dinner was deadly, nothing but a lot of inane chatter, with Jimmy right in the thick of it. Not me, though. . . . And I don't think anyone was amused. They all left early. . . . It was such a fiasco! I felt awful about it. It was all Jimmy's damn fault. . . . And you know something? This therapy is something of a fiasco too, because . . . when—oh when!—am I going to start getting better?

The defense is externalization of blame and responsibility, the self-image is the blameless one or innocent victim, and the transference combines the two. Each of the three interpretations I had in mind when I composed the study shares the same motif, but each has to be formulated in a different way.

The transference interpretation can be put simply and succinctly in the form of a direct response to the patient's final question (or complaint): "When I start doing my job right?" But that would only be snide and flip, perhaps conveying some defensiveness. Moreover, it flies in the teeth of his defense. But a student makes the point just as succinctly, and maintains a certain tact, with "I take it that part of you would like to blame me for that," and I'm not sure that it isn't a nice solution. Nevertheless, I prefer interpretations that include the theme of caring, because it's a transference motif that always merits special attention in a form of therapy that is marked by our extreme neutrality and impersonality. Here is a good example:

> I think your disappointment over the dinner party has disturbed you so much that other experiences, such as your therapy, seem like fiascos too. Perhaps you blame me as you blamed Jimmy for not caring enough, and you don't feel you can rely on me to help you, either.

Another example that underscores the motif of caring:

> Perhaps you are saying that just as Jimmy didn't care about how the party went, I don't care about how the therapy is going, and that in some way my not caring is responsible for its being a fiasco.

Notice how the externalization of blame was integrated with the theme of caring. That's a far more effective way to approach the defense, in the context of the transference, than the way this example does it:

> I appreciate the fact that you're very upset about what happened, but I wonder what you think of the possibility that you want me to be as unreliable and as thoughtless as Jimmy, because then you could blame me for therapy being a fiasco.

It is tactful enough, and has the advantage of suggesting that the patient "wants" us to be culpable, but I believe the formulation would be better if it implicated the theme of caring, which it could easily do. Here's one that does:

> When you said how Jimmy seemed so unconcerned and nonchalant during dinner, while you were upset, I thought you might be expressing some of your thoughts about how things are here—that perhaps you see me as being indifferent, or unconcerned, at times when you feel like a "nervous wreck."

—the implication being that the transference reaction was a defensive distortion stemming from the way the patient was feeling about himself. But notice how we didn't commit ourselves to a cause-effect formulation, and our patient can still insist that it was our "indifference" that caused him to be a "*nervous wreck.*" If he did that, I wouldn't want to say anything that he might construe as disputing his formulation. Instead I would proceed carefully and patiently, trying to exploit the dinner-party event (insofar as it provided a vivid analogue to the therapy situation) to find some evidence in it that he was externalizing the blame. And it will have to be evidence that he can accept without undue embarrassment or defensiveness, so that he can begin to take some of the responsibility at least for the defense itself. (How that might be done is examined below.)

Judging from my students' work, addressing this patient's self-image in an empathic and tactful way is likely to be difficult. For example, the same student who gave one of the tactful transference interpretations I cited above gives this self-image interpretation:

> You seem to see yourself as surrounded by incompetent people whom you blame for any failures. That way you can think of yourself as being able to do a really great job at anything were it not for the bungling of others.

(Such challenging, refutation-begging and fighting words!—can this be the same therapist?) Moreover, while students interpret the transference in a rather uniform way, this isn't true for their self-image interpretations. Many opt for a formulation based on the patient seeing himself as the perfect one (rather than the blameless one), and these formulations tend to be especially tactless. Here's a way to formulate the self-image with more tact:

The fact that you were so nervous at dinner because everything wasn't absolutely perfect, I think tells us something about the way you think of yourself and about the standards you set for yourself in life. Things have to be either 100 percent okay or else they're 100 percent awful, a miserable fiasco.

Unfortunately, it misses the point in a way that might lead the patient to hear little more than a challenge; it's too easy to imagine him objecting to the "absolutely" and the all-or-nothing characterization of his standards.

Students also attempt to go beneath the surface and explain his self-image as a cover for quite the opposite image—which is always a risky thing to do. An example that does it this way is:

You seem to feel that you're a competent, capable person, and it's other people's fault if things go wrong. Maybe this is your way of avoiding other feelings which you can't face in yourself, feelings of inferiority, failure and helplessness?

That kind of explanation runs the risk of either being a piece of critical evaluation or a piece of explaining-away. Those risks can be somewhat minimized if we wait until the patient begins to wonder why his self-image is the way it is. Therefore, I think the following interpretation strikes the best compromise and shows how a self-image interpretation can be maximally useful:

I appreciate how upset you are, including your pessimism about therapy, but I feel that one of the reasons for your despair lies in your intense feeling of being the helpless victim, doomed to be hurt and misunderstood by others and yet unable to do anything to make things better.

I would substitute "your wish to see yourself as" for "your intense feeling of being."

The defense interpretation, aside from its role in the transference (that is, discounting the final sentence of the transcript), is especially problematic. When a defense shows itself in therapy—where we are in a position to observe it in action, so to speak—we can work with it directly. But when it occurred outside the therapy and is being described for us, we cannot

analyze it the same way. In this study, we aren't in a position to
make an independent assessment of the degree to which Jimmy
was, in fact, responsible for the fiasco, nor, indeed, to know how
much of a *fiasco* it actually was. We have only our patient's
word for it. (To be sure, we usually have other words of his to
base our assessment on, and they can belie or support his word
here. But we have to use these other words of his with special
circumspection and care, bearing in mind that they are still his.)
And any intimation that we are passing independent judgment
on his word is bound to be a serious breach in our neutrality and
define us as the skeptical one. Consider: "Perhaps by blaming
Jimmy for the entire fiasco you can absolve yourself of all the
blame." Aside from everything else, it implies that Jimmy was
not, in fact, altogether responsible for the fiasco, for perhaps the
patient was. Similarly:

> It seems to me that you are getting angry at Jimmy to
> avoid getting angry at yourself for your own contribution
> to the evening's problems.

This presumes that the patient made some contributions. In
order to circumvent the problem, we have to have some basis
from which to infer that he was in fact partly responsible—and
be prepared to specify it. The following example has good form,
in that it suggests to the patient that he suspects the defense,
but then neglects to make reference to any evidence for the
claim:

> I understand that you are feeling very upset right now. But
> I think a part of you suspects that by being so upset about
> Jimmy's shortcomings, you are avoiding any painful real-
> izations about what might be some of your own.

While he is likely to appreciate our tact and care, he might
wonder what makes us think he "suspects" the avoidance—just
because he's "so upset"? (Form is good when we remark on a
patient's awareness of a defense, but we must not declare into
existence an absent inkling.) Here's an interesting variation:

> I wonder if by being the one to worry and suffer, you are
> alleviating guilt about your own responsibility for things
> going badly.

It implies a logic (or psychologic) that might be puzzling to him, and for that reason he'll wonder what makes us think so.

The matter of evidence is also germane to a formulation's diagnostic-ness. In fact, a handy measure of how diagnostic it was is how we could respond to the rejoinder "*What makes you think so?*" An answer that had to resort to normative or theoretical considerations is ipso facto a more diagnostic formulation than one based on evidence he had already provided. Consider:

> I sense that your vulnerability to what others think of you is so great that you defend yourself against the possibility of pain by blaming them before they can blame you.

It can be judged highly diagnostic on several grounds, and one them is that no evidence was alluded to—nor is it easy to see how we could provide any were the patient to say "*What makes you sense that?*" Similarly:

> I realize you're very upset about the party, but do you see perhaps that your blaming Jimmy is one way that you avoid responsibility? If you allowed yourself to think that the fault may be partially yours, you would then have to face certain feelings about yourself that are unbearable— feelings of failure, incompetence, and helplessness.

It is a tactful and altogether plausible formulation whose diagnostic features might be significantly attenuated if it included some evidence. And the narrative does, in fact, contain some evidence: the fact that he felt like a "*nervous wreck*" during the party, and he broke a glass and didn't participate in the after-dinner conversation, and perhaps also the fact that he only "*thought*" Jimmy didn't turn the oven high enough and slammed the oven door. This evidence can be pressed into service—but not necessarily to point to his contributions to the fiasco, because that isn't the best way to use it.

We can try to transform a diagnostic formulation into an empathic interpretation by suggesting to our patient that he purposely included these pieces of "evidence" because he intended to hint at his own part in the fiasco. Accordingly, I would structure a defense interpretation around the evidence and focus on the way they undercut his contention that it was all Jimmy's fault—and most importantly, I would speculate that he meant to do exactly that. In short, he wanted me to tell him that he was externalizing the blame, because he thought it was true.

Now, why he needed for me to tell him the truth is certainly a germane issue, and it can be viewed as an integral part of the externalization defense; after all, I am responsible and to blame for my interpretations. But this can probably wait until until the externalization onto Jimmy has been explored. I would begin, therefore, by drawing attention to the parts of his account where he alluded to his own culpability, and the parts where he had no direct proof of Jimmy's dereliction but only inferred it. Then I would suggest that he included them because "part of him suspected / believed / caught a glimpse of the fact" that the blame wasn't all Jimmy's, and it's painful for him to acknowledge this suspicion. I would then look for an opportunity to say:

> I think you realize that you are blaming him too much, that you are overdoing it, and I think you want me to say this to you. I think you want for me to tell you that you're defending yourself against accepting any of the blame and responsibility.

A student approaches the issue somewhat along the lines I am suggesting:

> Right now you seem most angry at Jimmy, but during the dinner party you took most of the responsibility on yourself. What I mean is you said you were a nervous wreck during dinner; perhaps you were already blaming yourself quite a bit then. Now you're focusing that blame on Jimmy. So maybe you've changed the direction of your criticism, because of how painful it was when you directed it at yourself.

Notice how this interpretation succeeds in elucidating the defense in a tactful and nonjudgmental way, and without very much diagnosis. (The diagnostic element is there, of course, but it's virtually impossible to avoid it altogether when offering a defense interpretation.) And above all, notice the absence of any pussy-footing around the issue, how directly the issue is being addressed. Being nondirective does not mean being indirect— and neither does tact.

Study 3
Making a Pass at Jayne

Jayne and I were alone then. She was waiting for me to make an overture. I'm sure she was expecting me to. But I couldn't. I couldn't make myself do it. I just sat there as if I was frozen. All I had to do was put my arm around her, make some sort of a move. I knew she expected me to; I knew she would accept it, but it was as if I was waiting for her to make the first move—even though I knew she wouldn't. She expected me to. . . . Oh God! (tone of anguish) *I wanted to be close to her, I really did. But I just couldn't start. I can't understand why not! . . .* (What are you thinking about?) *How I used to fight with my cousin Ellen when we were little kids! I've told you about that. I don't know why it comes to mind now. We fought in anger sometimes, but usually we weren't so angry. I guess we just enjoyed it. But whenever my mother caught us, she would give me a long lecture about how it's bad to fight. A gentleman never fights! And she expected me to be a perfect gentleman, perfectly gentle all the time. To be rough was the biggest sin of all. And all of us—not just me, my father and brother too—were always models of good manners and breeding. Never say anything critical to anyone! Never hurt anyone's feelings! Never impose yourself! The Jews, you know, were bad because they were so pushy. The Catholics were too uncouth, the blacks too aggressive. We were the perfect Protestants, WASPs. . . . I assume you are Jewish, and I feel bad I said that about Jews. I don't really believe it, you know; I'm no bigot—just a damn mouse! I really wish you wouldn't just . . . you'd just tell me why I couldn't make a simple pass at Jayne.*

And we could do it easily—too easily, in fact—because he had spelled it out clearly enough. His apparent equation of sex and aggression, together with his mother's insistence on nonaggres

sive gentlemanly behavior, provides ample basis for an explanation. So the study invites interpretations that are obvious and
useless.

During the course of the narrative there were at least two
opportunities to offer useful interpretations. After the first
pause, instead of asking for his thoughts, we could have addressed the defense by saying:

> You emphasize how much she expected you to make the
> first move. I gather you're thinking that this might have
> been why you couldn't.

Or if we wanted to speculate to a piece of internalization: "I
gather you felt a sort of hand inside you holding you back."
After the second silence, before the transference issue was
introduced, we could have articulated the self-image as defined
by his mother. But what interpretation might be helpful at the
end, when he is begging us to tell him why? I think a simple and
unencumbered one stands the best chance, and therefore it
should address his self-image; that's the form that best fits the
content. A student meets these requirements with:

> Perhaps it was impossible because it was something a
> perfect gentleman wouldn't do.

I would add "And you want to see yourself that way." And to
the following one I would add "And it doesn't fit your image of
yourself":

> I wonder if you see sex as some kind of struggle, some kind
> of aggressive imposition, something a gentleman doesn't
> do.

Here is a well-articulated self-image formulation:

> I think you would prefer to see yourself as a mouse, who is
> unable to take initiative, rather than risk being pushy,
> uncouth, or aggressive.

And here's an interesting variation:

Perhaps being a "gentleman," though it paralyzes you in some ways, helps you preserve the idea of being special, being better than other people.

But it is too diagnostic; self-image interpretations are usually most effective when they stop short of offering dynamic and functional explanations. In this case, however, it might be useful to suggest that he was struggling to shake off his mother's values and her hand in his self-image. The following interpretation has substantial merit:

I believe you're afraid to see yourself as strong and aggressive because you feel you might risk losing your mother's love.

Students also suggest a dynamic conflict among his self-images, and here's one that would be excellent were it not so speculative: "Is it possible you choose to think of yourself as an ineffective mouse because you're in conflict about whether you have the right to experience, and to act on, the same feelings of aggression and sexuality that other people have?"

Notice how the self-image interpretations I've cited speak only of the patient's "viewing" himself as unaggressive and inoffensive. I believe it's important to keep from suggesting to him that he was in fact unaggressive and inoffensive. Maybe he did, after all, hurt Jayne with his passivity? Maybe that's the reason for his guilty feelings?—not because his impulse was sexual-aggressive. This intriguing possibility is bolstered by the fact that he is feeling guilty right now for having insulted us, and perhaps because he is again taking the passive position. So a student formulates it this way: "I think a part of you is feeling guilty now. Maybe you think you have hurt my feelings and that I am angry with you"—but she doesn't stop there, but continues in a way that misses the point: "And now you may be anticipating a scolding or lecture from me, believing that I, like your mother, only expect you to be a polite gentleman." Better to suggest that he also felt he'd hurt Jayne. (For doesn't he already know that we aren't going to behave like the mother? Perhaps that is what's upsetting him.)

He might also be feeling guilty because he's asking us to do

something he himself should be doing—explain his behavior
with Jayne. To the extent that he has provided ample material,
he has put us in a perfect position to say, as a student does:

> I think you've already partly answered the question, and it
> has to do with the way you think of yourself—as someone
> who was taught never to impose, not to be pushy and
> aggressive.

Another student puts it more succinctly:

> So you think it's possible that you couldn't make a move
> because you were afraid of being aggressive.

In short, we can point out that he already has an answer—which
always, of course, raises the further question: Why does he need
us to give it? And students answer by suggesting that he needs
us to take the initiative in therapy in the same way he needed
for Jayne to take it. For example: "You want me to take the
initiative here the way you wanted Jayne to take it. Maybe it
would be 'imposing yourself' into my work, if you took the
initiative in explaining why you couldn't make that pass."

On the other hand, when things are as obvious as they seem
to be in this narrative there is the temptation to look for the
nonobvious, for an explanation that doesn't draw directly from
the material. Here's a good illustration:

> Perhaps you are living up to your mother's expectations
> with a vengeance. By acting the perfect gentleman so well
> with Jayne you may have hurt her. Yet you don't experi-
> ence any anger that you may have toward women.

Fine!—though I wouldn't have included the final generalization,
it can only deflect the impact of the interpretation.

But when we venture a nonobvious formulation, we run the
risk of defining ourselves as the shrewd and clever one who
doesn't take things at face value. Since I prefer to avoid that
role, if I thought it was useful to ferret out a nonobvious
explanation I'd go about it gradually and carefully. "I take it one
reason you felt bad was because you sensed that Jayne felt
hurt." That's a tactful way to begin, simply drawing attention

to the effect his action had on her. Of course, the fact that she was hurt doesn't mean that it had been his intention to hurt her, and he might say so. But if he was taken aback by the suggestion and wanted some evidence for it, I would offer two points. He stressed how much she expected him to make a sexual overture, and he believed I was hurt by his remark about Jews. (Whether or not it was his intention to hurt me can wait until he's explored the idea.)

Nonobvious interpretations are sometimes not only far-fetched but overly literal. Consider these examples:

> I think that here you have an urge to be closer to me, to put your arm around me; and you're waiting for me to make some kind of overture, to be the aggressive one.

> It sounds to me as if you're not sure now whether it would be fun to fight with me, like with Ellen, or whether I'd lecture you about it as your mother did.

Given his anguish, such interpretations are likely to jar the patient. They have the quality of using his words against him, and using them in a way he never intended. Notice how much more sensitive and empathic is this simple rendition of the same transference theme:

> I wonder if you aren't doing in therapy what you describe yourself doing with Jayne, unable to express and explain what you really feel and feeling yourself to be frozen.

Students offer similar transference interpretations. They stress his need for us to take the initiative or his expectation that we'll react either like his mother did, or in the opposite way, and some speculate that he wants us to tell him how to make a sexual advance "like a gentleman."

The defense reflected in the narrative is—what? Some would point to internalization, others to inhibition. "To be assertive and aggressive is bad, so when you're in a situation that arouses such impulses you freeze." That's the way a student puts it, and it's quite sufficient. It isn't necessary to spell things out as fully as all of these do:

In making a pass you would show you can be assertive, but displaying this kind of behavior might cause you anxiety because to act that way might be to impose yourself, and it's against what your mother taught.

I wonder if perhaps the feelings of being frozen and unable to move farther was in one sense a way to keep in check your desire to be rough-and-tumble, just as you had been with your cousin Ellen.

Your sitting "as if frozen" seems to have been a way of ensuring that you don't get carried away.

I wonder if you become passive and freeze when you feel anxious about what you might do. Perhaps you become passive when you feel like being more aggressive, but this frightens you.

Each of these interpretations may be valid enough, but none is empathic enough. And in my estimation, these are not promising ways to invite the patient's active search for the explanations he wants.

Study 4
God, I'm Such a Mess!

This patient—in his late teens—has recently been coming late to his sessions.

I don't know why I came late today again. I could have made it on time, but I just didn't try. It somehow didn't seem worth the effort . . . I bet you're angry at me for coming late . . . I'd ask you but I know you won't answer—probably throw me an interpretation, (slightly mimicking tone) "So you want me to angry at you, eh!" . . . Maybe I do, I don't know. . . . Everything stinks these days. I seem to be getting worse and worse. What's the use! (sighs and lights a cigarette) I had another fight with my father. This time it was about my sleeping late. It really bugs him when I sleep till noon. He gets all hassled. And I'm getting fed up with it. I wish he'd just

*resign himself to the fact that I'm an adolescent and
adolescents like to sleep late. . . . He really blew up when
I told him that—flew into a royal rage. And I got a bit
scared at how furious he got when I said "Tough shit!"
You know, I was afraid he was going to hit me. . . .
But what does he expect? Ever since I was little he's
always treated me in such an offhand way, as if I didn't
matter much to him. And he'd make all these big promises to me and then never keep them. So naturally I
wasn't going to be his good little boy. I mean, what'd he
expect? . . He always wanted me to do well in school, but
I guess I wasn't as smart as the other kids . . . And he
wanted me to learn to play chess but I hated it. And the
piano, too.* (puts out cigarette and begins to weep) *God, I'm
such a . . . such a mess!*

This study raises the same question the previous one did. Is it
likely to be sufficiently useful to offer the patient a simple
articulation of his self-image, or is some elaboration and explanation called for? Perhaps because the narrative provides the
material for it, students opt for more than a simple articulation.
Except, the narrative also provides us with a special reason to
prefer a simple articulation; we have to keep from exonerating
or faulting him, and there is also the risk of deflecting him from
his emotional state to an intellectual one. Therefore, for the
moment at any rate, while our patient is feeling acutely distressed and is weeping, I believe it's quite sufficient to suggest
to him that he believes he has no choice but to see himself as the
bad and disappointing one, the one who has to provoke disap-
proval and anger.

But a simple articulation needn't restrict itself to the form of
"This is your self-image." It can be embedded in a succinct
enough formulation that also takes account of what the patient
is feeling and the issues he's working with. Consider how this
tactfully formulated interpretation restricts itself to articulation
and uses the self-image to explain his despair:

I appreciate how upset you are, including your pessimism
about therapy. But I feel that one of the reasons for your
despair lies in your intense feeling of being the helpless
victim—doomed to be hurt and misunderstood by others,
and yet unable to do anything to make things better.

Another sensitive way to formulate an articulation and still take his weeping into account is shown by this succinct interpretation:

I think you're beginning to explore that aspect of yourself which feels you never lived up to your father's expectations. And it hurts.

However, this succinct interpretation is actually curt: "I think a part of you gets pleasure from feeling like the hopeless one who can't be helped." To suggest that he enjoys his self-image, when he's feeling so distressed about it, is bound to be provocative and add to the patient's distress. Notice how confronting the interpretation is, which usually happens when we are curt.

Students also cast their self-image interpretation into a form that sounds like a fatherly lecture. Here's a flagrant example:

Sometimes it's tempting to give in to feeling like a hopeless mess and unable to do things, because it's hard to always stand up for yourself and insist on your rights in the face of people's anger.

This, surely, can't be the right moment for such remarks—even though our patient "deserves" them, having not only "transgressed" by being late again but by giving in to feelings of hopelessness about therapy. Here's a more subtle variation:

I understand that you are distressed by feeling like such a mess, but perhaps it is more acceptable to you to see yourself as incapable of doing anything about it than as unwilling even to try.

I would venture the rule of thumb that any interpretation that included the clause "this is more acceptable to you than that" was bound to be a poor one. The same applies to "it is easier for you to do (feel/want/believe) this than that."

Students also construe his self-image as "the blameless one," and emphasize his sense of unfairness over expectations he couldn't meet. That, too, has to be done carefully, for we don't want to blame him for failing, or imply that there isn't a good basis for his self-image. But we also want to avoid making the obverse implication—namely, that he has every reason to feel about himself the way he does. (It's not his "*fault*" and it's perfectly "*natural*.") In fact, this is the chief danger in any explanation that is given in conjunction with the self-image interpretation. For instance, students suggest that his self-image was his way of punishing his father for the offhand treatment he gave him, or else it's a way of disappointing the father in retaliation for being disappointed by him. I see little merit in offering such tit-for-tat formulations; they might only justify and buttress his self-image. Thus, even a shrewd variation, like the following one, can serve the interests of defense alone: "I wonder whether you need to think of yourself as someone who is messed up and bad, because then you can protect yourself from being disappointed by others by disappointing them first."

Many teachers and practitioners advocate that we formulate a patient's self-image in cognitive terms. They suggest we do it this way: "You behave as you believe you are expected to behave; your self-image conforms to the image you believe others have of you." In our patient's case it can be put in terms of his father's having expected him to be a failure, as follows: "Perhaps in order to explain your father's offhand treatment of you, you need to see yourself as a mess and a failure." Without questioning its validity, I want to question its utility. Not that our patient isn't likely to welcome the formulation, but chances are he'll use it in the interests of intellectual defense rather than of making useful discoveries. In my opinion, the formulation runs the risk of explaining things away. It may, of course, provide some useful structure for his synthetic function, but it may also provide too much; it can be too purely a cognitive and intellectual construction. (To be sure, it will probably help him stop weeping.) Therefore, I prefer the way the following example articulates his belief about his self-image:

> I think you very much want to believe that you were forced to be rebellious and to do badly at school. But a part of you fears that it is all your fault—that you are a bad person, and that your father rejected you because there was something wrong with you.

Perhaps I am relying too much on intuition when I judge that this formulation, if it happened to be valid, would have an impact that wasn't purely cognitive-intellectual. (And that it *won't* stop his weeping.) Notice how it implicates the volitional

and affective realms of experience without slighting the synthetic function. Notice also how free it is of nomothetic overtones.

This study provides for a transference formulation that draws
a simple and direct parallel to the patient's father in the motif of
indifference. For example:

> Perhaps you're thinking that I, too, treat you in an offhand
> way, and so you aren't going to be my "good little boy" and
> come on time or get better.

It can include feelings of anger:

> I think that your wish for me to be angry with you for
> coming late means you wish I would care for you, just as
> you attempted—by doing poorly in school and hating the
> piano—to get your father to stop treating you in an offhand
> way.

It can speculate that a reaction of anger is better than nothing:

> I think you're feeling so sad and discouraged about therapy
> because you expect I'll be like your father, that you'll have
> to be a good boy here, too, and it still won't matter, I still
> won't care about you. Perhaps you come late to try to
> provoke my anger, because you feel that the anger would
> at least show that I cared about you—just as your father
> notices you only when you can provoke his anger.

It can infer a motive:

> I think you want me to comfort you and show you I really
> care about you, just like you would want your father to do.

It can infer an affect:

> I wonder if you could be feeling angry at me because I am
> becoming important to you, and you are afraid I'll disap-
> point you and let you down as you say your father does.

And it can speculate that we are seen as someone whose
expectations are so high, they cannot be satisfied:

> Part of you believes you can only disappoint me, that you
> can never live up to my expectations anyway—as you felt
> you couldn't meet your father's—so why bother trying.

All of them are good interpretations; but none of them, in my
opinion, is the best interpretation. They are more superficial
than they need to be and draw a superficial parallel between the
patient's father and us.

Now, transference phenomena needn't be complex, and it's
always a good technique to formulate them as simply as
possible. But there's a distinction between simplicity and su-
perficiality. A formulation that extends to an underlying level
needn't be complex—in fact, when we seek to understand at a
deeper level, matters often become less complex. Consider,
then, the direct parallel that students draw: our patient has a
need to cast us in the same image as his father—as the one who
disapproves and disappoints, who breaks his promises, who
reacts in anger. But consider further: we do *not* disapprove and
disappoint, we *never* break our promises and react in anger—
and the patient already knows it! This raises the possibility that
he is experiencing us not as being exactly like his father, but as
being exactly *unlike* his father.

Moreover, his transference has a distinctly resistive cast; it
seems to be serving a need to withdraw from therapy. (In fact,
this study could have been included in the next chapter, as one
of the Resistance Studies.) This suggests that he is experiencing
some danger in therapy and wishes to flee. The question now
becomes: What is he afraid of? And our potentially intriguing
and useful answer is that he is afraid we are not going to fulfill
his transference "needs." In other words, we are not, and are
never going to be, like his beloved (and be-hated) father. This
formulation of the transference isn't more complex than the
direct parallel, and it isn't as superficial.

A student captures the formulation in an especially tactful
and sensitive way. The interpretation begins along familiar
lines, but notice how it concludes:

> I know you're feeling very upset, and I think you're telling
> me that if I expect anything of you—as your father ex-
> pected things of you—I will only be disappointed and
> angry, as he's been, because you are such a mess. I

wonder, however, if you don't need to see things that way
because of the real possibility that I *won't* react as your
father has, and *that* is even more disturbing to you.

I doubt whether I could improve on it.

Finally, what about the fact that our patient is weeping? We
can infer from his tears that he is feeling afraid. A student
interprets it this way:

> Your tears suggest that maybe you are afraid that I will be
> angry; so you are telling me not to hurt you now. I have an
> idea about the reason for this feeling. You see me as being
> like your father, whose anger when you are a "bad boy"
> frightens you.

Spelling out the transference implications was perhaps quite
unnecessary, because the affect interpretation already says a
good deal. Another possibility is to interpret the tears as a
signal. A student does it and also draws an allusion to the father
with:

> Your crying might be sort of signaling me that you don't
> want me to hurt you—for coming late or for sleeping late.

These formulations overlap with the defense interpretation I
had in mind for the study, except I construed the weeping as the
patient's defense against his own rage. Of course, since he isn't
wondering why he's crying, telling him why is bound to be an
imposition, and chances are he'd either be perplexed or enraged
by any suggestion that his tears were anything but an expression of despair.

Still, he might be willing to work with the idea that his
despair was related to his self-criticism and derogation, and
perhaps he was defending himself by internalizing the blame
(or turning aggression back on himself). How to say this to him
is the problem. The following is a good attempt, but it resorts to
a solution that is flagrantly diagnostic:

> At first you were criticizing your father in what seemed to
> be an angry way, but then you turned the criticism on
> yourself, saying what a mess you are. This self-criticism,

which makes you feel bad enough to cry, seems to be your way of preventing yourself from getting really angry or critical towards your father, and perhaps towards other people too. (Meaning, of course, me!)

That is exactly the sort of formulation we ought to keep to ourselves and never attempt to verbalize aloud—not all at once, at any rate. Consider the way the following example restricts itself to the first part:

A moment ago you were very angry at your father for treating you as he did, and then you turned the anger against yourself as if to say you're just a bad boy, someone who isn't good enough to live up to your father's expectations.

That was still too diagnostic for me, so I might settle for a succinct remark that was altogether undiagnostic—such as: "You were furious at your father a moment ago, and now you are furious at yourself"—and then wait to see how he picks up on the observation.

Students' defense interpretations reflect a lot of unclarity. I resorted to the marginal comment "What's the defense?" more frequently than I did in the other studies. For instance:

I wonder if you use your anger at your father to cover up that you feel bad because you don't seem to matter much to him. (What's the defense?)

It sounds as if it hurt you when he didn't seem to care, but it was such an awful thing to feel you provoked him to anger, and when he was angry at you at least you felt he cared. (What's the defense?)

Students speak of his making others angry as a way to secure their love, or as a means of avoiding disappointment, or as a wish to be taken care of. In other words, the defense is "provocation to anger." Sometimes they construe his being bad as a defense:

I believe that you avoid being the good boy now so as not to be hurt all over again.

That could be an interesting variation on avoidance. And finally, they formulate a purely resistance interpretation such as:

> You seem to be saying that your performance in school and with the piano was a way of paying your father back for his indifference. I wonder if a part of you would like to fail at therapy because you believe I am indifferent as well.

And this is a good place to end the discussion of this study, because resistance is the subject of our next chapter and that's where the rest of it belongs. But it's also a good place for another dialogue.

On Caring and Neutrality

The relationship between caring and neutrality came up during my discussion of several studies, as it also did in Chapter 4—where I stated that the intensity of our interpretive stance guards us against the appearance and substance of indifference. I also mentioned that we must limit our neutrality to the act of understanding—in fact, it was vital to do so—but didn't explain what that meant, and this may be the time to do it.

From the perspective of caring and indifference, neutrality can be construed as not taking sides. One of its dimensions in psychotherapy has to do with taking sides in our patient's interpersonal relations and blaming or exonerating from blame. Blame, however, is not the same as responsibilty—or if it is, then a distinction has to be drawn between moral responsibility and causal, or objective, responsibility. Attributing causal responsibility doesn't necessarily entail being partial; responsibility can imply cause or determination, while blame implies fault.

Reader: That's an easy distinction to draw in theory. But say a patient was wondering why his brother was unfriendly to him, and I had offered the explanation that he, my patient, was hostile to his brother, or behaved cruelly toward him. I might have intended only to point out a determinant, to say that the hostility or cruelty was objectively responsible, but he might, and with some legitimacy, construe the explanation as having blamed or faulted him. Trying to persuade him that there's a subtle but real distinction between what he heard and what I intended might be quite futile and only provoke a philosophical dialogue. Does this then mean that I cannot maintain the requisite neutrality?

Author: Yes, in fact it may mean exactly that—but only if and when you make such interpretations. The inescapable conclusion, it seems to me, is this: if you want to remain neutral, especially in your patient's eyes, you will have to keep from making those kinds of explanations.

Reader: In other words, if I had reason to expect that an interpretation will have strong implications of fault-finding—or exonerating, scolding, advising, and the rest—then it wasn't a good one in the first place. And that means that before making an interpretation I must feel secure not only in my neutrality but in my patient's perception of it as well.

Author: In fact, I derive several technical guidelines from that principle. One is "Never make an interpretation during anything like an argument." Another is "Never interpret if emotionally aroused—when feeling irritated or defensive, and the like, or when caught off guard by a direct question." Chances are too great that under such conditions any interpretation will carry a heavy burden of nonneutral implications.

Reader: Doesn't it rule out all interpretations of interpersonal events and conflicts, especially if it's early in therapy and my neutrality hasn't yet been established?

Author: Not necessarily. If your patient was wondering why he becomes hostile to his brother when his brother has done little to provoke it, your suggesting a reason for his hostility—for example, "What do you think of the possibility that you have old and unresolved feelings of rivalry with him?"—doesn't imply that you've taken sides.

Reader: What if he responded with *"So it's really all my fault"*?

Author: You could then switch to the business mode and try to clarify the distinction between a determinant and a fault. Still, if it turned out that you were mistaken, and he remained unpersuaded, you would have to avoid that kind of interpretation until such time as your neutrality was securely established. The same is true, of course, for all the manifestations of neutrality I discuss in these chapters.

The same, however, is not true for a second dimension of neutrality, one that is more difficult to conceptualize. And it is especially germane to the kind of distress our patient was experiencing in Study 4. It has to do with taking his side against his suffering, against his psychological problems. Siding with "part" of a patient—with an aspect of his self, no matter how conceptualized—is often a tacit and subtle kind of position for us to take. Nevertheless, I believe it is an accurate characterization of our position. The harder question, for me, is whether it is a fair way to construe "neutrality," because I don't think it is. If we were constrained from taking a patient's side against his suffering, our work would lose its therapeutic efficacy, not to mention its ethical justification.

Reader: Couldn't we resolve the problem by again distinguishing between moral blame and causal responsibility? May we say that we remain neutral insofar as we never imply an ethical injunction when we "blame" his harsh super-ego or "fault" his neurotic habits; we only lay objective responsibility at their door

Author: Perhaps. But I would rather draw a line here and contend that neutrality does not really pertain to the intrapsychic domain. For we must, after all, take our patient's side against his psychological problems; to do otherwise is to fall into an indifference that could undercut the purpose of our service.

Reader: In order to examine the technical issues entailed in this kind of intrapsychic side-taking, let me present you with two cases. The first will deal with a problem that had an external origin, the second will have an intrapsychic origin. Let's suppose a patient is in a state of emotional distress; he barely manages to tell me that his lover has abandoned him in favor of another, then bursts into tears. I can hardly keep from sympathizing with his anguish and wishing there was something I could do to ameliorate it. But let's suppose that anything I think of saying will either vitiate my neutrality or be ineffective, or perhaps both.

Author: In other words, you have reason to judge that an interpretation is untimely because it could entail blaming the lover, or else the patient himself, and also that understanding—as distinct from "There, there, I do understand!"—will not prevail against the intensity of his suffering.

Reader: I will be tempted, of course, to abandon, at least temporarily, my role as therapist and offer the patient some sort of relief based on the traditional principles of healing. I could try to disguise such an effort by formulating a remark in terms that at least sounded like an interpretation—for example: "You are feeling devastated right now because not only are you feeling the hurt of rejection, you are also feeling rage." But that would probably convey little more than the message "You'll feel better soon."

Author: So would: "You're feeling especially devastated because you cannot imagine that you could lose your love for your lover and find it in another." The underlying message is "Patience and fortitude! Be strong! Endure your suffering and you will prevail!"

Reader: But what other alternatives do I have? Am I helpless?

Author: And is your sense of helplessness nothing more than an empathic recognition of his? And do you in fact believe that he is actually so helpless? These questions aren't rhetorical. They suggest a possible line of interpretation that can focus attention on the intrapsychic domain. You can articulate his helplessness with: "You are feeling utterly helpless, aren't you?—as if there was nothing you could do about your anguish."

Reader: And if he agreed, but asked "*So is there?*"

Author: You could respond: "I have no way of knowing for sure, but I think your sense of helplessness is so deep and pervasive right now that it is contributing to your suffering." In this way, you remain in his intrapsychic domain. Now, if you already knew enough about his intrapsychic life, you might find something specific on which to base your speculation about how and why his sense of helplessness was contributing to his suffering. For instance, you might be able to suggest that it was making contact, or combining, with feelings of impotency, or perhaps reintegrating memories of his father's having left him.

Reader: Your point is that I can address myself to the sources of his suffering that are internal and idiosyncratic to him—and there are bound to be some. If he accepted my interpretation and went on to reflect upon it, then the therapeutic process will have been brought into the work. But what if he cannot make that switch, cannot consider the possibility that his suffering was a function, even in part, of his inner reality?

Author: Then you mustn't press the issue. But neither do you have to abandon your regular neutrality—unless you judged that he was experiencing a serious crisis.

Reader: He was plunged into a dangerous depression, for instance?

Author: Yes, and if that became the case, then anything you can do to help must, of course, have all the priority— because it goes without saying that there's no sense in protecting long-range benefits when short-range problems are so severe there may never be a long range. When the therapy itself is in jeopardy, not to mention the patient himself, then short-term considerations become paramount.

Reader: And isn't there the danger that I will hold back too long and allow a situation to deteriorate before taking appropriate action?

Author: Here, of course, is where our clinical wisdom and experience count for everything. But I believe it's important to bear in mind the enormous benefits to our patient when we show him, with our business-as-usual equanimity, that we have faith in his ability to endure and overcome—when we show courage. And our faith extends to the conviction that our neutrality, when combined with a diligent and sensitive focus on intrapsychic determinants and conditions, can have profound therapeutic value both in the short and long run.

Reader: All right, let's move on to my second case. Now the patient suffers with a disabling symptom, let's say a phobia.

Author: Let's make sure to assume that he was well informed and decided he wanted a nonbehavioral therapy, knowing that it isn't the economical treatment for his symptom.

Reader: Yes, don't worry, I've already ruled out all doubts about his decision and his willingness to forgo a quicker relief from his disability. How shall I proceed from there?

Author: Under those conditions, you will work with two timing criteria: the one I've been describing, and the other that has a short-range goal of understanding the symptom as rapidly as possible. This goal might require you to offer interpretations that are directed at the phobia (and in that way caring about it)—caring to explore its roots, its meanings and ramifications, and trying to reach discoveries—all of which may help ameliorate it.

Reader: Don't you believe I must assume that an active exploration of his symptom has to await a full uncovering of his life-history or his personality?

Author: No. And neither do I believe that it's necessary to assume that the symptom must take a back seat while therapy is achieving its principal goals, nor must it even wait until the therapeutic process has been fully established. Which is not to say that it might not have to do that, of course; my point is that you needn't make the assumption in advance. Furthermore, if you believed you could give him some advice or guidance that could significantly weaken the symptom, then I might advise you to give it and introduce that "flaw" in the therapy. You could explain your decision to him in terms of the need to overcome his disability as swiftly as possible. I think you can rely on clinical judgment to guide you in deciding whether this flaw would jeopardize the therapy and "spoil" your patient.

Reader: But what if he prevented me from doing any of that? Throughout the first stages of therapy, let's say, he makes no direct references to his disabling symptom and seems oblivious to it.

Author: That would strike you as noteworthy, I'm sure, and you'd want to understand the meaning and function of his "avoidance." If you thought you understood it, and even if you weren't so certain you understood it correctly, you could venture to share that understanding with him, using the second timing criterion as your rationale and taking full advantage of the smallest opening in his narrative. To be sure, you'd be actively steering him toward the subject of his phobia. But you can prudently risk the harm to the therapeutic process because he might be imagining that the symptom would dissolve if he talked about his early childhood, for instance, or he presumed that once he had given you the full story of his life you would formulate an interpretation that would cause the phobia to vanish. Whatever the case, it can count as a piece of useful understanding to uncover and explore his beliefs and fantasies regarding the disabling symptom. Therefore, I would look for an opportunity to say something like: "I gather you are deliberately not talking about your phobia because you believe that it will do no good. Instead, you believe it might be more useful to work on your early childhood."

Reader: Let's suppose he agrees, but in these words: *"That's right. But are you implying that my belief is wrong, that working on my childhood isn't the best way to overcome my phobia?"*

Author: The subject is now your neutrality with respect to content, a neutrality to which you committed yourself when you gave the Basic Instruction. You will want to protect it. But there's a significant difference between that and "neutrality with respect to the intrapsychic domain," and you can try to explain it to him. After all, we are no longer dealing with narrative; this is clearly a business matter. I believe the appropriate response can be formulated this way: "No, I didn't mean to imply that. I can see where you drew the implication from, but I didn't intend to challenge your belief." That comes first, of course. Then comes: "The reason I drew your attention to it is because I was distracted by the fact that you weren't talking about the problem that caused you to seek therapy, and it's something that is causing you so much suffering."

Reader: What's the point of formulating the decision in terms of distraction, rather than simply saying "I was wondering why you weren't talking about the problem"?

Author: It stays consonant with the spirit of the Basic Instruction. After all, if I am distracted by a patient's behavior, and that distraction is interfering with my ability to listen and understand, then I am justified in treating it as business.

Reader: That rationale is nice and elastic, isn't it? Can't it easily be stretched to cover a wide range of directives?

Author: Yes, so it has to be used sparingly and judiciously, and only when the issue at hand is of substantial significance. I would reserve it for issues like the one we're examining, where the distraction originates from a concern about the patient's well-being.

Reader: Let's suppose my patient accepted the rationale and didn't quarrel with its formulation, but wanted to know whether I was distracted because his avoidance was surprising—and that meant his belief was mistaken. Or suppose he simply asked to know whether I disagreed with his belief.

Author: You would now have to decide whether to tell him that you believe, if in fact you did believe, that it might be better if he spoke about his phobia, or whether to say, no matter what your belief was: "I'm not sure what would be more useful for you and more helpful for overcoming your disability, whether it would be more helpful to talk about your childhood, or whether it would be more useful to talk about your phobia." Either response, in my opinion, is likely to be useful, although the one I cited has the added advantage of forestalling a didactic discussion.

Reader: —And the disadvantage of inviting his outraged *"You're the therapist! What do you mean you don't know?"*

Author: But chances are good, in any case, that he will now go ahead to examine his assumptions about therapy, and his assumptions about his symptom as well. And you've acted in a way that wasn't indifferent to him and his suffering.

7

RESISTANCE

Resistance in Psychotherapy

A patient seeks therapy because he wants to change, and a patient enters therapy because he wants to keep from changing.

Reader: You are referring not to two patients, I gather.

Author: Yes, and my point is that his motivation to change, no matter how strong, isn't likely to be conflict-free. However painful his symptoms, debilitating his inhibitions, and intolerable his condition, we can prudently assume that he has a substantial stake in staying the way he is. It can be conceptualized in a variety of ways and take a variety of forms, but however conceptualized and whatever its form, this stake can be so powerful a force that to lose sight of it and fail to give it the active attention it deserves—by articulating it at every turn, analyzing it in every form, and diligently working it through—is to imperil our patient and his therapy. Resistance is the broad clinical rubric under which this "negative" or inertial motivation is commonly classified. But there's a narrower definition of resistance that reserves the term for episodes called "flight from therapy," and it is these episodes to which we now turn.

Reader: You single them out for special study? Why?

Author: Because they confront us with special problems. Resistances against change are certainly fraught with technical problems, and all forms of therapy have them. But our nondirective format makes it especially difficult to deal with resistances that are directed against the therapy itself. And because these difficulties are so serious, I designed a set of studies for them.

Reader: Before turning to the studies, I have a question about the relationship between the two definitions. Resistance in the broad sense—those defenses that are directed against significant change and growth—derives from the evolution of our conception of defense. It was the phenomenon of resistance in psychoanalysis, as well as subsequent observations that the forms of a patient's resistance tended to correspond closely to his major defensive proclivities, that gave "defense" a metapsychological status. Insofar as it refers to the defensive measures a patient takes against the therapeutic process, this kind of resistance can comfortably be formulated in those terms, can't it?

Author: Yes, but that formulation is likely to have little practical utility if we didn't have specific criteria by which to identify defenses that also threaten the integrity of the therapy as a whole—the narrow definition. For otherwise we would have to contend, as many teachers and practitioners do, that since the therapeutic process—the "analytic process" in orthodox psychoanalysis, and specifically the quality of free-association—*never* achieves its full potential, our patient is *always* in a state of resistance.

Reader: I gather you regard this point of view as devoid of practical significance.

Author: Hardly. It reminds us that defenses have a high priority in respect to timing. Only, it doesn't help us distinguish between those resistances that only *may,* so long as other things are equal, command our attention and those that *must* command it no matter what—specifically, clinical manifestations of a significant withdrawal from both the work of therapy and the therapy itself.

Reader: And what specifically are those manifestations?

Author: They aren't so difficult to identify. Their characteristic feature is withdrawal or evasion, and for that reason the term "flight" is commonly used to denote them. When a patient becomes preoccupied with quitting therapy, or when he experiences a very strong sense of detachment from it, it is obviously a resistance. But it can also be a resistance if he falls into protracted silences, experiences a reduction of involvement in therapy or of urgency to speak, or has the conviction that there isn't anything worth speaking about. Similarly, we might infer a state of resistance if we sense that therapy has "slowed down" or reached a plateau—if our patient is speaking freely enough but not about matters that are vital to him.

Reader: But just a minute! What about our neutrality with respect to content?

Author: Yes, there's the rub! It's a serious problem for us. To be sure, no form of therapy places a premium on a continuous stream of speech—there is, after all, the phenomenon called "resistance in the form of free-association"—and since we supervise the therapeutic process in a way that promotes self-inquiry, we have a basis of expectation that our patient will speak of things that are meaningful to him.

Reader: But we still didn't define it as a task; we've never even implied that he might want to be reflective and involved, and therefore speak of meaningful things. I raised this issue in the first chapter, and you deferred it.

Author: I will defer again, but only till Study 4 and A Dialogue on Resistance and Neutrality. That's where I'll tackle the problem head-on. Let me mention here that, while aspects such as lack of involvement and reflectiveness are not difficult for us to identify, they are difficult to prevail against and still preserve the spirit and format of a nondirective therapy like ours. The same, however, is true for all forms of resistance, as narrowly defined; they confront us with technical problems that merit special study and practice.

Before we turn to them, I want to insert a cautionary note that may come across as moralistic and preachy. Resistance is perhaps the most notorious of all our concepts, in that it is widely regarded as both circular and self-serving. It has certainly been misused to fend off challenges to our theory, and I hope you agree that it ought not to be used for that purpose. But it can be subtly and egregiously self-serving in our clinical work too, and we must be especially vigilant against that misuse. There are, after all, many reasons a patient may want to quit therapy, and only one of them is resistance. Moreover, there are many reasons we might not want him to quit, and only one of them is because he's in a state of resistance. It goes without saying—but here I am saying it anyway—that we may have a great stake in "holding" the patient, as indeed we may occasionally have a stake in letting him go. More than any other feature of our work, resistance calls into play not only our clinical judgment and wisdom but our professional and personal integrity.

Reader: I get the point, and I don't begrudge you the sermon. But you are waxing moralistic—and you've come pretty close to it here and there in the book. Why don't we just wrestle with the technical problems and leave my integrity out of it. I'll deal with it in my own treatment, and under supervision.

Author: Agreed.

Instructions for the Resistance Studies

Each study presents a narrative whose underlying theme reflects a resistance phenomenon. What is involved in each case is a defensive move directed against the therapy and/or the therapist. Your task is to identify the resistance theme and then write an intervention that can be given to the patient. Each study is drawn from a different patient, and each occurs during the middle stages of therapy, after the opening stages have been completed.

Study 1
A Flight into Health

Boy, am I ever feeling great these days! I don't know what I'm doing here any more, everything is going so well. You know something? I've been getting to all my classes, even the morning ones. I finished the socio paper yesterday and handed it in right on time, and I'm working on the English assignment too. For the first time in a long time I can actually sit down like a real person and apply myself without getting all restless and jittery. And I can get my ideas down on paper; the words come, they feel right. Boy, is that ever a good feeling! . . . I spoke to my father on the phone last night, and for the first time in I

*can't remember how long he didn't get to me. You know
something? It was practically a human conversation! I
didn't get my usual feeling that he was bugging me about
every damn thing. He made only one remark that got to
me. When I told him how well I was working on the
papers, he said his usual thing, "You're a real macher
(achiever), eh? . . . But you know what? I just brushed it
off, didn't let it hassle me at all. I felt like saying back
"And you're a real shlemiehl (loser), eh!" But I didn't. I
just shut up. . . . I was rapping with Henry a couple of
days ago, and he said he never saw me so cool, so
relaxed. You know what he said? Therapy has done me a
lot of good. That's what he said. I'm a new man. I'm not
so tense and so worried anymore; I can laugh and fool
around. . . . And it's really true. It's marvelous!*

If this transcript reflects or depicts a resistance—and that, of
course, is our a priori assumption—it has to be a so-called
"flight into health." *"Because I am doing so well, because I
have improved so much, it is pointless to continue with the
work of therapy or the therapy itself,"* is the logic of our
patient's narrative. Students are glad to formulate interpretations that articulate this logic—and their only shortcoming is
that they aren't resistance interpretations. Here's a good example:

> Things in your life are going the way you want them to,
> you are feeling great, and you say you don't know what
> you are doing here. Could it be that you are wondering
> whether to continue in therapy, whether there is any more
> to be gained from therapy?

Articulating his message can be regarded as our first step,
perhaps a necessary preliminary step, in exploring the resistance itself, because when the patient simply concurs with the
interpretation (as he probably will), we will have to take further
steps toward the resistance. However, taking matters a step
further by inferring conflict, as the following example does,
doesn't make it anything more than a fuller articulation of the
initial message:

> I understand that you've been feeling good about yourself.
> But I wonder if perhaps your emphasis on it isn't a way of

saying that you feel you don't need therapy anymore. Perhaps you didn't come right out and say so, because a part of you thinks you still need therapy.

All it would take to transform this into a resistance interpretation would be to add: "And part of you thinks / suspects that it is a resistance—in other words, its purpose is to allow you to feel you don't need therapy any longer." The only problem, of course, and it's the key problem of this study, is that we have no evidence that the patient thinks (or suspects) it.

Given that *we* think and suspect it—in fact, the instructions give us no choice in the matter—we have the option of simply apprising him of the fact, perhaps with a few didactic remarks by way of tactful introduction. In other words, we can treat the matter as business. That's what many practitioners would do. To do otherwise, they might contend, is depriving the patient of their professional expertise. Basically I don't disagree. But I wouldn't take the didactic approach before I had attempted an interpretive one. My first goal would be to help the patient recognize for himself that his condition was serving a resistive function. I would rather he *discovered* the phenomenon than *learned* about it. To be sure, I may have to speculate more than I usually do. I may have to resort to confrontations more than I ordinarily do; but I would proceed under the conviction that in the long run (assuming, of course, that the therapy was not hovering at the brink of termination) an interpretive approach will be more advantageous than a didactic one. And Study 1 invites a number of different interpretive approaches. Many of them, unfortunately, may cause more problems than they solve.

As this form of resistance, a "flight into health," strains our neutrality (if not also our credulity), it invites interpretations that are diagnostic and confronting. We're bound to experience some skepticism at the rosy picture our patient is painting for us and also sense that the resistance will be recalcitrant to empathic formulation. Since it isn't an uncommon resistance— and puts us in a difficult position, if not a paradoxical one as well—I will devote a lot of attention to this study and examine a wide variety of interpretations that students suggest. I'll begin by criticizing their solutions and save my own until the end. The solution will have to emerge from a process of elimination.

Let's consider, first of all, the most direct, most no-nonsense, and no-beating-around-the-bush approach. It can only be the message "Look here, your remarkable improvement will only serve the purpose of getting you to quit therapy prematurely!" However formulated, it epitomizes the confronting mode. It is purely diagnostic; it isn't very different from didactic; and in my opinion it is bound to fail. Do we expect the patient to simply accept our judgment? Do we, in fact, expect him to understand it? It simply isn't realistic to expect that any attempt to meet the resistance head-on will promote anything more than an impasse. Yet there are practitioners who would venture an even more challenging message: "So how come you're still here?" A student comes close to it with:

> I hear a contradiction in what you're saying. On the one hand you say nothing is bothering you and everything is fine, but on the other hand you come to therapy. Perhaps you *do* realize that you have problems, things you would like to say but don't, things you try hard to brush off.

It should be obvious why I'd reject such an approach. But I would also reject a milder confrontation like:

> You are making a point of telling me how well everything is going. I wonder if you are trying to avoid talking about some of the things that *are* bothering you.

I suppose such a speculation could be justified as an attempt to promote the therapeutic process, in the sense that it might enable the patient to get back to work on his remaining problems (which, after all, he must still have). But the attempt stands a substantial risk of failing. It can just as likely promote an impasse. And an even more tactful formulation, so long as it remains confronting, runs a similar risk. Consider this example:

> I can appreciate the fact that you are pleased because you are feeling happy and productive. But just as you brushed aside your father's comment so that you wouldn't be hassled, I wonder whether you find it easier now to brush aside therapy for the same reason.

It isn't easy to imagine the patient responding in a useful and productive way to such fighting words. Given his state of resistance, he is apt to resist such a suggestion.

A second approach, which in my opinion isn't likely to be any more successful, entails suggesting to the patient that the improvements he has described are not genuine and / or permanent. Now, to be privately skeptical of his experience is one thing; it's quite another to lose sight of the fact that it can be authentic and contain no phenomenal hint of impermanence. I carefully avoided including any evidence in the narrative that our patient regarded his condition as anything but genuine and stable. My main purpose was to make it difficult for us to introduce an element of doubt. Had I ended the transcript with an expression of some doubt, or something to suggest that he might be aware that he was exaggerating, we could simply support it with "I take it part of you suspects that the way you're feeling may not be altogether genuine; it may be serving some other purpose—such as a wish to stop therapy, for instance." But as things stand, there's no reason to suspect any doubt. We must therefore take care not to doubt his experience or appear to question its authenticity.

In practice, I would want to wait for some evidence that he himself had some doubts. Until such evidence showed up, however, the following interpretation—which is a highly confronting version of a kind of formulation that many students suggest—remains unwarranted and inimical:

> I get the feeling you're trying to convince yourself and me
> that you no longer need therapy—everything is rosy.

It says little more than his claims are not to be believed and that he should come off it. The message is "Whom are you trying to fool?" Even a less challenging interpretation, like the following one, might convey that message:

> You are feeling good now, and I think you would like to
> stop coming to therapy before you encounter more
> changes that will involve greater risks and possibly be
> painful.

If there are more changes left to be made, then the ones he reported may be thrown into question. Moreover, he is likely to focus on exactly that part of the interpretation, wondering what further changes we have in mind for him. And what about the "greater risks"—does this mean the changes that he's already experienced were risky?

Before moving ahead, let's consider an interpretation that formulates the resistance accurately and yet subtly undercuts the patient's good feelings:

> I can appreciate that you are feeling good. But I wonder if a possible reason for your general good feeling is that you want to leave therapy.

Despite the introductory sentence, it is quite curt. Resistance is not a good subject to address curtly. The patient is obviously unready to give the idea thoughtful considerations—he's under the sway of resistance, after all—and is going to be surprised, to say the least. Therefore, a gradual approach is called for, a step-wise form that can allow for some modulation of the doubt and tempering of the challenge.

Some students cast their doubt by suggesting to him that not everything in his life is as good as he's claiming; he must still have problems. Such speculations are likely to intensify the resistance instead of opening it up for exploration. Not only do they draw a big inference for which there isn't any evidence, they also have a self-serving texture. "*Why such a specula-tion?*" he might wonder, "*For my sake or yours?*" Consider the following example in that light:

> It is marvelous that you are feeling so good today. But I wonder if there aren't some things causing you problems, things you are overlooking. Perhaps by telling me how great you feel and how you don't need therapy, you hope to avoid exploring areas that might cause you pain.

The opening remark is apparently meant to underscore the patient's insistence on how good he was feeling, but it could be taken as patronizing, if not sarcastic. Then the interpretation is both confronting and speculative. That combination, especially when a patient is in a state of resistance, can provoke him into defensiveness. Similarly, those interpretations that express their doubt by restricting their focus to therapy have the same shortcoming of making an inference from no evidence. For example:

You seem to be experiencing less anxiety and feeling more
in control of your life, yet I wonder if you are trying to stay
in control here by declaring yourself cured and therefore
not needing to look at some of the unresolved and more
painful issues.

What will we say when he asks "*What makes you think so?*"
What evidence can we appeal to? And notice the undertone of
skepticism in "You seem to be" and "trying to stay in control."
Students even speak of his feeling "uneasy" about therapy—
again, out of thin air. Given his great optimism and enthusiastic
gratitude, he's likely to feel second-guessed, put-down, and
otherwise misunderstood, even chastised.

In short, it's clear to me that we must accept our patient's
claims and not challenge the validity of his documentation, not
excluding even the telephone conversation with his father. His
description of that conversation is of a somewhat different order
than his description of his other gains, and his conclusion that
it reflected an improvement is open to question in a way that
they aren't. His father disparaged him, as he apparently always
does, and the patient mentioned having the impulse to respond
in a familiar way. But instead he did something new; he
brushed his father off and he simply shut up. This new behavior
was apparently a success, yet we might sense that it was forced
and artificial. We might therefore be tempted to exploit the
interchange and press it into the service of articulating the
resistance and defending an inference that all was *not* so well.
Moreover, it has dynamic content, along with intimations of
transference, which offer us something concrete to work with.
So it's an altogether tempting target, and students aim interpretations at it.

This, too, I regard as a risky choice, if not a potentially serious
error. For he intended the interchange as yet another illustration of his improvement. He regards it as a victory. That,
apparently, is why he described it to us, and we don't want to
make him regret having done it. We cannot ignore his appraisal,
and neither should we want to undercut it. At best, then, we
must use this material with special caution and circumspection.

In an apparent eagerness to suggest the transference implications, students fail to be sensitive to the implications of

having challenged the patient's attitude toward the telephone conversation. They proceed too swiftly and don't give him a chance to consider the fact that a different way of construing the interchange is being suggested to him. For example:

> It seems to me you might be handling your feelings here in therapy the same way you handled your feelings last night with your father—that by not saying what you really want to, by brushing things off, by shutting up, you will avoid feelings that might hassle you.

This interpretation simply brushes aside what he had claimed, and that, of course, is what his father did as well. (Our patients can be adept at provoking this kind of correspondence, which is what countertransference is about.) And consider this variation:

> I wonder if you are more bothered by your conversation with your father than you say. And perhaps you feel you won't allow yourself to be hurt by me that way.

We have apparently taken cognizance of the patient's remark that one of his father's comments did "get" to him, and we should have said so—"You mentioned that one of the things your father said *did* get to you." We might also move more slowly and amplify: "I gather you meant that it did manage to upset you, even though you thought it wouldn't," thereby allowing him an opportunity to react, and us the opportunity to gauge the reaction. Then our speculation would be limited to the second sentence. As it stands, the patient is too likely to respond: "*What makes you think I was more bothered than I said? I wasn't hurt by him. He just kind of got to me, that's all.*"

Whether or not the response to his father reflected an improvement, the father's attitude toward his successes may still have a direct bearing on the transference. And we might also draw the inference that the patient intended to provoke us to challenge him the same way his father did. In fact, we might even speculate that he included a description of his father's sarcastic mocking in order to evoke in us a similar reaction—or perhaps a dissimilar one. Students do formulate a transference theme along those lines:

> Are you trying to tell me that, since you can do your work
> and handle your father now, maybe you don't need to look
> into yourself any more? Are you a little afraid, perhaps,
> that I may bug you for every "damn thing," as he did?

I object to "trying to tell me" and "maybe," and I think our
patient also would. (It sounds a lot like the father, doesn't it?) So
I prefer this version:

> You were telling me of the many things you're doing now
> and finding satisfaction in, then you told me of your
> father's sarcasm at hearing about them. Perhaps you feel I
> will put you down for your attempts also. I wonder if you
> expect me to undermine the new changes in you, as your
> father did.

And if we wanted to suggest that he not only expected a reaction
like his father's but may actually have intended it, we can
choose this one: "I wonder whether you are trying to find out
whether I will react to you as your father did." But I wouldn't
want to formulate it as confrontingly as:

> It seems to me that you are setting up a situation with me
> in which I could easily disagree with you and undervaluate
> your progress, as your father did.

And if we wanted to suggest that he expected an opposite
reaction, we could say: "You want for me to give you the praise
that your father withholds."

All of them are sound articulations of a potentially important
transference issue, and they can be regarded as preliminary
steps to formulating the resistance, to which none of them
alludes. However, since the hallmark of resistance is the impulse to flight, and since flight is commonly motivated by fear
or apprehension, all it might take is to add, as one student does:
"Perhaps a part of you is afraid to go on and wants to quit now."
That, alas, is a pure speculation. There is no hint of any fear or
apprehension in the narrative—there is anything but—and
neither is there a good clue as to what our patient might be
afraid of. Yet students do infer that he is afraid to continue

therapy. Some attribute it to underlying feelings of anger, others to a conflict over dependency, and they use the one piece of evidence that might support such a hypothesis: the interchange with the father. Not only does this require them to cast doubt on it, it tends to lead them into a provocative kind of formulation. Consider this way of using the evidence:

> You report good feelings in general and that your father didn't hassle you; but when you described the conversation, it seemed as if you didn't notice the fact that his comments were as sharp as ever. What I'm wondering is whether your general good feelings are the result of such not noticing.

How is the patient supposed to respond? *"Yes, now that you mention it, I see your point—I was closing my eyes to the truth—your observation is most useful because it helps me question the validity of my general good feelings—which I will now proceed to do."* No, he probably knows how to match his father's sarcasm—*"And you're a real* shlemiehl"—and will proceed to do so. What will likely ensue is an argument, and the therapeutic process will fall by the wayside.

To be sure, it will fall by the wayside if his resistance isn't resolved and he quits therapy. Therefore, we have a find an approach to the resistance that is sufficiently active and still maintains the integrity of the therapeutic process. The approach will necessarily have to be confronting—our patient has no idea that resistance is afoot, so the idea will have to be imposed—and the process will be compromised to that extent. But our confrontation needn't be directed at his claims and documentation; instead it can address his feelings. In my opinion, that is likely to have the fewest disadvantages, and if it is done gradually and sensitively, the greatest chance of success.

Therefore I would approach the resistance by starting from an empathic understanding of what he was feeling—and that, it seems to me, is optimism. His optimism is intense and pervasive. Furthermore, it seems to be based on the current excellent state of affairs as well as a wishful assumption that the state of affairs will continue. The underlying logic is that of the optimist. So the question I would raise for myself is: "Things are going very well, yes, but what makes you feel so sure they will continue that way?" I wouldn't put this question to the patient—not only because it is too blatantly a challenge, but because I already have the answer. He feels so sure things will continue to go very well because that feeling subserves his wish to be finished with therapy. And notice that it isn't necessary to doubt whether things are indeed going so well in order to justify the explanation. The basis of his optimism is clear enough, only its logic is debatable—or vulnerable. The optimism could provide the point of leverage we need to articulate the resistance. This comes down to leveling a "challenge," not at the basis of his optimism, but rather at its form and function.

My approach can be schematized as follows: he is feeling optimistic and therefore is questioning the point of continuing the work of therapy; his optimism is also subserving a prior wish to be finished with therapy, or an impulse to flee from it (or from me). To put this schema into practice, I would begin with a remark that focused on the optimism:

> You are feeling well, doing well, and it is making you optimistic. I gather you are feeling so optimistic that you're thinking you don't need to work any more in therapy.

After he had responded, presumably in the affirmative, I would venture a doubt-casting remark directed not at the improvements or at the interchange with the father but at the optimism. It will necessarily be a confronting interpretation, yet it can be formulated in a way that minimizes the pitfalls and side effects of that mode:

> I want to raise a question about the way you are feeling optimistic. I can sense how marvelous the changes you've been experiencing feel, and I know it may be foolish to question the way they've made you feel so optimistic. But what do you think of the possibility that one of the reasons your optimism is so high is because you no longer wish to work in therapy but want to be finished with it altogether?

I'd be far from surprised if he heard me challenging the changes, and I'd be ready to make it clear that I wasn't. Neither would I be surprised if he misunderstood the resistance formulation, and I had to explain that I meant to be suggesting that it was his wish to stop that was "causing" his optimism, at least in significant part. And notice how my interpretation leaves him with a way out; he can agree that it is foolish to question his optimism. Say he put it this way: *"Yes, I do think it's foolish. But since it obviously isn't foolish to you, would you please explain yourself."* Or say he reacted with a baffled:

> *You're asking me to consider the possibility that I've gotten better in order to be finished with therapy, and I find that an extraordinary idea. As if there were something wrong with that! Didn't I come to therapy to get better? Frankly, it seems paradoxical, if not crazy, to me. So I wish you'd tell me how that could be.*

At this juncture I would have two options. One is to emphasize that I was not speaking about his having gotten better, I was referring to his optimism. The question I raised was whether it might be serving a wish to be finished with therapy. The second is to go the didactic route by notifying him about the "flight into health" phenomenon. Notice, however, that the didactic explanation, since he literally asked for it, won't necessarily be construed as a gratuitous act of supportiveness. It will, however, cast me into a teacherly role. So if I had so far avoided didactic explanations in the therapy, I would take the first option. To be sure, it transforms the resistance from a "flight into health" into a "flight into optimism," but this might be little more than a temporary expediency.

If the patient had reacted to my interpretation with resentment, feeling that I had thrown cold water on his improvements, then it might be possible to point out to him that he himself probably had some doubts about them—why else would he accuse me of something I didn't do? If, on the other hand, his reaction was little more than obstinacy—he had no sense that his optimism was suspect, and refused to entertain the possibility that his wish to withdraw from therapy came first and reflected a resistance—I might be able to prevail on him to suspect the intensity of his obstinacy. Then again, of course, I might not. But bear in mind that if my efforts failed, the outcome would be no different than if I had said nothing to begin with. He'll quit therapy. And within the limits of tact, judiciousness, and professional responsibility, I did all I could.

Study 2
A Flight into Despair

I can't see what good therapy is doing me. I just can't see how it can really help me. I talk about my hang-ups here and I get to understand them better, but nothing really changes. Last night I was lying in bed—unable to get to sleep, as usual—and I was thinking about therapy and about you. You know, I think you're a decent person, and you're very smart, and you listen all right. And I'm not saying that you tell me things that aren't true, because they are. Like when you said I was angry at my father because he wouldn't let me grow up and be a man— that's exactly the case. And I really didn't know how angry I was at him, and you helped me realize it. But so what? I mean, what good does it do me? Nothing has changed. I still can't talk to him for two minutes without getting stomach cramps. And I still can't sleep like a normal human being, and I am still self-conscious with people, and still can't talk to anyone for more than two minutes without getting anxious. So this. . . . This is not helping me. And I don't see how it can. . . . If anything, you know, things are getting worse instead of better.

Here we have the mirror image of Study 1; I tried to duplicate its structure with the obverse resistance. There isn't a commonly used name for this resistance. (We might call it a "flight into misery," but I prefer "flight into despair.") This patient's logic is: *Because I am doing so badly, because things are getting worse, it is pointless to continue with therapy.* Again, students simply articulate the logic and not the resistance, and again they find a way to cast doubt on the authenticity of his experience. As in Study 1, there is a documentation of claims that can only be taken at face value and should not be challenged, including an interchange with his father that can be pressed into the service of interpreting the resistance and defending the interpretation. For these reasons, both studies raise the same kinds of technical problems, and I believe their solutions are formally similar. Instead of optimism, this time it's his pessimism that provides us with the key point of leverage for a resistance interpretation. I would begin with an articulation of his pessimism:

> The discoveries you've made haven't helped, and the things I've told you haven't done you any good, so you're feeling that anything you may discover here, or anything I may say, is doomed to be useless. In other words: since things are getting worse, you don't see how therapy can possibly help you.

Then I would ground a resistance interpretation in the pessimism this way:

> But I wonder whether your pessimism isn't also based on a desire to stop therapy.

I would then emphasize that I wasn't challenging his documentation, and neither did I mean to put all the onus on the resistance:

> I don't mean to say that your experience of therapy not helping isn't true. I'm suggesting that your pessimism is partly due to something other than the fact that you're not getting better, even getting worse.

If the patient asked me what made me think he was resisting (what I had in mind with the "something other," for instance), if he wanted to know what else beside his poor condition was making him want to stop, I'd say I wasn't sure and there were several possibilities. One was the way his father wouldn't let him grow up and be a man. (Perhaps he mustn't let me be so different from his father; perhaps there's a danger in allowing me to be the agent of his independence and maturity.) A second possibility—which is at once more specific and vague, and also more speculative—is that there were certain things he wanted to avoid talking about because they were so painful. But I would

hold both of these speculations in abeyance and offer them only
if his reaction to my remarks required it.

Students start out with the speculation. Here are two examples:

> You say nothing has helped and nothing can. Perhaps you
> are taking this despairing position because it's your way of
> not facing some painful matters.

> You say I tell you things that are true and that you didn't
> realize before. Could it be you are afraid of what other
> things I might tell you and therefore doubting that therapy
> will help you?

Since they fail to articulate the resistance itself, these interpretations are somewhat premature and abrupt. They invite the
challenge "*What makes you think so?*" Or the patient might
wonder what "painful matters" and what "other things I might
tell you" we had in mind.

Let's examine a strong interpretation that contains a variety
of themes that could constitute separate interpretations. It is
fully cast in transference terms; therapy is the principal subject
and we are the main object; it begins with an articulation of the
patient's feeling of disappointment, it adds anger to it, and then
proceeds to speculate that the basis of these feelings is a set of
unrealistic (and immature) expectations, nothing more. Only
the resistance itself is missing.

> I think a part of you is very disappointed and angry with
> me for not being able to magically solve your problems. I
> believe you may find it difficult to accept the fact that
> change takes time, and that I cannot supply you with
> immediate answers. And I have the feeling that by saying
> things are getting worse you want to punish me.

Not only is it, in its parts and its totality, unresponsive to what
the patient has said, but it strongly implies a minimization of
the genuineness and legitimacy of his despair. Its overall tone is
judgmental and confronting; it has a defensive, if not retalia-
tory, tone; it reflects a countertransference reaction that is
problematic. And where is the evidence?

A surprising number of students infer that our patient is angry. He is certainly expressing disappointment. He is probably complaining. But does that provide a basis for inferring anger? A student offers this interesting variation:

> It sounds as if you should be feeling pretty angry that things aren't getting better, particularly since you are doing everything expected of you here.

Does that mean he is angry because he should be? Or have we suggested that he isn't angry but should be? He has taken special pains to exonerate us from blame (or at least I did when I composed the narrative), yet students infer that he is angry at us—and they have us say so. What they achieve thereby is a transformation of his message from "*I want to quit because therapy is not making me better*," to "*I want to quit because I am angry at you for not helping me get better.*"

Is it reasonable to infer that he chose the illustration of his anger at his father because he wanted to convey the message that he was angry at us? From a theoretical perspective, yes, but in practice it won't work. For suppose we told him that we inferred he was angry at us because he mentioned his anger at his father, and he protested with "*But I meant it merely to illustrate that knowing what I really feel is not helping me overcome my problems. Why do you use it in a way that I did not intend?*" And suppose he added:

> I am wholly unaware of any feelings of anger at you. As I said—or don't you believe me?—I think you are a good person and a good therapist. So not only do I not feel anger at you, but since I feel no sense of holding you or the therapy to blame for my failure, I have no reason to feel any anger."

How could we now proceed—back down with a tactful apology, or press ahead with our original formulation? I think we would simply have to apologize.

To press ahead would require taking his painstaking exoneration as evidence, and we could only claim:

> I think the fact that you took such pains to exonerate me from blame is an indication that underneath you do feel I

am to blame, and therefore that you do in fact feel angry at me.

If he now asked for some explanation of how that works—and he has the right to have the matter explained to him because it was we who raised it—we'd have to give him a normative and / or theoretical answer. (For example: "Because in my experience, and according to my theory of human behavior, when a patient does what you have done he is resorting to the defense of reaction-formation or disavowal.") But it is both unwise and therapeutically ineffective, in my opinion and experience, to ground an interpretation in evidence of that kind. Normative and theoretical formulations, after all, brook exceptions, and just because there's a probability that behavior X is a cover for experience Y doesn't mean it applies in every case and instance. So I believe the approach is likely to lead us into a difficult position—and given our patient's state of resistance, it may achieve less than nothing.

Students formulate the resistance according to its broad definition, and their interpretation tends to become a piece of diagnosis. A succinct example: "I think part of you fears changing and becoming independent." I find it hard to imagine how such a diagnosis could benefit the therapeutic process. Even if our patient accepts it, and even if it comes to him as news, he will most likely just add it to his list of complaints. ("*Yes, that too—and how is therapy going to cure me of that ailment?*") Here's a more complicated formulation of the same idea:

> You're discouraged and feeling helpless, and I think I understand why. Feeling helpless is a way of saying to yourself that you can't change. And I think a part of you is very afraid of changing and wants you to feel helpless so that you won't have to.

"*Yes, I do feel helpless, and maybe it's true I'm afraid to change,*" the patient might respond, "*So I guess therapy is not for me.*"

The same idea can be formulated in a more specific way, by including a reference to the father, the way this example does:

Perhaps you prefer to see the therapy as useless and ineffectual, because then you wouldn't have to do what your father did not allow—grow more independent, for instance.

This may be a better way to do it, because it invites the patient to consider the role that his father's attitude towards growth and independence may be playing in his conviction that therapy is useless. But in view of the fact that he's in the grip of a resistance (it's our ruling assumption), I would worry that any interpretation that had a diagnostic form would be perceived as a scolding. In this instance, the patient might also sense that it stemmed from a need on my part to rise to the defense of the therapy—and myself, too.

Since it challenges the efficacy of the therapy and indirectly our skill as therapists as well, and it attacks us where we are apt to be most vulnerable, such a "flight into despair" can easily shake us from our neutral position. It does that to my students. More than other studies, it causes them to—

Shift the blame onto the patient's shoulders in a defensive way:

You are feeling helpless and also feeling that therapy is not helping. Perhaps you would like therapy to change you in spite of yourself—that is, without your actively changing. (Look here, don't blame therapy for your plight, it's your fault!)

I think one of the reasons you feel things aren't getting better is because a part of you still construes therapy as a place where you come to tell me about your hang-ups and problems, and then expect me to solve them for you. (Look here, don't blame me, it is you who are responsible for your plight!)

Counterattack in an aggressive way:

You know, I bet your complaint is a lot like your anger at your father. Part of you is saying "Help me, damn it!" while another part of you is saying "Stop the therapy, let me do something by myself, leave me alone!" (Let me give you a good shaking up, get you to quit your angry whining, and face up to reality!)

Offer interpretations that make little sense:

I believe you are struggling with the idea of growing up. Part of you wants to grow up, so you are angry at your father for not letting you. But part of you doesn't want to, so you are angry at your therapy and at me for allowing it. (*What was that again?*)

Rather than using your increased understanding to change outside of here, you are protecting yourself against further exploration by blaming the therapy for your problems. (*I'm doing WHAT?*)

I'm thinking that you feel being in therapy makes matters worse because it allows you to avoid standing up to your problems. (*How does therapy allow me to do THAT?*)

To be sure, the question of therapeutic efficacy is never an easy one. But when we conduct therapy our position should be unequivocal. We assume that our patient's well-being will best be served if we calmly accept the working hypothesis that our method is the optimal one for him. Not that we dismiss the advisability of introducing modifications, or even of an entirely different form of therapy for him; but our short-run attitude remains one of giving our method the benefit of all doubt. We maintain a full faith in the treatment, along with the optimism that includes his ability to use it beneficially. This means we proceed in a business-as-usual way, doing nothing differently, giving the interpretive approach a reasonable chance. And it also means we don't defend the therapy; we defend the therapeutic process.

Students tend to defend the therapy, and they do it in several ways, some of which amount to telling the patient that it is actually working. For example:

Perhaps your feeling that things are getting worse is related to the fact that you are more in touch with your feelings—your anger at your father, for instance—and this

makes the repetition of the same old patterns more uncomfortable.

Interpretations along this vein want the patient to believe that it
isn't true he's getting worse and not improving; he's merely
feeling bad (uncomfortable or not good) as a result of therapy's
effectiveness. The implication is that's how it has to be. Getting
in touch with one's feelings is a mixed blessing. Now, this may
be quite true, but still be quite self-serving. Moreover, if we've
been avoiding didactic lessons until now, now is exactly the
wrong time to start giving them. They might even intensify the
patient's resistance by reinforcing his pessimism, because he
will have been successful in shaking us from our usual stance.
Or else he might hear reassurance instead of explanation. And
suggesting to him that he is experiencing no gains from therapy, and feels that he's getting worse, because that's exactly
what therapy entails, is quite different from suggesting that a
resistance to therapy is at work and that's what is responsible
for his lack of improvement. Or more precisely, his condition is
serving the prior and more basic wish to be out of therapy. And
even more precisely, in my opinion, his condition is serving to
bolster his pessimism, and it is his pessimism that is subserving
his resistance.

Study 3
A Flight into Distrust

*I didn't feel like coming today. I don't know why, but . . .
I just didn't feel like it. Henry asked me to go downtown
with him today and I was tempted to, but I figured I'd
better not, I'd better keep my appointment with you.
Anyway, he's a drag to go anywhere with. He's always
late and making phony excuses. Like he'll say he'll meet
me at two o'clock in front of Macy's, and at two o'clock I'll
be waiting for him, he shows up at two-thirty and makes
a phony excuse—like he thought we were supposed to
meet at two-thirty, or else he thought he said some other
store. It gets me depressed when he does that—when
anybody does that—doesn't keep their word. . . . Not that
I don't expect it to happen to me, because somehow it
always does, you know. I don't know why, but I get to*

thinking I must be sort of a bad person, in a way. Not a bad person, it's more like sort of . . . evil. Yeah, like someone evil who should be avoided, or something like that. There must be a reason why people don't keep their word to me. . . . (What are you thinking?) How my father used to make promises all the time that he didn't keep. That didn't used to really bother me so much, though, because I expected it from him. He was a weak person, as you know, and he could never say no to me. Anything I asked for, he would say he'd get it for me, and then, of course, he didn't. I never told you this, but he once promised to buy me a fancy train set, and I knew he wouldn't because it was too expensive and he didn't ever buy us expensive things because he didn't have enough money, really. So I didn't really feel so bad when he didn't. And then when I grew up, that's when I just avoided him all the time. We became these two strangers because I knew he would always disappoint me. . . . I guess people just do.

This study seems to raise fewer and less serious technical problems than the first two. For that reason, perhaps, students offer interpretations that fail to provide a sufficiently articulated and focused formulation of the resistance. The fact that the patient acknowledged a wish to miss the session invites the complacent assumption that he is aware of the resistance. Furthermore, the narrative provides the material for a range of good interpretations that are not resistance formulations, strictly speaking. A succinct example:

You wished not to come today because you feared that I would disappoint you.

A more fully articulated one:

I think you didn't feel like coming today because you are beginning to wonder whether I, too, can be trusted— whether I will keep my word—or whether I'll disappoint you like Henry and your father do. And as you said, when you begin to wonder about that, you get depressed.

As they don't go on to address his underlying wish to stop therapy, they apparently presume that his wish to miss the session wasn't merely the manifestation of the resistance, it was the resistance. My point here isn't theoretical, it has important practical ramifications. The patient may well respond as if he were fully aware of the resistance. (*"Yes, I didn't feel like coming today."*) But were we to suggest that he wanted to quit altogether, his response might be quite different. (*"No, no, I just didn't want to come today!"*) For that reason, I would develop a line of interpretation that led to "You didn't want to come today *because* you wish to stop therapy," and culminated in "You wish to stop therapy (not merely miss today's session) *because* you are afraid to trust me not to disappoint you."

But is that the most cogent, most potentially effective, resistance formulation? I believe it isn't. I can imagine our patient having no qualms accepting it—*"Yes, I'm afraid you will disappoint me like Henry, my father, and everyone else does."* And I can also imagine his welcoming the help I've given him to bolster his resistance—*"Yes, you're right, I guess I want to quit because I'm afraid you're going to disappoint me, too."* This, however, isn't the only reason I think the more cogent, more potentially effective formulation is to reverse the cause-effect sequence—namely: "Your fear that I, too, will disappoint you isn't the cause of your wish to stop, it's the other way around. Your wish to stop, to flee therapy, is what's *causing* you to feel distrustful of me and to fear disappointment."

In fact, I wouldn't speak of "fear," I would use the word "expectation," because I think he doesn't fear disappointment so much as he welcomes it. And I would try to make it clear that I was suggesting that the expectation was serving as the vehicle for his wish to stop therapy. To be sure, a formulation like that is bound to be provocative and tactless, and it certainly is highly speculative. It would have to be conveyed carefully and sensitively—and gradually. But it is altogether worth it. It is worth it because the other causal order presents a finished line of inquiry, whereas this order opens up a new and fruitful field. How does the patient transform his real desires, and why does he wish to stop in the first place?

The point is partly theoretical and partly practical, in that it comes down to a particular way of construing resistance. Just as the patient in Study 1 was using his optimism—and in Study

2, his pessimism—as the instrument of his wish to stop therapy, so does our current patient use distrust together with the conviction that he is doomed to disappointment. In other words, the resistance itself cannot be explained by distrust; it has to be formulated with respect to the therapy as a whole and especially to the therapeutic process. The therapy and the process contain the seeds of their own resistance; they have an indigenous inertia, an inherent counterforce against self-inquiry and significant change that enlists the patient's defenses into its service. As a working hypothesis, this formulation of resistance is likely to be a particularly powerful one, and often it's a mandatory one as well. Resistance can become a crucial issue in long-term therapy. It has to be respected.

No matter how formulated, however, resistance is best approached with a gradually evolving sequence of interpretations. A succinct interpretation will usually not suffice, for it may deflect the patient's attention from the phenomenon, or else explain it away instead of opening it up for further and deeper exploration. Perhaps because the narrative is so transparent that it invites no extended dialogue, students opt for a single interpretation to this study. But if we wanted a single interpretation, our best choice is to formulate it on the patient's self-image theme of the unworthy and evil one. Here are three good examples of what I mean:

> I wonder if you're thinking that I shouldn't be concerned that you considered canceling—because you're not really worth my trouble, you're some kind of evil person who isn't worthy of my concern.

> I wonder if you are afraid I am going to let you down as other important people in your life have, and as your father did. Perhaps you feel you must have been a bad person for him to have done that, and that it's risky to have those feelings of being evil and bad reinforced.

> In telling me you don't expect people to keep their promises to you, I wonder if you're letting me know that you're expecting me to break my promises to you also—because you think I'll find you unworthy, evil, and then you're

expecting to avoid me for it. Maybe that would partially
explain why you didn't feel like coming today.

My preference would be to put a special emphasis on his
expectation of disappointment, reserving the "fear" for the
resistance proper. Had the final sentence of the transcript been
accompanied by a smile or a gesture of victory, my impulse
would be to say: "Isn't that lucky! It enables you to be in the
enviable position of the one who is always disappointed, and
this nicely backs up your self-image as the evil one." I wouldn't
have said this aloud of course, but I'd use the impulse to help
formulate the theme in my mind. A student comes close to
articulating it:

> I am wondering if perhaps this feeling, that people let you
> down because something is wrong with you, doesn't allow
> you to feel disappointment and perhaps anger over being
> let down.

As a preliminary step toward the resistance interpretation, this
interpretation might be good and useful. I like the way it
suggests to the patient that he may secure gratification from his
distrust; it's a short step from there to the idea that he may be
using his distrust in order to bolster, and make sense of, his
resistance.

Another step that can be interpolated is the question "Why
today?" Why is he now feeling so mistrustful and anticipating
disappointment? Students raise the question by wondering if
there might be some topic on his mind that he fears discussing,
perhaps because it will reflect badly upon him. Instead of
alluding to "some" topic, we could be a bit less vague with
"And what you said a moment ago suggested that it (the topic
you want to avoid talking about) has something to do with the
fact that you are feeling unworthy these days, or *evil* as you
put it."

But the narrative invites further complications. Is it merely
an expectation of being disappointed? What about the possibility that beneath it lies the further expectation that we will in
fact *not* disappoint him in this respect? I would take this
possibility very seriously. I would infer that he may be apprehensive out of a sense that I was *not* going to be yet another

person who lets him down, and therefore his experience in therapy is going to threaten the integrity of his self-image. Now, there are two ways I can let him down, two ways to construe the "promise" I have made. One is that therapy will help him get better, the other is that I will understand him with compassion and neutrality. I'd be inclined to assume that he was apprehensive about both those promises, perhaps because they each threaten his self-image, so I would try for a formulation along these lines:

> I understand that you didn't feel like coming today because you're afraid I will disappoint you, as your father did. But I wonder what you think of the possibility that it would actually not upset you very much if I did that—and what *would* upset you is if I *don't*. I have a hunch that you are worried about that also.

From there I could go on to point out that he fears my unconditional acceptance because he feels threatened by it. It threatens his need to feel unworthy of trust and understanding. And because he senses that I am never going to fulfill that need, he wants to withdraw from me and stop therapy. This is a formulation with great potential for important discoveries and insights. It can set him on the way to autonomy in a way the confrontative student interpretations couldn't manage. If he realizes he partly wants the neurotic set-up, that part of him realizes it is free of the set-up, we have thereby created or at least enlisted that more autonomous part of the self in the work of therapy. If this succeeds in resolving the resistance, it will not only have rescued the therapeutic process, it will have promoted it.

Study 4
A Flight into Trivia

I went shopping for a new suit. Yesterday afternoon it was, and . . . I couldn't decide where to go. Henry went to Macy's last week and got an imported suit from Italy for 40 percent off. It was . . . it was originally marked at $180 and . . . uh . . . he paid only $108. But when he got home he found a small rip, about an inch or so long, in the right

*armpit, and took it back but had a lot of trouble over it.
Anyway, so I decided to go to Altman's. But I didn't get
there because on the way I passed a shop on Fifth
Avenue, just off Fifth on 48th Street, and in the window I
saw this beautiful suit, dark green with a fine yellow
stripe. It was marked down from $195 to $119.50. Henry
has one almost like it, except his . . . uh . . . his is grey
with an orange stripe. Anyway, I tried it on and it fit
perfectly, except the jacket was about an inch-and-a-half
too long, but it can easily be shortened. The salesman
was a tall, skinny guy, he must have been over six-
foot-four, with enormous thick glasses. And he kept
smiling all the time, and he had buck teeth. And the
reason I mention this is because he reminded me of a
fellow named Allen who was in my class in the eleventh
grade. Everybody used to make fun of him because he
had buck teeth and lisped badly. He had braces for his
teeth, but . . . I used to feel sorry for Allen, though . . . uh
. . . God knows, he was better off than I was. His father
was an executive in the telephone company, a vice-
president I think, and they were richer than anybody else
in our school. I remember how impressed we all were
with the colored telephones in his house. He was the first
person in the class to get his own telephone. And he could
make all the calls he wanted because his father got the
service for nothing. Allen had a friend who was at school
somewhere in the Midwest—in Illinois, I think—and he
used to just call him up and talk for hours. He once talked
to him for a solid hour and forty minutes.*

Reader: Before you go ahead, let me point out that your
transcript fails to convey what you intended. By packing in so
many irrelevant details, you have produced a caricature of a
"flight into trivia" that is highly ambiguous. And not only does
the patient remain unaware that he is resisting, he gives no hint
that he is speaking in a way that is unusual for him.

Author: Yes, I agree. For that reason I even hesitated to
include this study. Instead of relying on the presumption that
therapy would not have gotten past the beginning stages with
this kind of circumstantiality, and it therefore reflected not a
style but a resistance, I should have included something in the

narrative to suggest that he knew he was speaking in an unusual way, that the mentioning of so many details was remarkable. So it's no surprise that most of my students failed to spot the resistance. As I mentioned parenthetically on page 154, the titles were not given with the studies. Yet even those students who did identify the resistance failed to use it.

In any case, I could hardly leave the study out. The resistance itself is hardly trivial. And it's a resistance that is not only common to many forms of therapy, but it has a special relevance to ours. It flies in the teeth of our nondirective orientation and puts us in a paradoxical position vis-à-vis our neutrality with respect to content. After all, the Basic Instruction has granted our patient the full freedom to speak however he wants to, and we never want to abrogate that freedom. But can we keep from doing so and still deal with his decision to avoid the therapeutic process by speaking trivia?

Reader: I gather you believe we can.

Author: Yes, but only after having solved some technical problems that are especially delicate and difficult. The problems are compounded in this study by the fact that the patient shows no awareness of a resistance. Not only has he made no allusion to stopping therapy or withdrawing from the work of therapy, he hasn't alluded to therapy at all. Therefore, we'll have no choice but to introduce the idea of a resistance, and this is going to take a confronting interpretation. We will have to begin by interrupting him to draw his attention to the way he is speaking. And we may have to do it without recourse to any content in his narrative.

Reader: This will put a big strain on our tact and our neutrality, won't it? And won't our role definition be compromised?

Author: I'm afraid it may, to a degree. For there isn't a way to be fully empathic and purely interpretive and still address the resistance. Short of waiting for a suitable opportunity, we must resort to confronting interpretations with all their potential for tactlessness, directiveness, criticism, and the rest. In a sense, then, this is a study of compromise, an exercise in the use of confrontation.

Reader: Look, couldn't we begin this way?—

I want to interrupt in order to draw your attention to the way you are talking today.

Author: Yes, I think we have no other choice. Then we could pause briefly to see whether the patient recognized what we were referring to.

Reader: If he didn't, and asked what we had in mind, we could formulate the resistance this way:

> Do you notice how much detail you are going into about things—the exact prices of the suits, the exact position that Allen's father held in the telephone company, the exact state his friend lived in, and so on?

Author: Okay, but we shouldn't pause again and await his response, because if we stopped here we'd be left with all the risks that attend the use of confrontation.

Reader: The chief one being the message "So please cut it out already!"

Author: Exactly. In order to avoid that, we could go right ahead with a remark that had an interpretive cast to it, that sought to offer an explanation. And we have two options. One is to say something about the resistance itself, perhaps by suggesting the possibility of an underlying wish to withdraw from therapy. The second is to say, in effect, that it would be useful to explore the reasons behind his talking this way today. The first option is riskier than the second because it is bound to strike him as farfetched; we might prevail on him to accept the possibility that his circumstantiality was interfering with his work of self-inquiry, but anything more is hardly imaginable and bound to be premature. We would therefore want to choose the second option. But instead of saying "I believe it would be useful to explore the reasons behind your talking this way today," and thereby compound our violation of the Basic Instruction with a directive to explore, we should try to convey it in the form of an interpretation. In that way, we restrict ourselves to the directiveness that inheres in every interpretive act.

Reader: And it's the kind of directiveness with which our patient will already have been familiar. All right, what's wrong with saying?—

> I am wondering why you feel the need today to go into such details, whether it might be a way of avoiding talking about

something specific that you think might be upsetting to talk about.

Author: It is at once diagnostic, speculative, and vague. And not only is the speculation wholly unsupported by evidence, the interpretation doesn't make reference to any. It would obviously be better if you could have suggested to him what topic he was specifically avoiding.

Reader: But I deliberately didn't do it.

Author: Why not?

Reader: Because there is a fresh risk in picking something out of his material to serve as possible evidence—namely, a grasping at straws.

Author: Yes I think it's important to try and avoid even giving the impression that we had selected something from the content of his narrative for the sole purpose of backing up an interpretation—and more precisely in this case, for the purpose of transforming a pure confrontation into a less diagnostic interpretation. There's a subtle but significant difference between using evidence to justify and using it to rationalize.

A student offers a similar solution to yours, but finds a clever way—perhaps too clever—to integrate an interpretation with the narrative's content by picking up smoothly from where the patient had left off:

I think you're having to do the same thing here with me, because a part of you is afraid of what might happen if you stopped talking solidly.

Then, after allowing him to ask "*What do you mean, what might happen?*" continues with:

Well, I have in mind two things. Talking solidly might be a way of keeping the unexpected or troublesome thoughts from occurring, and it also minimizes the opportunities for me to say something. Perhaps either of those possibilities makes you anxious—and talking solidly is a way of avoiding that anxiety.

It is no less diagnostic than your solution but may have greater merit. Another student comes close this way:

I wonder whether you are going into such irrelevant detail in order to prevent yourself from getting into other things that might be more disturbing to you.

Not only does the resistance go unmentioned, but the interpretation doesn't stop at this point and continues in a flagrantly diagnostic manner:

I think that when you feel threatened by some thoughts, you tend to go into elaborate details about something else as a way of stopping yourself from having to confront whatever you are afraid of.

Unless this theme had already been discussed in the therapy, this formulation is bound to put the patient on the defensive. In a similar vein, a student begins with an unnecessary and imprudent apology, "Please don't take this as a hostile criticism, I don't intend it to be"—which the patient might take as nothing more than kind consideration—but it has at least two big faults. It gratuitously suggests that what's coming can be taken as a hostile criticism, and it sweetens the bitter pill artificially. Far better to let the chips fall and then work with the pieces. But the student now offers an interpretation that captures the spirit of yours:

I was impressed with the amount of detail in what you've told me so far, and yet all of it doesn't seem to relate to you on anything but a kind of superficial level. I am wondering if you're talking on this level because talking on any other level now might make you more anxious.

Another student offers a succinct (if not curt) continuation and then invites the patient to recognize what we had in mind:

It seems to me that you, too, would like to just talk for hours. I wonder if you see what I mean, or suspect what's behind this.

That's an attractive possibility too, although I doubt whether our patient is going to get the point. I am certain he would not get the point—unless the point was to chastise him—of this version of the formulation:

> You seem to feel you can talk on and on here, like Allen did on the phone, without using the time meaningfully—as if the opportunity was worth nothing.

It's no surprise that students betray an irritation with his chatter. Here's an example that reflects an undercurrent of impatience:

> I find myself wondering if there is some point you are trying to make, or if there isn't something you want to talk about with me more directly.

Notice how we have accused the patient of being indirect—and done it indirectly!—without offering any basis for the charge. Another student does the same, but draws some content from the narrative:

> I wonder if what you are saying is that everyone is better off than you are.

I doubt whether that lessens the sense of irritation.

When I composed the narrative, I deliberately avoided any usable content. I was trying to present a pure form of the resistance. Nevertheless, students do find material in the narrative and press it into the service of explaining the resistance. An interesting example is:

> I have the sense that you are feeling today very much like Allen with his telephone, who'd call his boyfriend and talk for hours. You seem to be in the mood to chat with me, much as you might with a friend over the phone, moving from one subject to the next, nothing too serious.

And here's a succinct version:

> Perhaps you want to do much the same thing here—just talk for hours to see if I'll allow it.

And—

Reader: And that's quite enough, Author! I think you might be suffering from a touch of countertransference, if I may be so bold.

Author: Yes, dear Reader. Your interpretation is a bold and confronting one, but accurate nonetheless. Before I release you, however, I want us to do a dialogue that is pertinent to "flight into trivia" and to resistance in general. I need to summarize a few things, and at the same time keep the promise I made you in Chapter 1 that I would examine the problem of our "neutrality with respect to content" as it relates to our fundamental neutrality. If you will play the role of patient, and imagine us during a session in the middle stages of our therapy, we can have—

A Dialogue on Resistance and Neutrality

Author: I want to draw your attention to the way you're talking today. Are you aware of speaking about things that are unimportant to you?

Reader: *Yes, I'm aware of that. But why do you want to draw it to my attention—to get me to stop doing it?*

Author: No, that wasn't my intention. At least, it isn't the best formulation of my intention. You see, I intended to ask next whether you were aware of doing it out of a wish to avoid talking about something that *is* important to you.

Reader: *Yes, I'm aware of that too. But look here, you've made a big point of my freedom to talk however and about whatever I wanted to. And this is what I want to do today— avoid talking about something that is important. Are you telling me I shouldn't? Isn't it perfectly all right?*

Author: Again, that wasn't my intention. I don't mean to be saying that you must avoid or aren't free to talk about unimportant things. I decided to raise the issue, and find out whether you were aware of it, because I thought it would be useful.

Reader: *I see. You thought it would be useful. And you have also made a point of telling me that you'll be saying "useful" things. I've got a fairly good idea by now what you mean by "useful," but what you just now said seems like a different ball game. What makes it useful to raise the issue* *you've raised today? Assuming I was unaware of it, why is it useful for you to point it out to me? I can think of only one answer: to get me to stop doing it and get me to speak of things that are important.*

Author: I can think of another possibility: to help you discover why you want to avoid talking about things that are important to you.

Reader: *Sure, but that amounts to the same thing, doesn't it? If I were to discover why, then I'd stop doing it. What other reason is there for trying to discover the motive?*

Author: Here's one: if you felt compelled to talk about unimportant things, understanding why might free you from that compulsion. And then you'd be free to do it or not.

Reader: *I see. Your point is that understanding can increase a person's freedom of choice. But I did feel that I was in fact freely choosing. So if I had let you know that I was doing it knowingly and deliberately—if I'd begun today's session by notifying you that I was planning to talk about unimportant things out of a conscious wish to avoid something important— then you wouldn't have had anything useful to say about it. Is that true?*

Author: Not necessarily. In fact I might not have said anything, but in principle there might be something useful to say, because there will be—and necessarily, I believe—aspects of your decision that are outside of your awareness. So, for instance, I might have judged it useful to wonder aloud if you were challenging me to a confrontation, or perhaps you were doing it out of a wish to withdraw from therapy.

Reader: *Hello! Then we're right back where we started from, aren't we? What message could that have had other than "Stop challenging, and stop withdrawing"? Am I not free to do those things?*

Author: Sure you are. I never intended to take those freedoms away. But once again, you see, there's the question of whether or not you were aware of wishing to do those things.

Reader: *Okay, so let's go around the bases again. Suppose I was fully aware of avoiding talking about important things out of a wish to challenge you and / or withdraw from therapy, what useful remark could you then make to me that would not amount to a request that I stop it?*

Author: I can think of a number of different possibilities, all addressing the question "Why do you have these wishes, and why do you have them now?" And some of the answers are bound to lie outside of your awareness. Insofar as they do, they wouldn't necessarily imply a directive, would they?

Reader: *Not necessarily. But if they did, in fact, lie outside my awareness, are you saying they'd therefore be useful for me to know?*

Author: Yes.

Reader: *In what respect?*

Author: In respect to discovering things about yourself that you weren't fully aware of, or didn't fully understand. And useful in augmenting and extending the zone of personal freedom you seemed to acknowledge as desirable a few moments ago.

Reader: *I see. I appreciate that you put it in terms of discovery and self-understanding. That has seemed like just about the only thing you care about. Otherwise, you've been very neutral. You've never judged or evaluated me, or anything like that. Even when I told you my suicidal thoughts, you didn't seem to care whether I was actually going to commit suicide—although I knew damn well you didn't want me to, if for no other reason than it would bring the therapy to an end. And I know you want me to get better, but nothing you've said has indicated it. All I could tell from your actions and your remarks is that you wanted me continue in therapy. Listen, I'm not accusing you of indifference, only of inconsistency. Whenever I've described my interpersonal relationships, you never took sides. Why should you be partial when it comes to my self-understanding?*

Author: Because I regard self-understanding as intrapsychic, and when it comes to that domain, I don't believe that such impartiality applies. You see, I don't think its useful—nor for that matter is it ethically defensible—to be impartial when it comes to matters that are therapeutic for you.

Reader: *I understand. But granting that self-understanding is important to me, even therapeutically "useful," where does it leave my wish to speak today of unimportant things? You would have forced me—as in fact you did—into speaking of important things. What happens to my freedom to* *speak as I choose, when you've forced me to widen the scope of my self-knowledge?*

Author: That's a difficult question for me. I'm not sure I can answer it adequately, but the word "forced" is perhaps too strong. I prefer to put it this way: I would have "encouraged" you to stop acting on your decision, and instead to explore the reasons for the decision. After all, if your talk was unimportant, as you agreed it was, what harm is there in encouraging you to make it important?—as long as you remain relatively free to resist my encouragements. I don't believe, for instance, that I've forced you into this discussion we are having.

Reader: *All right, say I agree with you on the distinction between "forced" and "encouraged," the fact remains that it was you who encouraged the discovering, not me; it was you who moved me in the direction of understanding why I made the decision.*

Author: And that's one of the ways I construe the term "useful." Listen, this may seem harsh, but it's crucial. You have been free to stay away from therapy, free to terminate your work here. This is crucial because it means, to me at least, that your coming is a voluntary submission to the unavoidable breaks in my nondirectiveness and skill in understanding. And I take it for granted, you see, that one of your reasons for coming to therapy is to make discoveries about yourself. I further assume that you're likely to have conflicted feelings about it, and part of you doesn't want to discover anything new about yourself, since it might be painful and unsettling. But I regard it as useful to ally myself with the part of you that does want to discover and risk the consequences. I never meant to be impartial in that respect. It's one of the chief ways I try to be useful.

Reader: *I've noticed how you like to divide me into parts. That, I gather, is your favorite way of talking about my conflicts. But I won't quarrel with it. I'll even agree that there's a part of me that wants to discover and to widen the scope of my self-understanding, and the rest. But I'm not entirely sure what it means concretely for you to "ally" yourself with that part. It's a fine metaphor, but what else does it entail other than encouraging me to explore and persuading me that it's a beneficial activity to engage in? And isn't that a paradox? Don't you necessarily infringe on my freedom of choice in order to enlarge on it?*

Author: Yes, the paradox is real. But there's a distinction between short-term freedom and long-term freedom, and it's only the short-term one that I infringe on in this particular way—hopefully in the best interests of the long-term one. And even when it's your short-term freedom that's at issue, I try my best to keep from infringing on it more than I feel I have to. It's a matter of balance and judgment on my part, when you come down to it.

Reader: *I see. You abrogate my short-term freedom only insofar as you can enlarge my long-term freedom; you side with me against my neurosis, thereby violating your neutrality, only insofar as it can make me stronger and my neurosis weaker. It makes a certain sense. Okay . . . so I guess I should now talk about the important thing I was consciously planning to avoid today.*

Author: "Should?"

Reader: *Hey, lay off already! It's going to take some time.*

Author: I appreciate that. But the reason I repeated your *should* is to suggest to you that you are still in a state of resistance.

Reader: *You mean because I didn't "discover" anything about myself, only about Psychotherapy, this has been what you call "business"? It's all been beside the point, outside of "narrative," important but not therapeutic?*

Author: Yes. And this entire book, as well.

INDEX

Activity-passivity, 14, 74,
106–107, 116–118, 134,
206
Advice, 31, 104, 251
Affects and feelings
articulating vs. explaining,
210
articulating vs. naming,
148, 165, 194
expressing of, 148
as impulse and wish,
147–148
and introspection, 148–149
role in psychotherapy of,
107–109, 111–112
signaling function of, 107,
111–112, 138, 147–148,
211
and suggestion, 109
and tact, 42–43
Altered state of
consciousness, 117, 159

"Analytic experience," 159
"Analytic process," 9, 256
Anger, 43, 49, 145–146,
194–195
Anxiety, 138, 147, 211. *See
also* Affects and feelings
Apprenticeship. *See*
Supervision
Argument, 30, 52–53, 58, 63,
115, 151
Assessment. *See* Diagnosis
and assessment
Authority, 114–115
Autobiography Study:
purpose of, 54–55
Autonomy, 8–9, 28, 74, 77,
88, 92, 107, 169, 282.
See also Freedom of
choice; Patient, freedom
of
Awareness. *See*
Consciousness